The Disastrous 1990s in Russia

The Disastrous 1990s in Russia

Emulating the West Paved the Path to Putin

Konstantin Sidorov

Algora Publishing
New York

Library of Congress Cataloging-in-Publication Data

Names: Sidorov, Konstantin (Pseudonym), author.
Title: The disastrous 1990s in Russia : emulating the West paved the path
    to Putin / Konstantin Sidorov.
Description: New York : Algora Publishing, [2022] | Includes
    bibliographical references. | Summary: "The 1990s' dive into cowboy
    capitalism and "democracy" with advice from the West led to an utter
    breakdown in the former Soviet Union. Shocking concrete examples of the
    corruption, chaos and misery are related by an eye-witness. Facing
    destruction, they chose a strong, smart leader...and so we have Putin"—
    Provided by publisher.
Identifiers: LCCN 2022022243 (print) | LCCN 2022022244 (ebook) | ISBN
    9781628944884 (trade paperback) | ISBN 9781628944891 (hardcover) | ISBN
    9781628944907 (pdf)
Subjects: LCSH: Russia (Federation)—History—1991- | Russia
    (Federation)—Social conditions—1991-
Classification: LCC DK510.76 .S53 2022 (print) | LCC DK510.76 (ebook) |
    DDC 947.086—dc23/eng/20220509
LC record available at https://lccn.loc.gov/2022022243
LC ebook record available at https://lccn.loc.gov/2022022244

Printed in the United States

TABLE OF CONTENTS

1. A Fuller Picture: Foresight and Hindsight

Introduction From the Editors

One day in 2000, we received an email from Mr. Sidorov, a Muscovite who was fed up with the appalling decline of his country over the past dozen years. He sent a manuscript enumerating cases of corruption from one end of the country to the other and decrying what appeared to be insane misjudgments by the leadership. Then he sent a small update and announced that he was leaving for the West — and that Sidorov is a pseudonym he used for his own safety. Not a word more.

He and others like him thought the new Russia was "just like the USSR but stupider. And who thought stupider was even possible."

But by now, everyday people will tell you that "In reality, the USSR and what was going in my country never was stupid before Gorbachev and it only became stupid as a pretext to destroy the country, brainwash the population to steal resources and to turn the country into a capitalistic hell." Many former Soviet citizens now acknowledge that "what the Soviet media used to say about capitalism turned out to be true. There is nothing attractive in current state of world affairs after [the demise of the] USSR. Degradation of humanity is in full swing. It's wrong to say that the USSR was stupid. Naïve yes. Stupid no. It was naïve to believe that coexistence with the West is possible."[1]

---

[1] Comment by Serge Krieger, March 5, 2022, in *The Unz Review*. "Russia Ukraine 2: The World Order Has Changed," by Patrick Armstrong at https://www.unz.com/article/russia-ukraine-2-the-world-order-has-changed/#comment-5212885

Looking back today, it's clear that Mr. Sidorov, too, was not stupid — but he was naïve. A number of his predictions came true, and yet a number of the strategic decisions that he felt were wildly off base turned out to be correct. Like most of the educated elite of his time, he admired the West and fell for the propaganda.

Thus, when Gorbachev began to open up the society in the late 1980s, the changes were greeted with enthusiasm. In just a few years the Soviet Union split up and the Communist system was abandoned. Cowboy capitalism, or gangster capitalism, was established under Yeltsin. The transition to a market economy led to unimaginable levels of corruption and caused an economic and demographic catastrophe in the 1990s.

Sidorov mistakenly thought the West was immune to many of the profound problems he saw, and he derides a number of the military and political figures' concerns and theories about the international conjuncture — theories that conflicted with the popular image of America and a bright future of collaboration rather than competition.

Now, the concerns of those officials look prescient rather than idiotic. Russia is indeed still being challenged on all sides as the US and NATO foment instability and worse in its closest neighbors. The pace has quickened, from Victoria Nuland's coup in Ukraine (2014) to the coup attempt in Belarus[1] (2020), Biden's precipitous abandonment of Afghanistan (August 2021) that sent refugees and armed militants fleeing across borders, the coup attempt in Kazakhstan (January 2022), and the accelerated arming and incitement of Ukraine in the lead-up to 2022.

Thus Sidorov's exposé is even more useful in retrospect than it was at the time it was written. It reveals in many different ways how the pressure to privatize assets and adopt "the European dream" and "democracy" have been used to weaken sovereign nations, including Ukraine. This book sheds light on far broader issues than the history of just one country at a turning point in its history.

Steeped in the day-to-day reality and recording actual facts in real time, the author was unaware of the broader context that shapes our interpretation of events today. At the time this book was written, at the end of the 1990s, George Soros and his Open Society foundations had been active in Russia and all of Eastern Europe and the former Soviet republics, including the Caucasus republics, for over 10 years. Their message has always been extremely attractive, especially to younger audiences: No more being told

---

[1] "Anatomy of coup attempt in Belarus," *Indian Punchline*, by M. K. Bhadrakumar, August 30, 2020.

what to do. "Democracy" (never clearly defined), less focus on engineering and economic realities and more on "self-expression," throwing off convention and indulging in social experiments. The funding and encouragement that Western organizations provided looked like a gift from heaven. There was a long standing belief that joining the West would be a magic elixir that would turn their homelands into "normal countries," automatically generating the standard of living seen in America or Germany. One can easily imagine, however, that while the bulk of program participants were earnest do-gooders inspired with lofty thoughts of "democracy" and "liberty," those designing and funding the projects had more political objectives as well, including undermining social values and weakening the social fabric, promoting identity politics, stirring discontent, and encouraging protests that lead to overthrowing the government.

With help from the US State Department, USAID, The National Endowment for Democracy, the World Bank, and major US and international corporations, such groups laid the groundwork for color revolutions wherever Moscow still had allies. They continue to operate as a fifth column in the Russian Federation to this day. Like "Occupy Wall Street," the Capitol Hill Autonomous Zone (CHAZ) in Seattle and various actions by "Black Lives Matter," peaceful protests and legitimate demonstrations can blur into radical mobs and a threat to security, threats the security forces eventually have to counter.

As soon as the Soviet "empire" broke into 15 newly independent republics, the young American lawyers eagerly volunteered to help them write new constitutions for themselves. One innovative feature they recommended was to set international law above national laws — which sounds laudable for others, but it is the US and its allies who control the UN, World Bank, IMF, WHO and other international agencies. US law does not provide for these bodies to over-rule its own sovereignty. In innumerable ways, the evolving situation as Russia felt its way forward to a new system left it vulnerable to often well-meaning but often unwise influences. The results are detailed in the grim reading below.

This is the context in which Vladimir Putin came to power in 1999, and this is important background for readers analyzing how and why a strong leader often comes to the fore during tumultuous times. When that leader keeps his own country's interests first and foremost, and succeeds in bringing order out of chaos, rival countries will gnash their teeth. They will do all they can to regain their hard-won access, to meddle and weaken the other while profiting from new markets.

Since the book was written over 20 years ago, from an embittered and limited perspective, we have aimed to convey mostly the facts and statistics the author presents, as these data may be useful in illustrating the dreadful conditions that prevailed during this intermission in Russia's history. Here and there, we offer a bit of perspective on some of the judgements offered by the author.

The translator of this book has been studying Russia and the Russian language for 40 years. She has 20 years' experience working with (and in) the Soviet and Former Soviet republics to seek common ground, to foster contacts at higher levels and also at the citizen-to-citizen level, including leading exchange groups for academics, professionals, amateur sports groups, and student groups to Russia and most of the other 14 republics.

In 1989, she met with George Soros in his Manhattan office and his Fifth Avenue apartment as he was beginning to work with branches of the US Department of State and USIA to cultivate contacts in the Soviet republics. As it was clear that the older Communist leadership was on the way out, Mr. Soros's initiatives enticed the next generation of leaders with trips abroad and flattering get-togethers with US senators and others. The relative luxury of the American lifestyle, still coasting on the economic gains due to two world wars that were not fought on US soil, and the unprecedented attention, naturally engendered warm feelings.[1]

This manuscript was competed in 1999, when the hardships were fresh and raw. Russians knew something was terribly wrong and were hungry for answers. One observer noted, "People lived under conditions of tough deficit and crisis. The tense situation gave rise to criminality and dissatisfaction with authority in general. The reasons for intentional homicides could be thefts of such simple goods as a rag that cost less than a dollar, etc. In the early years of the reform, the minimum wage fell significantly below the poverty line. In 1992, it accounted for 33% of the poverty line for able-bodied persons and by 1995 it had decreased to 14% of that level. Additional jobs have been used to compensate for the low wages."[2]

The new waves of information and opinion flooding in from abroad under Glasnost and in the early years thereafter were intoxicating. In the 20+ years since, many Russians have matured in their understanding of international

---

[1] Now Mr. Soros is involved in the US, too, and helping to decide who will be our next leaders. "George Soros Pumped $125 Million Into His Super-PAC. Here's Who's Getting The Money," *Forbes*, by Michela Tindera, Jan 31, 2022, at https://www.forbes.com/sites/michelatindera/2022/01/31/george-soros-pumped-125-million-into-his-super-pac-heres-whos-getting-the-money/?sh=4a5230d170dc.

[2] "Life of Russia Of The Mid-1990s," EnglsihRussia, June 11, 2011, at https://englishrussia.com/2011/06/14/life-of-russia-of-the-mid-1990s/

relations and have begun to see that all sides offer both positive and negative aspects, have their own agendas, and use sincere, pleasant, credible-looking individuals to deliver their messages...although those messengers may be naïve themselves, and while being perfectly honest, they may be misleading their international counterparts.

In countries where international travel is practically impossible, the irritation and frustration of intelligent people are compounded by their lack of real information and experience by which to judge reality. They are left only with promotional images. Clearly, Mr. Sidorov has never tried to get an apartment, make a left turn, or commute to work in Manhattan or many other "civilized" cities.

In addition, he overlooks many parallels between recent American history and the political, social and economic trends he decries in Russia. We've had our own share of presidents drawn from the CIA or whose parents were active in the "services." Nothing unusual in that. We've had our own share of wiretapping, corruption, state violence against demonstrators and extremely suspicious deaths of inconvenient news reporters or natural-medicine advocates.

Far more important are the structural factors that led to the decline of the United States and yet were promoted vigorously abroad: lack of investment and de-industrialization. As one observer puts it, "the United States has abandoned [its] traditional industrial policy since the 1980s. It is imposing on its own economy the neoliberal policies that de-industrialized Pinochetista Chile, Thatcherite Britain and the post-industrial former Soviet republics, the Baltics and Ukraine since 1991. Its highly polarized and debt-leveraged 'prosperity' is based on inflating real estate and securities prices and privatizing infrastructure. This neoliberalism has been a path to becoming a failed economy and indeed, a failed state, obliged to suffer debt deflation, rising housing prices and rents as owner-occupancy rates decline, as well as exorbitant medical and other costs resulting from privatizing what other countries provide freely or at subsidized prices as human rights — health care, education, medical insurance and pensions."[1]

There are surprising parallels between the Russia of the 1990s and today's America. And the general population, in both cases, is looking from a fishbowl into a world it cannot fathom.

---

[1] "Michael Hudson: America's Real Adversaries Are Its European and Other Allies," Naked Capitalism, February 7, 2022, by Yves Smith at https://www.nakedcapitalism.com/2022/02/michael-hudson-americas-real-adversaries-are-its-european-and-other-allies.html.

A Short Annotated Time Line [1]

Russia since the disintegration of the USSR

1985–1990: The Gorbachev era.

Mikhail Gorbachev becomes head of the USSR in 1985.

Between 1989 and 1991, Gorbachev lets the Berlin Wall be pulled down, Germany be reunited and all the "captive nations" of Eastern Europe go free.

> "In the late 1980s, Mikhail Gorbachev's policies of openness and reform, *glasnost* and *perestroika*, unleashed an unexpected epidemic of independence movements within the Soviet Union. People were, technically, free to speak their minds, demonstrate and protest. *Perestroika* opened the door for the leaders of the collection of states to demand more control over their individual regions and, eventually, sovereignty from the Soviet Union.... Gorbachev may have envisioned a second revolution in Russia but never a coup attempt. After his election as president in February 1990, many feared the onset of another dictatorship. In fact, Gorbachev's actions seemed to contradict his policies of perestroika....Gorbachev was re-elected as president in February 1990."[2]

---

[1] Where not otherwise noted, the text in this time line is drawn from "Five key dates for post-Soviet Russia," AFP via Yahoo News, March 17, 2018, at https://www.yahoo.com/news/five-key-dates-post-soviet-russia-012335498.html.

[2] "August 1991 Coup Attempt," by Linda Delaine in *Russian Life Online*, 2001 (updated by *Russian Life* August 19, 2016), at https://www.russianlife.com/stories/online/august-coup-attempt/

1991: The Soviet Union dies.

A humorous snapshot suggests "the story goes something like this: a pro-Western faction of Soviet party elites imploded the USSR. Nationalized assets became private, i.e., up for grabs overnight. Communist Jews called up their capitalist cousins in New York who sent briefcases full of dollars to buy up state assets for pennies; a new caste of Jewish oligarchs rose up to rule the country thanks to the inept drunken rule of Boris Yeltsin; Vladimir Putin emerges as a compromise leader — a puppet of both the KGB and the oligarchs — someone who would be pliant and obedient; the new president surprises everyone and turns on part of the oligarch faction and starts arresting them while simultaneously crushing a CIA-funded Chechen uprising."[1]

June 1991: Boris Yeltsin is elected President [of the Russian Republic, not the USSR] at the first multi-party ballot.

This inaugurated a "disastrous decade-long rule of Boris Yeltsin, who ran Russia into the ground.... In that year, 1999, Putin watched as America conducted a 78-day bombing campaign on Serbia, the Balkan nation that had historically been a protectorate of Mother Russia... That year, also, three former Warsaw Pact nations, the Czech Republic, Hungary and Poland, were brought into NATO."[2]

August 1991: The Coup

The Soviet Union is about to be transformed into a confederation when the August 1991 coup strikes:

"December 8, Yeltsin agrees with his Belarussian and Ukrainian counterparts to replace their union, the USSR, with a commonwealth.

"As the Soviet Union disintegrates, USSR leader Mikhail Gorbachev resigns from the presidency. The USSR ceases to exist in international law on December 31, 1991.

Yeltsin launches a raft of free-market reforms and ruthlessly expands his powers, presiding over rampant corruption and a sell-off of assets to allied oligarchs. "This elite effectively privatized most of Russian industry: the lucrative oil and gas sector, the largest aluminum, nickel, platinum, and palladium plants in the world, and that giant but

---

[1] "The Retreat of the Oligarchs," *Unz Review*, by Rolo Slavskiy, March 23, 2022, at https://www.unz.com/article/the-retreat-of-the-oligarchs/

[2] "Did We Provoke Putin's War in Ukraine?" February 24, 2022 by Patrick J. Buchanan, at https://buchanan.org/blog/did-we-provoke-putins-war-in-ukraine-159120.

creaky Soviet flagship airline, Aeroflot. A stock market appeared, then soared to become the best-performing financial market in the world (1996-97) before crashing in 1998....in August 1998, leaving billions of dollars of debt behind)."[1] [2]

April 1, 1992–December 14, 1995: Bosnian War

After "popular pressure" [from whom?] the UN asked NATO to intervene in the Bosnian War after allegations of war crimes against civilians were made. The result of the war was the break-up of Yugoslavia, a multi-ethnic and multi-confessional parliamentary democracy, with one of the highest standards of living of socialist countries. NATO illegally used depleted uranium in its bombing campaign. Residents were interviewed on video saying that they saw snipers firing on houses of both sides simultaneously, in areas where good neighborly relations had prevailed. The net result was the break-up of a successful country into weak and impoverished fragments and the vilification of Serbia without proper evidence.

1992–1997: Russia dismantles its social welfare and defence budgets as required by the IMF's borrowing terms.

Finance Minister Anatoly Kudrin and Deputy Head of the budget department Anton Siluanov "delayed payment of pensions and public sector salaries to paper over the revenue shortfall; and dollarized Russian public finance in place of the ruble.

1994 to 1996: The First Chechen War resulted in Chechnya's de facto independence from Russia. "The incredibly rundown Russian army... Despite being heavily equipped, hundreds of tanks lacked any means of communication. Strategic planning and information sharing were disastrous. Training and morale were at their lowest. Instead of professional soldiers, inexperienced conscripts were deployed."[3]

---

[1] "From Yeltsin to Putin," by David Winston. *Policy Review*, The Hoover Institution, April 1, 2000, at https://www.hoover.org/research/yeltsin-putin

[2] The term 'oligarch' became popular in the 1990s, when dozens of ultra-wealthy Russians who schemed and swindled their way to control of Russia's most lucrative industries. These entrepreneurs and hustlers [mostly not of Russian ethnicity, many holding dual citizenship] took advantage of the sudden privatization of the Soviet economy to buy up natural resources and formerly state-controlled assets, using rigged auctions and other tricks. A few even took control of companies based on ownership documents they'd produced on home printers. "How did Russia's oligarchs become so powerful?" Yahoo, *The Week* Staff, April 3, 2022, at https://news.yahoo.com/did-russias-oligarchs-become-powerful-095211697.html.

[3] "The First Chechen War," CaesariusStudios, by Caesarius, undated, at https://caesariusstudios.com/the-first-chechen-war/

August 1998: The economy crashes.

Russia defaults on its debt and devalues the ruble. The severe financial crisis leaves millions of Russians in poverty, with the health and education systems collapsing. This sparks a political crisis that culminates with Vladimir Putin replacing Boris Yeltsin.

> "In 1998, when the commercial banks were unable to meet their foreign exchange wagers and the Central Bank declared a default on repayment of ministry bonds to service foreign loans, Siluanov was the ministry's overseer of banking and macro-economic policy; he reported to Kudrin who was first deputy minister at the time. Their roles in the 1998 default and the simultaneous disappearance of several billion dollars in IMF money, have never been disclosed."[1]

> "Russia had more or less completed the privatization of its manufacturing and natural resource sectors by the end of 1997. In February 1998, the annual inflation rate [appeared to be coming under control, which] should have cemented macroeconomic credibility, lowered real interest rates, and spurred investment. Instead, Russia suffered a massive public debt–exchange rate–banking crisis just six months later...This turn of events unfolded [due largely to] the interaction among Russia's deteriorating fiscal fundamentals, its weak microfoundations of growth and financial globalization... Russia's external debt increased by $16 billion or 8% of post-crisis GDP during this time. [Here,] financial globalization might actually hurt and a cutoff in market access might actually help.[2]

1999: Vladimir Putin arrives.

March 24, 1999–June 10, 1999: NATO bombs Yugoslavia [a Russian ally] during Kosovo War.

August 1999: Second Chechen War begins.

Wahhabi (Chechen) militants invade Dagestan and several apartment blocks in Moscow are blown up. These shocking events provided a direct justification for the invasion of Chechnya.

---

[1] "Gresham's New Law – In War There Is No Law," by John Helmer, May 30, 2022, at http://johnhelmer.net/greshams-new-law-in-war-there-is-no-law/

[2] "Financial Globalization and the Russian Crisis of 1998," by Brian Pinto, Sergei Ulatov. The World Bank, Europe and Central Asia Region & The Managing Director's Office, May 2010, at https://openknowledge.worldbank.org/bitstream/handle/10986/3797/WPS5312.pdf

As Yeltsin's prime minister, Putin had overseen the launch of a second war to crush separatist rebels in Russia's North Caucasus region of Chechnya, sealing his image as a strongman. The war began when Islamist fighters from Chechnya infiltrated Russia's Dagestan region, declaring it an independent state and calling for holy war. The separatists had carried out a series of bloody attacks which traumatized Russians. Tens of thousands die in the bombing of the regional capital Grozny before the conflict ends in 2009.

December 31, 1999: Yeltsin resigns, naming his prime minister, the ex-intelligence chief Vladimir Putin, as president.

March 2000: Putin is elected president, and then again in 2004.

During his first two terms as president, Putin asserts his dominance over parliament and regional governors, imposes control over the media and empowers the security services.He also sidelines influential oligarchs from politics, including Kremlin critic Mikhail Khodorkovsky, the ex-Yukos chief, who is jailed for 10 years.

Russia's economy recovers, thanks to high energy prices, a strict control of monetary policy, and reform.

Author's Preface

Sometimes a person feels a burning desire, the need to do something that does not give him rest until it is expressed in words or on paper. I, too, have felt such a desire. For several decades I lived in Russia, all over the country; in the end, I had to leave. But my departure helped make it possible to, and impelled me to, write this book. I have tried to be as objective as possible. I had no wish to slander the country, but facts are facts — even if everyone else has kept quiet about it. And that is not slander but the truth of life.

Much of our world is absurd, whether in Russia, or in the East or in the West, but when state policy is built on such absurdities, when people brought up on these absurdities come to power — then it is high time to talk about where these absurdities lead and what they mean. It's painful and embarrassing to write about what is happening now in the country and in the ever so "mysterious" Russian soul. But it must be written. Because of its huge size Russia has always attracted attention. She was either helped or hated, but she was never left to her own devices. Without looking the truth in the face, a people has no chance of becoming better and kinder, or to really change in any way. The Russian people should also take their dose of truth, that bitter tonic, without which society is liable to slide into an even deeper abyss. When the situation is as dire as this, people tend to say there is no place further to fall; but surprisingly enough, there always is. And having hit another new low, the country is opening deeper and deeper chasms into which to drop the Human Spirit.

This book is also written for those people who, having tried everything possible to change the situation, simply don't know where to turn; those who see with their own eyes that everything the Russian and the Western press write about it still fails to reflect what is really going on around them; those who, no matter how bad things get, are not relinquishing their moral standards, who don't kill and don't steal; as well as those who left their native land long ago (those whose education and training made that possible) and are living in the USA and Europe, Brazil and Mexico, Australia and New Zealand, Canada, Costa Rica, Nepal, India, Thailand and many other countries; those who have requested political and humanitarian asylum in various countries; those who are slowly dying in their cramped little apartments stinking of mold, piously saving their last dime for a decent burial and proper, if modest, clothes to be buried in. Forgive me, all those whom I do not mention here, since it is simply impossible to enumerate every category.

I hope that this book will help readers understand what was left in the wake of communism, during a collapse that most people did not see coming, a break-up that left more than the economy dismembered. People who are not burdened by morals, a conscience and an understanding of the laws that rule the development of society, can ruin an enormous and potentially rich country.

The actual material for this book was gleaned from ordinary every life in Russia, from police and official documents, sources in the government and the ministries, and reports from Russian news agencies and the media. This book does not give a complete picture of Russia. These are only basic outlines that should enable any interested person put together his own picture of what happened in the country. I also hope that Americans, Europeans and others will find a way to help the Russian people and help revive a truly great Russia that could serve as a bridge between the East and the West and that could show the world a model of wisdom and heroism, as it has done more than once in the past. Hope, as we know, is the last to die.

Konstantin Sidorov

Moscow, 1999

2. Ideology and Psychology

The history of Russia shows that the country has always been prone to foreign cultural influence. Power and its attributes, religion and social structure were copied from more developed neighbors, and later they were mechanically replaced by attributes of even more successful countries. For example, the current Russian white–blue–red flag was established by Peter I in analogy with the red–white–blue Dutch flag. The Tsar thought that the Dutch were the best sailors and shipbuilders in the world. However, later he became convinced that the British had surpassed the Dutch and he wanted the symbol of Great Russia to be more like the symbol of Great Britain, so the old flag was relegated to the archives. Peter's preference was clear when he introduced a new design — a blue oblique cross on a white background, reminiscent of the white oblique cross on a blue background included in the flag of great Britain — the cross of St. Andrew. The familiar red flag of the Soviet Union, with the hammer and sickle, was symbolic of the people's profound sacrifices and heroic victory in World War II. Introduced in 1922, it was retired in 1991. The white–blue–red flag was re-introduced as the flag of the Russian Federation after the dissolution of the Soviet Union, but and it took years for the public to get used to the change.

Many Russian holidays, including Independence Day, are highly contrived and were established specifically for some event, like a new Constitution (it changes frequently in Russia) or the proclamation of a new group coming to power. It's impossible to name any holiday that has remained the same for the last hundred years, except, perhaps, New Year's. The rest of the holidays are easily changed when the government changes. Even if the Commissioner for Human Rights in the Russian Federation, Oleg Mironov, called the day of the adoption of the Declaration on State Sovereignty of the Russian Federation a symbol of its emergence as a democratic state, you need to understand that this is nothing but words.

There were revolutions and upheavals in many countries in the late 19th and early 20th centuries, but in all of Europe, communism was only able to establish itself in Russia as a state system. In the rest of Europe, despite the left-social leanings of a large part of the population, communism was not sanctified by the state, and in Eastern Europe it was actually imposed by the USSR. This was shown by constant uprisings and demonstrations in Hungary, Czechoslovakia, Poland, etc.

Communist ideology, contrary to many claims, did not change the psychology of the Russian people; it just landed on fertile ground. According to the latest scientific data, even in a state of hypnosis a person will not do something that he considers taboo. He may have hysterics, but he will snap back into consciousness and will stop at the last moment. Conversely, if a person is ready to do something, anything can serve as the trigger. It is not that communism was imposed on the Russians — it reflects the peculiarities of their psychology, which is based on the well-known principle: "What do you think, we need to take everything and share it (equally)." By definition, no one should be richer, smarter, more capable, more successful than the rest. No matter how hard a person works, if he makes good money, he is a bourgeois and an oligarch. If he has built himself a private house, he has to share it. People will say, "Well, you're living well, you have a lot of money, but we have nothing. That's not right, everybody has to share, give us some money!" You can tell them, "What about you? Work, do something, you'll have money." But their answer is always the same: "Buddy, we're not talking about us but about you. As for doing something, that's what we did — we came to you. You're a rich man, and the rich are supposed to share. And if you don't divvy up what you have, we'll divvy you up, yourself!" Justice means taking everything and sharing it. The legendary times of "Prodrazvyorstka," when the Bolsheviks confiscated all supposedly surplus agricultural products in the 1920s, went as far as taking the last pot of food off the stove from the "bourgeois"; this left a deep impression on the memory of Russian Champions of Justice.

Private property is a joy, of course. But Russia makes life difficult. Even building a country house. A man saves literally every penny. Then he builds a little summer place and turns his patch of land into a blooming garden. And one fine day, a homeless man, gets into the property and takes the old TV set, the simple furniture, the vegetables from the garden, and on top of all that, he cuts down the trees in the yard — for firewood. And he takes with him everything that can be eaten (Half of all thefts in the countryside consist of stealing food, while apartment thieves head for the fridge Worst of all, the guy may very well set fire to the house. And the *dacha* is burned to ash. They set fires because they're angry, desperate, dead drunk. Dachas and houses are burned down by the dozens, and if there's no watchman, no one finds out until it's too late. Many other problems are caused by uncontrolled burning of dry grass and the constant burning of garbage. Some people give up taking care of their summer places because there's just no use in continuing this fight.

In Russia, with the sudden introduction of "democracy" and "the market," many people immediately dropped the survival skills that had been passed down from generation to generation, the culture of poverty, the knowledge of how to eke out a meager but sober and calculating life. Instead, theft on an epic scale proliferated. Overnight, casinos and boutiques cropped up like tumors, squeezing out less tawdry businesses in the capital. Moscow boasted the largest number of Mercedes in a single city; palaces and villas with elevators were built outside of town, so close together that they could see in each others' windows. But there is no culture of wealth in Russia, either. The Russian capitalists of tsarist times had too much personality. The millionaire Shchukin, for example, sent his shirts to be washed and starched in London, which did not exactly strike either the intelligentsia or the ordinary people as a great idea. Perhaps that's why Russian capitalism of the early twentieth century ended so quickly.

Even in our time the "new Russians," who were primarily secretaries of Communist party and Komsomol groups, were stunned by the sudden opportunity to earn big bucks. They thought this would solve all their personal problems — physical and emotional. But outwardly they expressed only crude aggression, directed at everyone at once. They only wanted luxury in order to flaunt their power and dominance. History has turned back the clock. There is something prehistoric about it, like when the chief of the tribe was the strongest man, painted, and decorated with ornaments. Primitive symbols of power were what mattered most. Such a regression in behavior cannot be explained simply by their being ill-bred. The great Russian soul, having suffered such great losses, so much humiliation and impotence, wanted to shake off this burden at once and take revenge on all offenders, acquiring more and more attributes of power.

Russian millionaire Boris Berezovsky induced the governors to unite and create a party of "muzhiks" ("peasants," or "regular guys"). Minister for Emergency Situations Sergey Shoigu, for example, was perfect for this role — he can open a bottle with his teeth. The top three members of the political movement "Unity" included, of course, Shoigu, Olympic wrestling champion Alexander Karelin and police major General Alexander Gurov. Power is the main factor when assessing the abilities of anyone in Russia. A civilized, prosperous people will never think of putting a military leader or state security officer in charge.

There is only one way to solve problems in this country — interdiction. They know how to resent and despise, to deny and demand, to cry and beg. But they do not know what it is to support and help. Noticing homeless children or homeless adults, of course the rest of the citizens feel sorry for them. That's easy, because pity does not cost anything. But no one is going to do anything concrete to help them or keep them warm. The Russian post office charges for sending charitable packages. If you are looking for support at the societal level, you probably won't find it. And if you do, you will soon find out that it was just words, and no one was thinking about actually doing anything. The Social insurance agencies spend 20 times more on maintaining their staff than they spent on victims of the Chernobyl accident and children with disabilities. Instead of paying money to those in need, the funds all go to building luxurious administrative offices in the center of town.

The Communist Party, through Stalin's repressions and the subsequent processing of the consciousness of all Russians, has given rise to people who start with loud statements and end up keeping quiet. They think about their families, and about their dachas, and they shut up. Thanks to this long-standing tradition of suppressing dissent in modern Russian history, no social protest is expressed. This applies to ordinary citizens, and generals, politicians, and various types of leaders. Sociologists and political scientists are still looking for the answer to the question: Why are there still no social explosions in Russia? Neither the destruction of the population's savings in January 1992, nor the looting of the national wealth under the guise of "privatization," the firing on the lawful parliament in October 1993, the slaughter in Chechnya which killed more than 100,000 in the first Chechen war, or the unpaid wages and pensions — none of this generates a strong resistance or a powerful protest.

Three times in recent history, the state has ruined its people, and in response — nothing. The brutal beatings of demonstrators by the Moscow OMON (special militia detachment) on 23 February and 22 June 1992 and 1 May 1993 and the firing on the White House on 4 October 1993, were acts of intimidation, as well. This revived in the souls of the people their inherent fear of power, which had already begun to wear off over the years of perestroika. Hence the depressing political apathy of the population. People who were thinking, active, able to protest during most of the Bolshevik rule were mercilessly destroyed and later expelled. Because of this, there is nobody to lead active protests in Russia. And 70 years of communism undermined the solidarity between people. In addition, a person has a certain threshold of social activity. His strength goes into survival. What are moral principles, moral authority? Such words as pity and compassion have left the Russian lexicon.

In fact, only harsh measures are popular in Russia. Russian governors are calling for a reconsideration of the agreement with the Council of Europe to introduce a moratorium on the death penalty. The governor of the Sverdlovsk region, Eduard Rossel, and the Governor of the Omsk Region, L. Polezhaev, and the Governor of the Krasnoyarsk Territory A. Lebed all are behind it. They are collecting signatures to hold a referendum on the death penalty. For the first time, authorities of the Russian Federation have openly the Constitutional Court's ban on the death penalty. Citizens enthusiastically signed on; the Omsk region has already collected nearly half a million signatures. Moscow Mayor Luzhkov agrees with this. Russian doctors are willing to support the initiative of its governors. And no leniency.

Russians aren't much concerned about political despotism. This country has lived for centuries under despotism and political terror. Russian politicians attack each other like religious soldiers of the same faith attack other soldiers — especially when the victim is on vacation, and they think they can get away with it without an immediate reaction from the other side. Therefore, in Russian political life August is the busiest month. The vacation statesmen dream of — the sunlit pine forest, fishing, staying at the dacha with friends and a bottle — tends to fall apart.

Tolerance for, and even believing in the necessity of violence in solving anything, was one of the main features of the mentality of the Russian people. Since the days of Stalin, when the masses took to the streets in rallies with banners and unanimously demanded that "enemies of the people" be shot, little has changed. Compared with Stalin, many dictators just look pragmatic. But Stalin did not spawn despotism in Russia. On the contrary, Russian political intransigence and thirst for a "strong hand" led to his rise. Many Russians just say they want to live in complete freedom. But freedom also means full responsibility for themselves and their actions, and reliance on their own strength. But no one wants that. They only recognize the part about free education, health care, etc. etc. No matter if the quality is abysmal; at least it's free. And do not think wow. No one can conceive of to do something, if for it there will be no concessions. People who enjoy discounts on public transportation are getting more benefits than people who do not have these privileges. And it is mostly the young who are not accorded such bene-fits, while it falls on their shoulders to actually fund the transport system.

In Omsk alone, a city with a population of under one million inhabitants, 600,000 are on public assistance. Public transportation carries 67 categories of passengers for free. In fact, this approach has built entire industries in the inefficient national economy and the service sector.

The idea is, everyone owes you, but you don't owe anything to anybody. This is how millions of Russian pensioners across the country think, and they mercilessly elbow other people as they shove their way into buses, trol-leybuses, or trams:

— To a young person sitting in a bus: "Get up! You owe me, I busted my gut for the Soviet government for decades!"

—"I hate these crowded buses!"

— "Take a taxi, then, you yuppie bourgeois punk!"

The class struggle never loosens its grip on the minds of most of these people. A unanimous buzz applauds the long horn blasts as the tram driver beeps at the driver of a private car stuck on the tracks. "Crush it, crush it!," the crowd shouts, "what a bastard, he owns a private car — these guys robbed our country blind and bought cars for themselves." A car is an unac-ceptable luxury for many Russian people, an object of envy and hatred. There is an idea out there that any capital purchase, including a car, can only be made by stealing money, and in no case by actually earning the money. This is partly true. And even those who demand that the unfortunate owner of the car be crucified would not mind stealing themselves, if only they had the opportunity.

Even trolleybuses can't be left on the street if, for example, the electricity is shut down. Once in the city of Vladimir, the trolleybus authorities risked leaving cars on the streets so they could be returned to service as soon as the power was back on. However, in the intervening four hours, the windows of three cars were broken, and two drivers and one conductor were injured by passenger attacks. As if it was their fault that the trolleys were stopped in their tracks.

Fights among retirees are often seen; for example, when there is a rumor that clinics and hospitals will only be accepting patients who have the health insurance policies that can only be obtained through the Social Secu-rity Committee. Although the relevant order has already been received by the medical institutions, the forms have not yet been delivered to the social authorities. This leads to long lines, hype and a scandal.

In every branch of Sberbank (Savings Bank), there is a huge line at the only window marked "Monthly Payments," while the other five employees are dying of idleness. Women of a respectable age, starting in the early morning, stand all day waiting to pay the bill for their apartment, utilities or phone. Arguments often break out, and then when the line begins to move, there's a lot of cursing and poking each other with their elbows. There isn't even a machine spitting out numbered tickets to clarify who is next in line. And you can't get anywhere with the bored staff at the other windows.

Criminal psychology, which actually is pretty applicable in Russia, generally views an offer to come to an agreement as a sign of weakness and an invitation to aggression. Prison wisdom says that "marked cards won't help if you're playing with thieves." So you must never rely on the authorities to play by the rules. If the Constitution gets in the way — it will be corrected. If any appointees get in the way, they'll be terminated. If they feel threatened by the current system of state theft — they will declare that the Fatherland is in danger, etc. Shocking stories about the death of famous businessmen and bureaucrats are often explained by very a mundane motive — envy. Criminals follow the money; they're lured by the victim's success and power.

Contrary to all the stories about Russian hospitality, the Russian nation is rather suspicious and envious. This is compounded by the poor material condition of the country, but not only that. The principle of paying for good-will is widespread in Western-style civilization, such that it is better to pay a person so that he can meet his minimum needs without destroying society and other members of society. This includes "mandatory" smiles on the faces of saleswomen or officials. You won't see this in Russia. The principle of free hostility thrives here. A stranger on the street may tell you to go to hell. Transferred to Russian soil, things may look the same while in fact under-going a subtle but significant change from the original. Even when you visit an elegant exhibition by a Swiss watch company in the city center, don't expect to be greeted with a smile and full attention.

If you try to get your photos printed, you can expect to get back only some of the pictures. Maybe the rest didn't look interesting to the operators. If you want to get all the pictures you took, you will have to write in the order: "no complaints." And this may mean that artists behind the scenes can save a little on developers by squeaking out a few extra prints from the chemicals. No complaints on your part, no smiles on the other.

The Western habit of constantly smiling when meeting people, without saying a word about your life, about what really excites you or worries you, is perceived in Russia as one of many manifestations of the Western lack of spirituality, as well as callousness, coldness and formality. Meanwhile, Westerners consider this a matter of tact and non-interference in someone else's spiritual life. You can't burden another person with your problems — they have their own worries and fears.

Why do many prominent Russian politicians, performers and businessmen prefer to go abroad for medical treatment rather than go to the best Russian medical centers, which are known around the world for their excellent doctors? Just look at the quality of the patient care. No private or semi-private rooms; just crowded wards. The staff is openly rude, and often they expect tips in order to provide basic care. There are no flowers, of course, and neither are the floors swept; and don't expect a pleasant word.

The myth of the deep Russian soul is just an attempt to avoid looking at what is really going on. What is the "deep Russian soul"? The ability to pour out one's failures and disappointments, in all the gory details, in a quick ten minutes over a beer? This is the worst kind of violence, using another person as a garbage can. Just dump all your problems on him so you feel better yourself. It's a standard Russian scene, frequently reflected in police reports: "We were sitting there drinking, I opened my whole soul to him, and he punched me in the face." A person goes on and on, stubbornly unloading his burdens on the other person, who tries to fend him off any way he can. This is the depth and openness Russians are so proud of. It takes far less energy to meet even the greatest challenges of everyday life than to soothe a needy soul. The "deep Russian soul" will not rest until it squeezes dry everyone around. Until it turns everyone into a trash can. The famous depth of the Russian soul is, first, the glorified readiness to immediately bare their souls to the first person they meet, and second, the desire to impress people with how bold and how cool they are. This latter pattern masks the reality: it is merely the habit of solving all life's problems in a flamboyant, bold way, that is, a reckless, thoughtless way, which means that it is extremely ineffective. The aching for all of life's unfulfilled promises is drowned in a sea of partying, in chummy chatter and kisses on the cheek, vows of eternal friendship, with the inevitable blow-up at the end.

Most Russians are unbelievably infantile. They have low self-esteem, constantly insist that they are "backward," did not go to university, and don't know European culture. Their wandering attention is easily caught. They feel the call of the herd instinct: the urge to join a group, do something, at least to direct their energy and aggression somewhere, to have someone promise something. The most important thing is to avoid responsibility, identification, truth. Most people prefer not to hear anything different from what they have already been told. People are afraid to overload their brains. The ability to endure and to adapt to difficult conditions in general is characteristic of the Russian nation. The flip side of this is that Russians are showing increased aggressiveness, which is expressed in pathological cruelty. This is also a defensive reaction, a way to insulate oneself from the changing world situation. It is like a snake that crawls, bites everyone in a rage, and then puts its head on the train tracks, thinking that this is a good way to cure their headache. Russians are less adept than Westerners at self-management and getting things done, and this is due not only to totalitarianism but also to the peculiarities of Russian history and national psychology.

The consciousness of Russian people is mired in countless myths. They take all kinds of forms, but they all boil down to one thing — It's someone else's fault, not mine. We are not to blame in any sense. In the summer of 1915, when Russia was defeated by the Germans, there was little talk about the fact that that war was a fundamentally different war than the previous ones, a world war and a total war; little was said about the fact that the training of Russian generals was unsuited to the new means of conducting warfare. There was a much deeper explanation for the severe defeats — the tsarina had a direct line to Berlin in her bedroom, and she used it to send the Kaiser the most important military secrets.

True to their best traditions, Russians still turn to such legends and urban myths even today, not wanting to face the truth, not wanting to admit their weaknesses and therefore be faced with correcting them and improving their own behavior. The weakness of state institutions is re-cast as being the fault of unscrupulous entrepreneurs, who take advantage of the situation to make higher profits. Put an end to this and bring these "biznesmen" to justice, and everybody's standard of living would improve, effective demand would go up, and the reforms could go forward. It's these malicious entre-preneurs who are destroying Russia!

Despite everything that's going on, Russia continues to drink with full confidence. If you are not plied with vodka at every party, it seems incred-ible, even inhumane! In provincial cities that have long lost the ethical stan-dards of everyday life, they will understand it even if you do something strange, but they will never understand it if you fail to offer a glass of vodka or wine. Sooner or later, everybody who produces or sells products in Russia are forced to switch to vodka or go bankrupt. This even happened to the famous businessman Vladimir Dovgan, who was kicked off the management team of his own company, which was trying to create a sales network for high-quality products in Russia. Dovgan has resigned from the company's shareholders and from here on will be engaged primarily in the production of vodka, as well as goods associated with any gatherings where the Russian national drink is consumed. In addition to alcoholics themselves, there is a huge number of drunkards, that is, those who do not have a physiological addiction to alcohol. The two million drug users in the country pale in comparison with the 27 million Russians who abuse alcohol. They account for the staggering statistic of 18 liters of vodka consumed per year for each resident, including children and the elderly. More than half of murders are caused by drunkenness. Drunks burn down countless apartment buildings.

In Chechnya, tanks and armored personnel carriers raid vodka stands every day throughout the military control zone. It is not only the Defense Ministry units, but the special police detachments (OMON) and special rapid reaction detachments (SWAT) that are particularly "distinguished" in this respect.. But the military is also involved. There are even stories of fights breaking out between different Ministry of Defense groups over the right to "clean up" a village where a booze factory was located.

In Russia, corruption is strongest where there's vodka. Knock-off brands of vodka sits on the shelves of a vast number of shops. No matter how hard authorities try to crack down on this counterfeiting with unannounced inspections, the shops are usually already waiting. The underground factory that was making the vodka from industrial alcohol may close one day after it opened, and will have a 100% profit. Therefore, competitors and inspectors are eliminated immediately. In 1999 alone, there were more than 600 explosions in Russia, most of them connected with the illicit production and sale of vodka. Indeed, the vodka problem is worse than the drugs problem. Russian truck drivers, locomotive engineers and even ship captains consider themselves entitled to drive their vehicles while intoxicated. This causes a huge number of accidents, and not only on land. The ship "Mania," under the Jamaican flag, sailing from the port of Falkenberg on the Atlantic coast of Sweden with a drunken Russian captain at the helm, first ran aground and then crashed into the quay wall. Almost simultaneously, a similar accident occurred off the east coast of Sweden, where they have a joke about such things: What stops two Russian captains from crashing into each other, if one is navigating in the Atlantic and the other in the Baltic Sea? Answer: Sweden, which is located in the middle.

About 400 tons of fuel oil were spilled into the waters of the Neva River, which flows through the center of Russia's second largest city, St. Petersburg. This occurred because of an accident on an oil tanker. According to the inspectors who were first to board the tanker disaster, the captain and navigator were drunk.

It has also been said that there are drunks at the controls of some strategic bombers. One such case was as follows: An intoxicated team climbed to a bomber through the cargo door and shut it tight behind him. When the plane depressurized at high altitude, the pilots, due to high alcohol content in the blood and lack of oxygen, fainted. For a few hours the plane was hanging in the air on autopilot, disappearing from the radar screens. Miraculously, one of the pilots regained consciousness and was able to land the craft with nuclear weapons on board.

Drunkenness has also penetrated the top levels of the Russian state. According to Yeltsin's guards, incidents like this were frequent: Yeltsin would pour himself a glass of vodka, and his senior guards would try to stop him, begging and cajoling. Yeltsin would angrily respond:

— Am I the "Tsar" or not?

— You're the Tsar, you're the Tsar, they'd all agree.

— Then I do what I want. Go to hell!

Despite the fact that Russia is already eight years into the reforms, the country still does not have a "vision of the future." No, not even in the most general terms: no notion of what social, economic and political models the majority of the population is hoping for and that, at the same time, could realistically be achievable. There is a vacuum, no feedback at all, between those who are developing fundamental strategic objectives and the general population. Experience shows that when implementing social and economic reforms, anywhere in the world, every nation needs a unifying idea, and Russia is no exception. At the heart of the American, German and Japanese "economic miracles" lay clearly articulated and widely popularized principles of national unity, around which all social strata rallied. Ordinary Russian citizens are wondering why no one is paying any attention to them, and all their initiatives are blocked. Even middle-class businessmen are surprised that generally accepted business practices are very poorly inculcated on Russian soil. It's all very simple. People in Russia are considered mere material for the Great Evolution of the country, its exclusive purpose. People are seen as inputs, counted like objects. Ordinary Russian citizens have to be braced at all times for the machinations of the state, not to trust the authorities under any circumstance, and to rely only on themselves. Everyone knows about the weird games that go on in the Federation Council or the State Duma when it comes to adopting virtually any law. The Russian parliament is not only uninterested in protecting citizens' savings, their health, and general welfare, it constantly fails to pass laws intended to achieve those ends.

Lonely and feeble in their old age, people with broken dreams, lost souls in a drunken daze. This is not a grim dystopia — it is a reality for many Russians. They firmly believe that in the 70s and 80s, there was no binge drinking and banditry going on, and that it's all the result of perestroika and

Yeltsin's reforms. They think the "reforms" were primarily undertaken to rob the people and enrich the "reformers" themselves.

But their memories of those happy days under socialism — those are also just dreams of a social utopia. I grew up in the "heyday of socialism" in one of the standard cookie-cutter residential developments in one of the standard regional cities of Russia. My family lived in a standard gray high-rise building. I went to a big gray school which was designed for 500 students. There were 44 children in my class. My whole childhood was thoroughly permeated with violence. Despite assurances from the Party and government that socialism was flourishing and communism would soon be here, people were mercilessly robbed on the streets and in doorways, teenagers looked up to people who had been in prison, and residents of the barrack-like apartment blocks drank heavily, killing and raping one another along the way. The only thing missing was drugs.

"Where we live, a man's authority is not determined by the number of sheep in his flock," observed General Lebed. In Russia, it's not who has the sheep that matters but who has the shears. This is a country where power and authority over people are very highly valued, so that the average man cannot stand it if he has none. He looks for any position where he can control people. If he's got to be a maintenance worker, at least he can try to be the man on duty at any given time so that he gets to decide whether or not to let people in — a decision which is often based on a whim. The desire to control people extends far beyond the gatehouse and encompasses all possible areas of human life. And this is not only for the sake of a bribe, but also in order to feel power over other individuals. One might even conclude that violent crime in Russia is a form of protest against the state's brutal total control over all spheres of life.

The average person in Russia firmly believes that everyone is stealing, but while those in the lower strata will be penalized for the least infraction, those at the top can get away with anything, scot free. This is why the public consciousness in Russia is no longer just criminal, but moribund. People can easily be bought and manipulated. They won't dig into the origins of events. They will believe any scenario dictated to them. They will follow anyone who is firm and tough. Even Putin's speechwriters are forced to include criminal slang in his speeches, or people don't understand him.

Western people are generally law-abiding. They do not need to be told why, for example, they should pay for the subway, even if no one is checking on them. Law-abiding people benefit society and therefore themselves. Why maintain an army of inspectors and other supervisors when you can just pay your fare? For Russia, it is always a matter of choice. They may consider it expensive, when, in fact, by paying for public transportation, you acquire the right to a certain amount of comfort, cleanliness in the train car, and to the right to know when you'll arrive at your destination.

People in Russia do not know how to count and do not know the value of money. People who don't have a cent and have never had enough money in their hands to live decently set ridiculous financial conditions when they try to get a job, thus putting off any employer. If they try to do any kind of business, they scare off everyone with their prices. Don't be surprised if someone turns down a job offer for good money, when he hasn't been paid at all for a long time. Even so, he can afford to spend six months participate in protests over low wages for six months.

Russian (in fact, still "Soviet") people live an intolerably complicated social life. Other nations, where they don't make things unnecessarily complicated, legalize various situations in life once they have already become very common — as long as no crime is involved. But the Russians are surrounded by a myriad of taboos. This extends to virtually every sphere of life, from sexuality to government administration. Long years under the reign of socialism got everyone used to endless rules and instructions. Now, people who appear to resist all this, and seemingly strive for freedom, punctiliously repeat the Soviet regime's regulations: "Forbidden," "Prohibited," "Not Permitted." This is the basis on which relationships between children and parents are built, and even among adults in many families. The Soviets endowed the nation with their legendary clichés very powerfully, and even many years after their departure from the scene, many young people are being brought up on exactly the same principles and in exactly the same atmosphere of double standards and double morality.

As soon as any politician receives the prefix "ex," which gives him a halo of being persecuted by the Kremlin, he is immediately sought out. In record time after a major official resigns, the governors and leading federal politicians call him up. In Russia, it helps to be persecuted, to be unhappy and to demand compassion. Exposing one's sores in this country is an even greater bonus than criticizing other people's sores.

Processes and behaviors that were typical of Russia during the siege during World War II are once again emerging: the organization of "people's squads," the creation of tenants' councils, stricter control over housing, night watchmen at entrances, the strengthening and increased funding of all law enforcement agencies. Some deputies have even expressed nostalgia for 1941, when those suspected of committing terrorist acts and espionage were shot right in the streets.

Stalin is the most "natural" political synonym for law and order. It took decades to filter out who was who in the wake of civil war, world war, reforms and counter-reforms. At every turn, power and money changed hands; radicals posing as nationalists often turned out to have other motives and foreign influence was always present. Those who failed to win that round called Stalin's era "an order built on blood and bones." But under present circumstances (the 1990s) not only the people but the presidents of republics that make up the Russian Federation dream of returning to Stalin's methods of management. In an interview for the Mariyskaya Pravda newspaper, the President of the republic of Mari El, Vyacheslav Kislitsyn, said: "Do you think it's a coincidence that Stalin is being remembered now? If we had his firm hand on the steering wheel of power, the economy would be stronger and there would be fewer crime victims." Such revelations from a top official do not cause much protest, in spite of all the democratic changes in the country.

In a matter of weeks, terror has turned Russia into a country with a police regime in which many people, especially those from the Caucasus, live in constant fear of arrest, and amateur "house committees" are closely monitoring all the tenants of residential buildings, just like in the Soviet era. Little old ladies sitting at the doorways have time and energy to watch all the comings and goings, relentlessly asking every stranger who tries to enter where, why, and to whom they are going. Society needs their relentless vigilance, their knowledge of every person, which they spread far and wide. People crave curfews, the registration of all residents and visitors at the nearest police station, and the temporary detention of everyone who is not properly registered. Groups of retirees, parliamentary deputies tell us, should participate in the immediate inspection of all empty premises and in the inspection of all outbuildings and automobiles located near residential buildings.

Unlike the Western public, which rebels against any military action, the majority of ordinary Russians are driven by a thirst for revenge. No mass protest movement against the Chechen war has yet been mounted and, apparently, none will be. In NATO countries, public support for the Kosovo operation has gradually waned after several bombings hit the wrong targets. In Russia, however, there is simply no public to which the military would have to answer for the "collateral" damage they might cause. The military, meanwhile, promises not to fall into the trap of peace negotiations and makes no distinction between peaceful and military targets, systematically destroying not bridges, airfields and military garrisons, but entire towns and villages as well. Only mothers whose sons who want to throw themselves into the war in Chechnya protest. In the capital, everyone who looks like they're from the Caucasus Mountain region is considered to be a Chechen, and everyone who resembles a Chechen must be a thug — although there is no evidence yet that Caucasians were involved in any terrorist acts committed in Russian cities. Russia has already engaged in a second war with Chechnya, forgetting what happens when colonial empires fall. Crises can only be resolved by political means, not by sending in the military.

Russia insists that its actions in the Caucasus are like NATO's actions in Kosovo. But as the world learns about Russia's methods of warfare, it becomes clear that such a comparison is out of place. The Kremlin constantly seeks to find some justification for military actions in order to quietly destroy its own people under the pretext that this is an internal Russian affair. It is impossible to live without hypocrisy in Russia. Despite the streams of refugees from Chechnya and the large number of civilian casualties, not a single major Russian politician condemns the military operation in the North Caucasus. More than half the Russian population takes a favorable view of the missile and bomb attacks on Chechnya by federal troops. These are called "constructive" solutions.

Just as in the memorable years of repression, the authorities are appealing to citizens to be vigilant and to monitor everyone and everything. Putin has asked veterans of the Armed Forces and law enforcement agencies to "take it upon themselves" to help out with that. One way or another, they want to impose the idea that there is a state of emergency. Vladimir Putin has a fine sense of the public mood: a strongman with tough rhetoric is what the Russian people like to see in an era of turmoil and terrorist wars.

A wave of "telephone terrorism" swept the country, from Bryansk in Siberia to Petrozavodsk in the northwest. There were countless calls reporting neighbors for suspicious activities, strangers lurking near such and such building, etc. Then the hotlines were flooded with calls stating that a bomb had been planted in the kindergarten, children's hospital, government building or apartment block. Most of these calls were, of course, false alarms or hoaxes. Finally, the hotline had to be closed down.

Several generations of young people in Russia have lived through one war syndrome after another. The dismal succession of generations traumatized by war have suffered social consequences and psychological trauma. The two latest, the Afghan and Chechen wars, have alienated young people to the point that they are unmoved even by the Great Patriotic War, the memory of which was honored by everyone because almost every family suffered losses. So many were killed that bones are still sometimes found in the woods and fields. They died for their homeland, and this enabled their loved ones to stay alive. The younger generations are losing pride in their heritage, they don't know their country's past, they don't remember those who saved it from fascism.

The growing hostility toward the West among Russian young people poses a great danger. One can imagine how strong the ideological pressure is if even young people, who can be considered the first messengers of peace due to their plasticity and openness to different cultures, are drawn into the atmosphere of confrontation and tension. Some summer camps have adjusted their programs to focus on military games, with military-sports and political training in the field. At one military training camp, in which city and district leaders also participate, the officials review their own combat training, practice shooting, and improve their knowledge of their military registration and enlistment specialties. With such sentiments now dominating society, we see that young, promising candidates focused on democratic reforms have no chance. Perhaps a new Cold War is on the horizon.

Russia knows how to "catch up and surpass" the West again. Just as we saw during World War II, when some collectives and even individuals bought an airplane or a tank for the Soviet army, during the war in Yugoslavia a group of Russian businessmen suggested to equip another regiment with Topol-M strategic missiles (NATO classification: SS-X27). The public began to feel like a "besieged fortress." The city administration of Norilsk (a major center for nickel, copper and palladium production) asked non-working retirees to help out by organizing watch committees in their own buildings' entrances. As an encouragement, there was even talk of exempting them from rent payments. The 50,000 workers who are supposed to be smelting metal are busy welding shut sewer manholes all over the city. The Norilsk Mechanical Plant is already fulfilling an order to produce 4,000 grates for manhole covers.

Thousands of those who make up the Russian political class and are well-informed about what is really going on prefer to fool themselves (and others) in order to support their own invented geopolitical notions, such as the idea of an "Orthodox Christian brotherhood." In Moscow, it's politically correct to sympathize not with the Bosnian or Albanian women and children who suffered during the war but with those who shelled them. The Russians are mobilizing to fight an internal enemy, which they identify as Islamic terrorism. However, the real enemy is themselves. The anti-Islamic zeal of the "new Orthodox" Christians is a dangerous trend in a country where 18% of the population is Muslim.[1]

---

[1] According to the Pew Research Center, there were about 13,600,000 Muslims in Russia as of 1990. By 2010, there were over 16 million, with estimates of 18 million only by 2030.

A kind of shadow Islam survived even during the Soviet era of religious persecution, and by the early '90s they had resumed active operations. At the same time, in order to join forces against the Kremlin, political strate-gists of the Caucasian Islamists are looking for allies in Russia itself — first and foremost among Russian nationalists and national-communists. The self-proclaimed "Islamic government of Dagestan" called on "patriots of Russia" to stay out of military adventures against Muslims in the Caucasus but to unite against "oligarchs, democrats" and other protégés of the West. According to the Islamists, the main common enemy is the "Zionist capital. "The Islamic Committee of Russia has called for a "fight against the dictator-ship of the Berezovsky clan," and for the sake of this noble cause they have already made an alliance with the national-patriotic "Movement to Support the Army." A united fundamentalist front is being created in Russia, uniting national patriots, communists and Islamists. Russia is between the hammer and anvil of neo-Bolshevism and pan-Slavism, sunk in nostalgia for the lost empire. Communists and nationalists believe that they should get their hands on the totalitarian government again, which they failed to manage properly before. The only result would be a confrontation between Russia and the rest of the world, and the country would be dragged into war. As the radicalism of both the left and the right opposition grows stronger, it is unclear whether there will be room for moderate politicians anywhere in the government. The same applies to future presidential candidates. It seems that communists and nationalists will be the most influential forces in the future.

Communist leader Gennady Zyuganov makes no secret of the fact that he has agreements with Evgeny Primakov and Yury Luzhkov to develop a unified approach to the country's main problems. They believe that Western humanitarian aid to the Russian people consists of the proverbial "Bush legs," chewing gum, and junk that even the last American vagrant would hesitate to touch. (During the shortages of the early 1990s, President Bush offered Russia a deal on cheap chicken leg quarters, which were quickly dubbed "Bush legs." Shortly Russia became the largest importer of U.S. chicken. There were controversies over the use of antibiotics, disinfectants, proper labelling, etc., but by flooding the market with these big, plump, processed chicken parts, the U.S. wiped out the local chicken producers.)

The worldviews of Primakov, Luzhkov, Shaimiev, and Zyuganov, all former Communists and modern de-facto nationalists, are wolves in sheep's clothing. All of Russia's "new" leaders are old Communist Party function-

https://www.pewforum.org/2011/01/27/table-muslim-population-growth-by-country/

aries, but that's been forgotten. Dmitry Ayatskov, governor of the Saratov region, made a statement proclaiming that the ideas of communism should be implemented in Russia as soon as possible. After promising, at the beginning of his term as governor in the spring of 1996, that "not a single Communist will join the parliament while I'm here," Ayatskov made a U-turn. At a meeting with local branch secretary of the Communist Party of the Russian Federation (CPRF) Valery Rashkin, he said that he had never betrayed the ideas of Communism and that he had never thrown away his party card. Each subsequent politician, often a former Communist, claims to be an alternative to the current system, while the model of power he proposes is fundamentally no different from the previous authoritarian system. Either the clan system will be destroyed, or this system in which the people have no voice and a few oligarchs hold a monopoly on power will gradually spread to all of Russia and the country will be in a terror state.

According to opinion polls, the overwhelming majority of Russians, people of almost all ages and residents of all territories, think the country as a whole is in a crisis. A whole stratum of society (15–20%) has pretty much adapted to extreme conditions and perceive the crisis as natural. In Russia, they are so used to all kinds of threats of explosions and terrorist acts that they are quite calm whenever such things come up, as long as it no one at the top is involved. The police and the FSB scarcely bother to investigate such incidents. One in seven inhabitants of the country is in a state of apathy. He has nothing to rely on morally. His own live story certainly is not inspiring.

The Russians buried the royal family in the Peter and Paul Cathedral of St. Petersburg on July 17, 1998, in order to demand the royal's assets in the West. The sum at issue is approximately $400 billion. Half of the city of Nice, including the port, was once the property of the Russian Empire, as well as the Athos Monastery in Greece, the Russian Cathedral in Denmark, and a number of holy places in Israel. In London alone, there are 5.5 tons of personal royal gold sitting in the Bering Brothers Bank. Advisor to Deputy Prime Minister Boris Nemtsov Aksyuchits, who headed the government commission for the burial of the royal remains, was immediately sent to London to demand money from the Bering brothers: they said, we've buried the tsar — give us back the gold! More than a year has passed since the burial of the remains of the royal family. No one goes to visit the grave, and it's not well maintained.

The religious component of Russian life is exhausted by the constant nihilism, the denial of anything and everything, which is evident everywhere. According to an all-Russia poll conducted in September 1999 by the independent ROMIR research center, the least important thing for Russians is to practice their religion (50.8% of the population). Only 1.9% of respondents said that practicing their religion is the most important thing in life. At the same time, the majority of Muscovites dream of holding a ministerial position, and some would love to join a criminal gang or become prostitutes for foreign currency.

In Zheleznogorsk, Krasnoyarsk region, blatantly pro-fascist and chauvinist leaflets and newspapers are sold and distributed quite openly near the main movie theater. They say things like "Attack the bourgeois!" and "We support murderers who kill businessmen and TV presenters. Hired killers are workers, just like miners, and what they're doing will make it easier for us to clean up the planet. Much more effective than mere strikers." The Zheleznogorsk FSB and police don't do anything about this rampant political extremism. And this is not the only place where fascists and nationalists openly gather and demonstrate all day long. Extremists gather near the popular Gostiny Dvor shopping center in St. Petersburg, and near the Revolution Square metro station in central Moscow — that is, practically in every city in Russia!

The fascists are going after young people, too. "If we don't get their attention now," nationalist activists explain, "then tomorrow they'll only be thinking about Snickers, lollipops, and Disney." In Volgograd, the National Bolshevik Party (NBP) created a children's organization named for Lavrenty Beria, said to be Soviet Russia's bloodiest executioner, the chief of the NKVD (analogue of the KGB) at the time of Stalin. It is hard to believe that anyone would volunteer to join this organization, but already more than ten kids between 10 and 14 years old are wearing armbands with National Bolshevik symbols, repeating that Beria was the coolest and that everybody was afraid of him: he helped Stalin, stole the atom bomb from the Americans and beat the Chechens. The teenagers are engaged in propaganda; some of them write articles in the nationalist newspaper Limonka and publish their own homemade newspaper, Limonka and Dynamite.

If this continues, who knows which form of extremism the West will be fighting in the 21st century — Islamic radicals or a form of Slavic "Nazism"![1]

---

[1] Little did the author know how intensely "Slavic Nazism" would be pushed in Ukraine!

3. It's All the West's Fault

Most Russians think that it's time to get rid of the petty and alien politicians oriented toward the West. The West has cheated and robbed Russia. Western bankers helped hundreds of financial speculators and crooks take billions of dollars out of the country. Russia has become worse off and poorer than it was 10 years ago, and its debts to the West have multiplied. Now, Russia must grovel and beg for new loans in order to pay interest on old ones. And they don't see that this is because the Russian authorities have failed to create a legal basis for a normal financial situation in the country. No. Nor do they think that much of the money from the International Monetary Fund and humanitarian aid is stolen or injected into unprofitable businesses. That is not the point at all. It's the West, the West that has been talking so long about the benefits of democracy and a market economy that would quickly provide Russia with prosperity and abundance; talk intended to destroy Russia's economy and turn it into an appendage of its raw materials. [Thirty years later, it's plain that this is exactly what was planned, and it very nearly worked.]

The Central Bank of Russia's official report on currency regulation and capital flight suggests that the main reasons for capital flight are the liberalization ofthe Russian economy in the 1990s and the policy of the IMF, which does not allow the Central Bank to block the exporting of money abroad. The Central Bank is testing the ground before a possible tightening of currency control. And it names the main enemy of all such good intentions — the International Monetary Fund.

According to them, the shocking rise in prices should not be blamed on the native government but on the International Monetary Fund, which gives loans to Russia. It is their fault prices are going up. The IMF's demands for tougher financial policies and liberalization of the currency market are at odds with the direction Russia is taking. The country is being led by a stubborn hand and not in the direction where the IMF's model applies (in the direction of open markets and free enterprise), but toward the concentration of all the assets and efforts to make a new leap in the struggle for world domination. Well, they say, we need the money, and the government has no other option but to comply with the IMF's conditions. However, passing laws is a time-consuming procedure. You can make promises and then not fulfill them. Moreover, the money can be spent on other things than what was agreed upon. The main thing is to get it, even if means the country will face economic and political isolation. You can always say later: "And what did we tell you, didn't the IMF get an order to crush and destroy Russia financially?" Nevertheless, America must give Russia more and more loans because "it is she" who ruined the economy and brought the country to this state.

The West is artificially imposing a system of values on Russia. It is doing this for one purpose only: to reduce Russia to a miserable and insignificant state, with the help of an alien and sordid culture, ideology, and system. There is even a specific goal — to reduce Russia's population (147 million in 1990) to 50 million people. What Hitler failed to achieve, the West is now doing by means of cultural and humanitarian aid. The State Duma deputies see it, and they blame the International Monetary Fund, the International Bank for Reconstruction and Development, the Organization for International Cooperation and Development and the European Bank for Reconstruction and Development for the reduction and genocide of the Russian population.

Such views are shared by most of the country's intellectuals, including economists. In their understanding, the West has been working on this hard and long, deliberately and painstakingly. The famous economist and philosopher Alexander Leontiev, the writer Solzhenitsyn, etc., come back home saying that they would never have returned to Russia if things were as good in the West as we are told. Leontiev, for example, said that he could not stay in the West after all that the West has done and is doing to Russia.

[Leontiev and Solzhenitsyn eventually changed their minds, but many members of the fledgling middle class, scholars and others with international contacts have been seduced by the relative prosperity shown in American movies and TV programs, a prosperity that is inevitably associated with "democracy" and "free markets," despite the facts.[1] The friendly smiles and

---

[1] By contrast, the US economy in the early years focused on mercantilist, protectionist policies — high tariffs, which particularly benefited the industrial and banking centers.

naïve, trustworthy do-gooders who are sent over in cultural and academic exchanges reinforce the idea that these people have only good intentions. But the bulk of these individuals do not represent Washington; and Washington is only using them.]

When Zinoviev returned home to Russia in the mid-1990s after years of absence, he said that as long as the Soviet Union existed, Western Europe had been protected from the Americanization that has been so destructive of the best achievements of the Old World: liberalism, creative pluralism, freedom of thought. To pro-Westerners, that was heresy. Yet already at that time, Western Europe had practically capitulated to the United States. The cynical US and NATO aggression against Serbia finally convinced him of the need to return to his homeland. History has become predictable and projectable. Bombing Yugoslavia was second nature, like going to the store for a bottle of vodka. The fate of Serbia may well befall Russia too: the American masters and their Western European servants will stop at nothing to break Russia's resistance, to wipe it off the face of the earth and erase it from the memory of humanity. Their aim is to reduce the Russian people to the condition of an ethnic tribe of no more than 30–50 million people, not even capable of self-government.

At a press conference in Moscow, Alexander Zinoviev showed signs of suffering from the opposite illusion, inspired perhaps by homesickness and an idealistic patriotism. He stated that there are more people with a high level of intelligence in Russia than in any other country; while he concluded that Russians need a dictatorship. Dictatorship and dictatorship again, he stressed. But he qualified that, specifying an intellectual dictatorship. But please note that there has never been an intellectual dictatorship in the history of mankind. Dictatorships most often turn bloody and evil. So you have to look very carefully at the man who calls for a dictatorship. At the same time, Zinoviev asked not to confuse him with that other returnee, the writer Alexander Solzhenitsyn: "I am not Solzhenitsyn. There is a huge difference between us. He is a man from the past, and he carries obscurantism with him wherever he goes." Zinoviev sees himself as a man from the future.

However, immediately upon his return to the country, Alexander Zinoviev came face to face with the harsh Russian reality and shed some of his starry-eyed nostalgia. He even accused the Central Election Committee of practicing persecution for political beliefs. The writer was number one from Moscow on one party's federal list. The Central Election Committee found a way to deny him registration: due to his failure to provide his 1998 income certificate (according to the tax service, Zinoviev was supposed to show more than 30,000 rubles). The Supreme Court of Russia declared the decision of the Central Election Committee legal. The philosopher promised to appeal against the Supreme Court's decision to the board of cassation and then to the European Court of Human Rights. Olga Zinovieva, the writer's wife, was so outraged by Russia's lawlessness that she declared that she was "ready to challenge the members of the election committee to a duel. This is how all the nationalist appeals of intellectualizing philosophers end up with threats to seek the truth in Europe or America.

In today's Russia, the real politicking is not done out in the open, in the State Duma, the government, or the presidential administration. It evolves in various formal and informal associations, united around the principles of anti-Western ideology and bearing the patina of a kind of elitism. The guiding and inspirational composition of such associations consists of former Party (communist) and Komsomol activists, KGB and FSB employees, and directors of military enterprises, who were once those same Party or Komsomol functionaries themselves. They have free access to state officials and criminal bosses alike, and use the services of one or the other when necessary. These associations are usually involved in accumulating money and developing an array of military technologies — from missiles to military parapsychology.

Bank funds and state subsidies are used to run such centers, but they also accept contributions from companies that have accumulated their own working capital. If this does not work, but the firm has a lot of money, then "their" officials from ministries and departments step in. They try to use restrictions, fines, delays in issuing permits, and sometimes direct threats to force the firm in question to cooperate. Friendly criminal groups can also be involved in the process. If even this fails, they may call in the "heavy artillery": former and current officers of the all-powerful KGB / FSB with their connections and skills. Any entrepreneur in Russia knows that while you may be able to pay off gangster racketeers, and even pay monthly protection money to save your business, you can't pay off the gangster structures associated with the former KGB. This is revenge on the part of ideological opponents and, as a rule, it goes all the way: the enterprise is bankrupted, the money is transferred to other accounts and the person is destroyed morally or physically. If a businessman suspects that these people are after him, he drops everything and flees abroad, taking the cash with him. Numerous directors of banks and financial companies, as well as politicians who are no longer in office, offer striking examples of this. But well-run businesses also go under from time to time because a significant portion of their finances go to ideology, and there is no way to patch up those financial holes.

It should be added that these organizations are closely intertwined with each other and their leaders know each other. They collect information about any inventions that might have military applications. Their numbers include engineers, inventors, and philosophers, as well as people who develop psychotronic weapons and methods of psychic influence on people. As a rule, they actively maintain contact with various kinds of armed groups inside the country, often using them as the basis for security services for banks and reputable Russian firms, thus penetrating into legal businesses and gradu‑ ally bringing them under their control. The data show that as much as 70% of businesses are thus controlled. These associations are a real force to be reckoned with, ready to throw real support behind any official whom they consider to be close to them in spirit. This is where well‑known political figures in Russia seek support, and this is why they go for nationalist and anti‑American slogans.

The Council for Foreign and Defense Policy (SVOP in Russian) was registered as a public organization on 25 February 1992. It was created by a group of people connected with the defense industry and security agencies, and then a group of editors and journalists joined them. Dmitry Rurikov, former presidential aide on international affairs, helped register the orga‑ nization. *Nezavisimaya Gazeta* became SVOP's political mouthpiece. When SVOP members are accused of having links with the special services, they say: if we are the elite, we should serve our state, and the special services and law enforcement agencies are the foundation of this state. And no apologies for that!

Members of the Council call themselves the "political elite of Russia" and they swear not to harm any other member of the Council — they do not "turn in" their own. This dictates many of the SVOP's foreign and domestic political initiatives. It was the SVOP that led the October 1993 military confrontation in Moscow through Rutskoy's closest aide, Andrei Fedorov, who was a member of the SVOP; under the supervision of Primakov, head of the Foreign Intelligence Service (SVR), they initiated the dismissal of Foreign Minister Andrei Kozyrev, and they directed Primakov's U‑turn over the Atlantic during the Yugoslav crisis and the threat that Russia would use its nuclear weapons.

The most important thing for the members of the Council for Foreign and Defense Policy is to make informal contacts between its members and civil society groups and organizations, and to support the useful activities of members of the Council — not "socially useful," i.e., useful to society, but mutually useful to the members of the Council. Sometimes, political conflicts in Russia are nothing more than theater. The extensive list of SVOP members includes former and current employees of the presidential administration — Yastrzhembsky, Zverev, Shabdurasulov, Prikhodko, etc.; employees of the

Foreign Ministry, headed by Deputy Minister Karasin; numerous bankers and businessmen, including Tsikalyuk, the general director of the Military Insurance Company. Among the politicians in the SVOP, we see Glazyev[1] and Livshits, Zatulin and Khakamada, Podberezkin and Murashov, and members of rival information teams of Gusinsky and Berezovsky.

The organization is built on Masonic principles and is notable for its internal discipline. One of their most secret goals, which they try to disguise as a joke, is that by 2010 all ministers appointed in Russia must be members of the SVOP. That is when they will be able to control the real work of the regime. One can guess what kind of regime this will be, bearing in mind that the leaders of the security services are standing right there behind the members of the organization.

In sum, a narrow socio-political caste of former functionaries of the Communist Party, the Komsomol and the KGB has formed in the Russian state, which attracts young people to its ranks on the principle of "whether they accept the idea of the great mission of Russia," which is understood as the superiority of Russians over others. Jews are conspirators, people from the Caucasus are thieves, Americans are decadent, but Russians are deeper souls and guardians of the world's intellect. Weren't the Russians behind all the most significant inventions, weren't the Russians the first to say so? At the same time, oddly enough, nobody points out that in order to become famous and to bring something forth into the world, to receive the Nobel Prize, a Russian must at the very least get out of Russia. There are certain groups within the government that cultivate these attitudes and are eager to pass them on to one another, to impose them on the rest of the people, pushing out anyone who doesn't share these views.

In fact, it's almost impossible to break into Russia's ruling circles if you don't share this mindset. Russian philosophers are pushing the government to play on the differences between the United States and Europe. Russia can play a part in protecting Western Europe from "total Americanization," they write, putting Russia on the list of countries committed to the ideals of Western European civilization. Russia is at war with savages in Chechnya, ultimately trying to do the best thing for Europe. Mikhail Margelov, head of the Russian Formative Center, called Russia "an outpost of world civilization in countering the most serious challenge of the late 20th century,

---

[1] By 2022, Sergey Glazyev once a darling of the West, had woken up and was fighting Central Bank head Nabiullina and demanding major changes, insisting that "much remains to be done to strengthen national sovereignty in the economy." *Sanctions and Sovereignty*, by Sergey Glazyev, February 25, 2022 at https://rentry.co/sanctions-and-sovereignty

international terrorism. Russia plays an exclusive role as a shield between two hostile races."

At the same time, ethnic Russian politicians believe it is the West that is trying to set Russia against the Muslim world, so it should reinforce ties with Iran, Iraq, and also China.

Anti-Western sentiments are particularly strong in the army, security agencies, defense industries, and veterans' organizations. Retired army, police and special services men meet across the country in organized councils and committees. The All-Russian Organization of Veterans of War, Labor, Armed Forces and Law Enforcement Agencies was established more than 20 years ago and now has forty million people. That is enough people to transmit their opinions to the entire population of Russia. Russian society, like American society, generally absorbs nationalistic clichés like a sponge and is keen to designate a common enemy. Russian historians still believe the Allied forces destroyed Dresden in 1945 and used atomic bombs in Japan mainly as a show of force to intimidate the Soviet Union, since those actions were completely unnecessary from a military standpoint. The Soviet Union never viewed the confrontational position of the West as a confrontation between the West and the USSR, per se. Great Power politics viewed it as a confrontation between the West and Russia specifically. That is why the other 14 republics of the USSR were considered unreliable and their leaders' actions were closely monitored. The same thing is going on now: Russia supplies President Lukashenko (of Belarus) with all kinds of advisors on how to influence the population. Ironically, it was the Belarusian leaders who suffered the most during the Soviet period because of their desire for closer integration with Europe. Two chairmen of the Central Committee of the Communist Party of Belarus died in Soviet times under unclear circumstances.

As our economy is being prepared for the privatization of public property, property not intended to steer profits to individuals but held for the public good, Russian newspapers are full of the passages like this: "We are all subject to powerful manipulative, disruptive technologies from overseas 'experts on Russia.' As an example, there is continuous meddling from abroad in the process of making fundamental state decisions on the budget and the Tax Code. Westerners are constantly telling us what to do and how to do it, in every sphere of public and economic life. It was they who required the implementation of disastrous economic policies as a condition for obtaining future loans. It is they who issued management directives (including downright instructions) that are sent to the ministries, obviously hasty translations from English. All this limits Russia's defense capability, paralyzes its economy, reduces people's standard of living, and destabilizes the sociopolitical situation in the country. All in accordance with the interests of our foreign 'friends.' Every year, starting with Yegor Gaidar,[1] our country adopts a budget according to a formula (that even in the abstract is obviously destructive) imposed by advisors from Harvard and other laboratories, including the CIA…" It's true, massive amounts of money were also squandered on unthinkable economic and ideological experiments, theft, and the war in the Caucasus.

Not surprisingly, a decade after "democratization" Russia is even more isolated from the world than the Soviet Union once was. Today's friends of Russia include Belarus, Serbia, and Iraq. China's totalitarian regime with a market economy is a dream come true for Russian officials of both the old and the new breeds. For the sake of friendship with China, Russia has taken an unprecedented step: in the final declaration after the meeting of the five countries bordering Bishkek, human rights violations were declared an internal affair of each state. Boris Yeltsin, who was the last to arrive in Bishkek, arrived for his morning meeting with Jiang Zemin five minutes before the Chinese leader, although the latter was the first to arrive in the Kyrgyz capital. Thus Yeltsin demonstrated to the West the potential for rapprochement between Russia and China. To quote Yeltsin: "I am ready for a fight with everyone, especially the Westerners."

Russia plans to increase trade in all types of weapons in all major world markets. The goal is to regain lost ground and increase activity in this area. No one in Russia seriously believes that weapons supplied to Iran or Iraq, for example, could ever be a threat to Russia via Islamic fundamentalists. At the joint Russian–Iranian diplomatic meetings, they say that "Russia and Iran, remaining the leading countries both in the region and in the world, can and must do everything in their power to prevent a third force, NATO, led by the US, from coming to the Caspian basin. But an imperfect rebellious state is not only unable to stop terrorism, but with its actions only encourages and strengthens it.[2]

The waves of terrorism, generated by the authorities themselves, make us look for foreign saboteurs inside the country. A "plan to destroy" our largest

---

[1] Upon the break-up of the Soviet Union, Gaidar was responsible for the Shock Therapy reforms that caused hyper-inflation and plunged the population into profound poverty. He was advised in this by Milton Friedman's acolyte Jeffrey Sachs, who was also instrumental in Bolivia's 1980s shock therapy reforms. "As always happened with economic shock therapy, a small group of wealthy elites became far richer while everyone else became much poorer," Darya Sinusoid has observed.

[2] Clearly, their crystal ball failed to warn that Islamic terrorists could be instrumentalized by the West; but these leaders did foresee the increasingly brazen Western incursions into the Black Sea and the Azov Sea, which seemed unthinkable 30 years ago.

shipping company on the Pacific, Vostoktransflot, which has hardly been a shining success in recent years, has been uncovered. The company's board of directors claimed that a secret operation by foreign special services was going on, aiming to totally annihilate the Russian fleet in the Pacific Ocean. Meanwhile, the company is on the verge of bankruptcy due to mismanagement and theft. It is very simple — the special services are selling ships cheaply, stealing money from the company, stealing equipment and products, and kicking foreign shareholders out of the company. Similarly, a powerful information campaign has been launched in Chelyabinsk in favor of liquidating the newspaper *Chelyabinsk Rabochiy*, which has allegedly sold out to the Americans and threatens to reveal defense secrets in the region. This is all because 1% of the newspaper is owned by the American Foundation for the Support of Independent Media, which made Andrei Kosilov, vice-governor of the Chelyabinsk region, suspicious.[1]

There is one more addition to the picture of American-phobia in Russia. The authorities of the village of Rovenki ordered organizations and residents to destroy the American maple trees which had been thriving in the village and had become a breeding ground for American white butterflies. The "American aggressors" were to be replaced by the Russian national birch trees.

The government agencies are just as quick to shift the blame. The State Duma can unanimously pass a resolution (with one or two abstentions) that would have made the bloody prosecutor of the 1930s, Vyshinsky, jealous, condemning the United States for state terrorism against Saddam Hussein's regime, independent of any norms of civilized international communication. The Foreign Ministry is seriously accusing the United States of undermining the post-1945 world order established by the United Nations, i.e., the years of the Cold War.

But while Russian politicians threaten punishment to the rest of the world and hope for a miraculous economic revival, the children of the country's previous leaders are taking American citizenship. "This is a great country, and it is an honor to live here," Sergei Khrushchev said of the United States in a *New York Times* interview four decades after his father pledged to bury capitalism. Some time later, Sergei Khrushchev took the oath of allegiance as an American citizen.

---

[1] *Numero Cinq* has an entertaining exposé on this and far more, at http://numerocinqmagazine.com/2014/06/04/the-world-aristocratic-governor-of-the-year-report-from-vladivostok-russell-working/

4. On Exclusion and Exclusivity

No socio-political formation, such as a state, can survive without a unifying idea. Figuratively speaking, communist ideology in Russia had its own religion (the religion of a bright future), temples (the mausoleum, places associated with Lenin and Party activity), clergy (leaders of Party cells), compulsory rituals (enrollment in the October Children group, Young Pioneers, Komsomol, formal processions, parades, Saturday volunteer work), service books (*A Short Course of the History of the Communist Party*) and other attributes, and held the minds of the masses firmly in its hands. After the collapse of Communist ideology, Orthodox Christianity did not have time to fill the vacancy in people's minds. In fact, because the vast majority of priests collaborated with the KGB, and people simply did not believe them. Fantasy beliefs took their place. The notion that Russia could shake off the burden of seventy years of Soviet rule and become a full-fledged democratic state with a market economy in just ten years was not realistic. The country had been in decline since Soviet times, and the Gorbachev and Yeltsin regimes only masked the further deepening of the crisis. Ten years after the collapse of communism, Russia still has no free market, no capitalism, no rule of law. Billions of dollars allocated have done little to transform Russia into a prosperous democratic state governed by the rule of law, and it is among the countries with the highest levels of corruption and crime.

The main ideological legacy that communism has left Russia is nationalism, a desire to pit its ethnic and cultural identity against others, to demonstrate its superiority and to proclaim it has a special historical mission. Contrary to the illusions of the West, most Russians see the West not as a partner, but as a potential adversary. And this is not the fault of the Yeltsin regime's incompetence and corruption alone. "There is a deep conviction in Russia that it has its own historical mission," are the words of former U.S. Secretary of State Henry Kissinger. Russian diplomacy continues to pursue its traditional goals in the international arena, seeking in every way to undermine American influence. The Russian mediator in any conflict, whoever he is, [correctly] assumes that by helping NATO, he will damage Russia's prestige on the world stage. The U.S. has helped Russia integrate into the international community economically. Foreign policy was not given the attention it deserved and, as a result, Russian citizens had the impression that their country was under colonial tutelage . The Russian march on Pristina during the Yugoslav war was also supposed to show that the Russian army was not a mass of underpaid ragamuffin soldiers, generals and officers, selling their equipment on the black market. The speedy redeployment of Russian paratroopers to Pristina airport was hailed in Russia as a heroic deed, restoring Russia's military glory, which faded after the fall of the Soviet Union. At the crucial moment of the Kosovo negotiations, Clinton and Yeltsin appeared to be deciding Europe's fate by telephone, as if the Cold War were just around the corner. Not the United Nations, not the G7, not the European Union, not even NATO, but, as before, the two warring powers — the United States and Russia — are playing the main game on the European continent. That is, in fact, their confrontation continues. Nevertheless, in Yugoslavia, Moscow once again deceived itself and others, presenting failure as a "brilliant" success and thus cutting off the possibility for itself to at least partially remedy the situation. What "brilliant" participation of Russian troops in the peacekeeping operation in Kosovo can we talk about? Either they have lost all contact with reality, or they are deliberately whipping up hysteria of national exclusiveness and invincibility.

Many Russian thinkers see America as an unnatural, technocratic civilization, where the people are not "a people" that grew up in their own homeland but came as migrants, raw material, inputs for processing. In Europe, first there was nature, then there was a people, then there was culture; in America, everything was planted artificially. That is why America is always opposed to Eurasia as a whole — technical, artificial civilization against life. Wars are virtual for Americans; they do not see the bloody results of their actions. For them it is just a game. From the point of view of Russian scientists, the Americans arranged mass ethnic cleansing, destroying Indians in order to build their artificial civilization.

But... The Russians and Americans have never been at war with each other. It was America who first gave the Soviet Union a helping hand when the Germans were at the gates of Moscow. It provided considerable aid under the Lend–Lease Treaty, invited Russia along with the rest of Europe to participate in the Marshall Plan, and, in the early years of Perestroika, opened a line of concessional lending and humanitarian aid. The Russian response was to boast that America had managed to steal the secret of the atomic bomb, that a mass of Soviet spies worked in every conceivable American government agency, and that there was a time when everyone was afraid of the Soviet "nuclear club." As *Trud* [Labor] newspaper wrote on December 7, 1999, that the beginning of perestroika in the USSR was characterized by a ruthless crackdown on secret agents among our politicians, diplomats, big businessmen, and career officers of the KGB and GRU. Two dozen officers known to be spying for the United States were hastily arrested and shot.

Today, Russian economists are talking deliriously about plans to deliver a crushing blow to the dollar by transferring Russian debts into euros. Deputies and ministers are constantly planning ephemeral "triangles" and other "multipolar world" political figures to curb American hegemony. Anti-Americanism in foreign policy today has become akin to anti-Semitism in domestic policy. No one seems to mention that the story of the creation of the NATO bloc dates back to the months-long Soviet blockade of West Berlin. They also prefer to turn a blind eye to the fact that it was America's help that transformed post-World War II Germany and Japan into what they are today. [The author seems oblivious to the fact that those two nations are still under occupation. The US has about 40 army installations in Germany and 84 military installations in Japan.[1]]

The socio-economic situation in Russia today is deteriorating. One budget after another is adopted for political reasons, leading to one crisis after another as expenditures always exceed revenues. The government tries to plug the hole in the budget by seeking big loans. The budgets are drafted in near-total secrecy by both houses of parliament - the Federation Council and the State Duma. In addition, each year's budget is developed by the Ministry of Finance of Russia without taking into account the recommendations of sectoral agencies. The budget ignores the interests of the subjects of the Federation. And the regions' budgets are adopted according to the same vicious logic. Even anecdotal evidence makes it clear that cash flows are cut off from the real production sector, and tax collection for the federal budget becomes predominant while the regions have to literally survive.

The demoralized state and the army are going downhill. This is primarily due to Moscow's inability to admit its weakness. Russia is hurt by the fact that it is no longer considered a great power. Russia can no longer count on easy military victories. The situation could worsen if the Russian authorities

---

[1] https://en.wikipedia.org/wiki/List_of_United_States_Army_installations_in_Germany

do not abandon illusory notions of their own power. Despite the external stability of the Russian economy, we have to wait for the next crisis. Any postponement of payments increases the debt, it doesn't reduce it. Plus, the strengthening of the ruble does not help Russian exporters: we have to sell more oil! On top of this, Russia has had crop failures every year. And we have to get our winter provisions from Canada and the U.S. again.

The West should be aware that Russia will not be an equal partner in the foreseeable future. And in the event of another upheaval that could entail the collapse of the Russian state, the International Monetary Fund loans will not help either. All the Russian officials who negotiate are skillfully using Western naïveté and fears to get more and more cash infusions. It is very much like the condition of an addict, only the whole country is in this role. It has its own highs and its own withdrawal pains, which no one else can understand. Moscow is ready to make any promises to the West just to get new loans, but it is not going to fulfill them. For all this, it is argued that if Russia is far from pursuing a sensible economic policy and none of the Russian governments has implemented its own economic program, it is all the fault of the IMF, which imposes its solutions and does not take into account Russian peculiarities.

What are these Russian peculiarities? Maybe virtual state activity? This is when the TV shows a lot of meetings going on, or there's a huge amount of verbal activity in newspaper articles, a lot of promises and stern faces, but nothing happens in the real sector. Or everything that does happen is done wrong, in the wrong place and by the wrong means. Everything is virtual, from the budget to the stabilization of society and the political skill of various political figures. Virtual activity has clearly replaced all other activities, not only in government but in all other branches of power. Talks, meetings, interviews, press conferences, statements, rebuttals, and televised debates have all successfully and effectively supplanted the real business that numerous participants in the governing process are so strenuously urging simple-minded citizens to pursue.

The constitutional process is being adjusted to the interests of certain individuals, and this undermines the population's already marginal trust in the authorities. So far in Russia, they are still trying to hand down power by inheritance. The active part of society has not yet developed any clearer system of resistance to this than consistent "self-reliance" and spontaneous patriotism. The unfolding election campaign exacerbated the already difficult situation, as the political parties and public associations have increasingly looked to violent methods to achieve political goals. Criminals enter the political arena and successfully merge with the political state structures. Criminal groups spend a lot of money to promote their protégés in the legislative and executive branches. They are most interested in the fuel and energy complex and the banking sector. Corrupt authorities create a favorable condition for the development of organized crime. The expansion of the shadow sector of the economy and the growth of criminal structures inevitably lead them to a struggle for power.

Many parties willingly list as candidates bosses of the shadow economy, even those who are wanted and have left the country. They like to have leaders from the shadow economy among their ranks because they represent a real, powerful economy. This is also a condition of Russian society — electoral lists including people with a criminal past (and present). They can do anything: they can show up drunk or in the most dubious surroundings. They can be infiltrated into the power structure quite quickly. First, a commercial structure is created with a name like "Supplies and Sales Department." Within a few months, the director of this firm becomes deputy mayor of the city in charge of the same supply and sales. Moreover, this position is created especially for him. Following this logic, he goes on to create a company called "Regional Duma," and then the "Government of the Russian Federation," and then the entire country is embezzled or sold. The government in Russia is not a political entity but a commercial firm and ideological grouping. People are competing to gain a controlling interest in the form of responsible positions in government posts and in the management of large para-state monopolies.

The political machinations at the court of any Soviet or Russian ruler can be likened to the intrigues at the tsar's court. Politicians are busy consolidating their own power and popularity, even if their path is strewn with more and more political corpses. The victims of these machinations are officials, especially prime ministers, who are appointed, dismissed, rehabilitated, and dismissed again. But the most important victim is the country's population, whose needs are completely ignored. As a result of the constant dismissals of moderate politicians, the Russian authorities have succeeded in making sure that the main contenders for the presidency are the opponents of democracy.

Following the crisis of socialism, as a social and economic system in Russia, various kinds of religious and moral concepts and pseudo-concepts began to spread. The spiritual sphere is becoming more and more primitive with a concomitant narrowing of opportunities to find options for moral and ethical guidelines. There are dozens of pseudo-parties in the country that do not express anyone's interests but their own. These parties ignore the socioeconomic interests of any electoral groups of the population.

The position of the intelligentsia take the position that it is possible to live in a pigsty full of filth and not get dirty, keeping oneself out of reach of humiliation and dumbing down. At the same time, people are losing what little self-respect they have left. At one pole, there is the super-smart and super-mannered intelligentsia; at the other pole, there is the unhappy common man mired in drunkenness, theft, and crime, whose well-being the same intelligentsia seems not to care about. And this is not the last problem of Russia. Considering themselves the bearers of a special spirit, the "intelligent stratum" of Russia endlessly spins theories, each one more fantastic than the last, but not for practical application and not for the well-being of the people. All of this is as virtual as the idea itself: to live in a pigsty without getting dirty.

The creeping revenge of the communist idea with elements of coercion and class struggle — this is how the reality of our day is defined. A gradual slide toward total control of every inhabitant, toward a world of controlled distribution, rations and coupons, toward a world of ruthless extermination of those who doubt the truth of the only true doctrine. Today, the pro-communist majority in the Duma and the government are like-minded and partners in the effort to return Russia to its totalitarian past. The ideology of totalitarian grandeur calls for brandishing weapons, throwing billions of rubles at weapons systems, and covering up unresolved social and economic problems with militant rhetoric about threats from foreign and domestic enemies. Western loans are of no use if the country squanders its economic resources on a pointless war in Chechnya, the victory of which, as it always turns out later, is highly questionable. The Russian military is driven by a desire for revenge and a desire to retaliate for the shameful peace that ended the last war in Chechnya. Politicians, on the other hand, are more concerned about the upcoming elections and are willing to risk inciting a major conflict in the Caucasus in order to achieve their objectives. Neither of them is embarrassed by the huge military losses, the numerous civilian casualties, the international isolation of Russia, and the flows of refugees.

Moscow builds its foreign policy in its own image — based on a strong personality. That is why the Russian establishment has so many friends among dictators in the world. Anti-democratic regimes commit their atrocities with the tacit consent of Moscow. Russia's leaders prefer to close ranks in a vague solidarity with regimes like Slobodan Milosevic.[1] This is evidenced by the general tone of Russian politicians and the media, who see literally

---

[1] They intervened to oppose another color revolution, wherein a thriving multi-ethnic country saw its internal divisions fanned to the point of combustion; the country was broken into statelets too small to demand a seat at any table. Logically enough, Russia sided with the Slavic, Orthodox Christians against Western-backed separatists.

everything as just a figment of Western propaganda. The war in Yugoslavia and the Caucasus are not the cause of Russia's increasing destabilization, but they have undoubtedly given the process a certain boost. Once again, the underlying anti-Western and anti-democratic sentiments in Russian society have clearly manifested themselves. Russia's weakness poses too grave a danger to be ignored. Moscow cannot give up its imperial ambitions, which contrast sharply with its economic and military potential, which does not allow Russia to effectively defend its national interests.

Whenever there is a political or governmental squabble, as the unforgettable Russian bard Vysotsky sang, "the Jews are to blame." Many observers point out that there are more and more Jews in the power structures, especially starting with Yeltsin's entourage. The *Boston Globe* proudly pointed out that Harvard experts were advising Russia in shifting to capitalism.[1] The head of Harvard's program, Andrei Shleifer, was is a protégé of Treasury Secretary Larry Summers. "Privatization stands as the centerpiece of Russia's economic-reform program," the *Globe* eagerly noted, promoting the groundless belief that privatization of public assets is equal to "reform" and that market capitalism is equivalent to the magical twins, democracy and prosperity. Arguably, the direct opposite is true.[2] [It's considered to be knee-jerk anti-Semitism to mention it, but outsiders generally overlook how Jewish Russian oligarchs stole state assets and spirited the funds abroad.]

The groups of Westernizers (i.e., those who insist on a common path with Europe) and Slavophiles (those who stand up for their own special path for the Russian nation and Russian state) that have historically emerged since the last century still exist in a very modified form today. One of these, called the "family," includes Yeltsin's daughter Tatiana Dyachenko, media mogul Boris Berezovsky, and Anatoly Chubais. [In 2022, Chubais finally, publicly, showed where his loyalties lie by passing his major real estate holdings to "friends" and emigrating to Israel.]

All are known as ideologues of pro-Western liberalism. This is one of the reasons for their constant denigration in the "patriotic" press and in "patriotic" society. The other, conditionally Slavophile grouping includes

---

[1] *Globe*, (9/22/92), "Red Square Turns to Crimson."

[2] See also: FAIR https://fair.org/home/harvards-best-and-brightest-aided-russias-economic-ruin/ "But the so-called reforms were more about wealth confiscation than wealth creation. Privatization, which had substantial input from U.S.-paid Harvard advisers, fostered the concentration of property in a few Russian hands and opened the door to widespread corruption and funneling of monies to Western banks.... Harvard appears to have benefited from HIID's Russia connection... the university's endowment fund, was allowed to participate in choice auctions of Russian government property, despite the fact that foreign investors were supposed to be excluded under auction rules."

former Prime Minister Yevgeny Primakov (a Middle East expert, family name originally Finkelstein), associated with Moscow Mayor Yuri Luzhkov, who, in turn, maintains close relations with another media mogul Vladimir Gusinsky. The long-standing struggle between Slavophiles and Western- izers in Russia has become extremely aggressive, with the former holding a clear advantage. According to public opinion polls as of January 1999, 43% of Russians support the National Socialist groups, of which there are already over 200. The specifics of Russian history are such that ever since the Civil War any compatriot living abroad has been regarded as a traitor to his home- land, a renegade. At present this is not entirely true, but nevertheless this stereotype is very stable.

As a kind of unifying philosophy, designed in the minds of its creators to reconcile the Westerners and Slavophiles, in the '20s of the 20th century, there was Eurasianism, and this was associated with the works of the first wave of Russian emigration. Eurasians proceeded from the fact that Russia geographically belonged to both Europe and Asia and absorbed elements of European and Asian cultures. The peoples inhabiting it have Slavic and Turanian roots, and in terms of religion they are Christian and Muslim. This cultural and historical peculiarity of Russian society prompted Russian emigrants to put forward a new idea called "Eurasianism." Based on this understanding of Russian history and culture, the Eurasians developed their concept of historical development, in particular, the peculiar path of Russia. Eurasianists believed that "Russia cannot follow wholly European cultural development as a certain model, and cannot indiscriminately, servilely bow to European civilization. The roots of our Russian identity, our culture, our way of life are in the village, preserving and developing it, we preserve the origins. If the world civilization, which has taken over our cities, comes to the village, we will lose Russia." This is from the position of Eurasianism.

Nowadays the concept of Eurasianism has been turned upside down. The Slavs are more ancient than all other peoples, maybe even more ancient than the ancient Egyptians — all Russian newspapers are filled with this, it is on the lips of many Russian cultural scientists. Even in the twentieth century BC, the Slavs washed their feet in the Indian Ocean. Slavs taught the builders of Babylon to read and write. They built the walls of Troy and stole the beautiful Helen. They lived in Siberia, in ancient Greece and even on Easter Island. For three thousand years, the Russians were advising the ancient Vedic masters. Russian rock concerts are held according to the ancient Vedic matrix, and the mechanism of collective rejoicing that purifies the psyche is incorporated into them. The ancient Vedic knowledge of the Russians is in no way simpler, it is even more complex than Indian yoga or Chinese philosophy. It is possible that yoga, philosophy and the ancient Egyptian civilization came precisely from the ancient Slavs. Today, no matter what, Russians consider their homeland a highly developed industrial country with advanced science and technology and strong intellectual potential, rich natural resources, and a highly professional workforce. It cannot be put on a par with the backward African and Latin American countries and accept the model of reforms proposed by the International Monetary Fund for such states. Russia does not need to go through such a painful path of market transformation as those countries "enjoyed."

Such ideological postulates are used to raise the young generation. First, a promising young man, who often comes to Moscow from the provinces, is introduced into the circle of assistants to various functionaries and deputies. Then he is offered a trip to one of the Orthodox monasteries. There, he will be told that Russian history is much older than what they say, and that Orthodoxy is the only true faith, which has always saved the country from the invasion of Western hordes and helped to preserve its independence and national spirit. A high-ranking official will explain to him that Catholicism and Protestantism are perversions of the "true religion. The adherents of these religions will be punished by disasters, flooding, and other misfortunes." More than once I have had to observe the reaction of responsible officials to news, for example, of a flood in Europe. "Hooray!" — they exclaimed, "The Catholics are flooded again!" When asked, "What good is that?" they would say, "They're Catholics! Serves them right, let them stay out of our business!"

But there is no emphasis on Orthodoxy, either. It exists as if in a parallel world, selling vodka and cigarettes and fighting for oil quotas; because of its strongly secularized activities it cannot serve as a spiritual ideal for these people. After visiting a monastery, the "initiate" is usually told that "Russia is strong even now, it has special facilities to respond to the creeping Western aggression," alluding to special technology. Once a person has swallowed these attitudes about the West's pernicious influence, he can be introduced to any of "their" officials, all the way up to the chairman of the Central Bank or a minister, depending on his abilities or patrons. There he will be patted on the shoulder, told friendly words and allowed to perform the economic activity he has been waiting for, lending him a budget of a couple million rubles as "one of our guys." In most cases, a person who has internalized this ideology, having been nourished financially, is a lousy businessman and the money — which is invested in absurd projects, and often simply transferred from one account to another — quickly runs out. The man, however, is firmly in the circle of "his own" and begins to make a political career. "It's okay, it's okay," he is told, with a preliminary scolding, "Money is not a problem. These problems can be solved. The main thing is that you understand the situation correctly and are a true patriot of Russia." Along with the direct embezzlement of public funds, this problem, while not visible, is one of the major internal causes of the budget deficit. All of this is replicated in one way or another throughout Russia. Money actually goes to ideology.

This "progressive"-thinking bureaucracy is concentrated in Moscow. It becomes clear why the population of the capital shows unprecedented activity in defending the point of view "Moscow is for Muscovites," in the face of a flood of immigrants from all over the country who come seeking jobs and more. A large number of Muscovites think that everyone else should be thrown out, including those who come from the provinces, and certainly "colored" people: those from the Caucasus, Asians, and Blacks.

Unfortunately, this is true not only in Moscow. According to journalists, Governor Kondratenko of Krasnodar Krai, a friend of Russian Human Rights Ombudsman Oleg Mironov, said during a visit to Washington: "It's a nice city, only there are too many blacks." All the famous moralists: the poet Yevgeny Yevtushenko, the writer Solzhenitsyn, other cultural figures, and a considerable number of human rights defenders are silent in Russia today. No one hears their voices.

5. Russia's Main Problem

Almost everyone steals. Deep in the minds of the people there is a deep-rooted idea: if you don't steal, you don't live. In Russian it sounds even worse. The authorities' plundering of state property, i.e., nobody's property, seduces the people into doing the same. Barbarism flourishes wherever it is allowed to flourish. The country is in the throes of a "metal mining" boom. Never mind that trains run on the rails, electricity flows through the wires and heats the houses in which the thieves live. Nor does it matter that the stolen and scrapped monuments are more than just a piece of metal. What matters is that it pays money. Dismantling railroad tracks and dismantling power lines has become commonplace. In the Republic of Komi, over 40 kilometers of high-voltage wires, weighing 13 tons, were stolen from one of the backup power lines. Although the line was kept electrified to avoid being stolen, the attackers managed to de-power the section without the control panel detecting it. In Chelyabinsk, the paramilitary guards of the Chelyabinsk Tractor Plant were left without telephone service. Unknown persons stole more than 750 meters of telephone cable in underground networks and wells. The thieves were children — 10 and 12 years old.

In just two months the "scrap collectors" in Yakutsk turned the high-power main telephone network into scrap metal. The employees of the Yakutsk City Telephone Station's line shop had to work day and night to restore the pieces of cable cut by the thieves. For several days the National Medical Center, the republican and city military registration and enlistment offices, the national airline Sakha Avia, the fire department and even the inhabitants of the government dachas were without telephone service.

In the Yaroslavl region there were attempts to strip a bridge for scrap. There is a railroad military unit in the area. Next to it, on the bank of the Volga River, are metal structures for bridge piers designed to install a pontoon bridge across the river in case of emergency. Three "entrepreneurs" cut the parts of the "unnecessary" bridge to pieces with an autogen metal cutter for three hours. The military unit only noticed the fire in the evening, and the perpetrators were detained by the police.

In the settlement of Belsky, Tver region, five local residents stole more than a mile and a half of heavy rails from the railroad track of the quarry.

In the Nizhny Novgorod region a whole Remtransformator plant fell victim to metal hunters; in the village of Touzakovo a kilometer and a half of electrical wire was stolen; in Sharapovo they took the coil of electric motors from the boiler house of rural administration. In villages they even took apart tractors.

In several neighborhoods of Angarsk, about two kilometers of telephone cable was cut in a short time. The restoration of the stolen communications is like Don Quixote fighting windmills. The telecommunications workers had no sooner replaced the stolen cable of one of the apartment houses than it was stolen again. In the same Angarsk, one of the main highways of the city was left without traffic controls when the criminals disassembled 7 traffic lights in search of precious metals. In the city of Kovrov, Vladimir region, teenagers tried to scrap almost half of all the city's historical relics. A bust of gunsmith V.A. Degtyarev, the inventor of machine guns, was stolen from the memorial tomb in Pushkin Park. Three metal plates with the names of the city's residents who died during World War II were taken from the Eternal Flame memorial. A total of 39 such plates were stolen from all the city's memorials.

In the city of Nakhodka, Primorsky Krai, the bronze statue of Mir (Peace), depicting a woman with a pigeon in her hands, has been taken from its pedestal more than once and, in an attempt to sell it as scrap metal, its arms and head were sawn off. This statue was presented to Nakhodka by its Japanese sister city Maidzuru in honor of the 30th anniversary of the twinning of the cities. Nakhodka is considering a proposal to put the statue in a museum —it "will no longer greet the ships entering the bay, but it will not have to blush in front of the Japanese," say the authorities.

In the city of Pervouralsk there is a shortage of garbage cans, which were made of aluminum. The city administration made an order to make new urns that will be made of cast iron. Since it is not possible to nail them to the asphalt, it is hoped that not everyone will be able to lug the product weighing more than 50 kilograms.

It got to the point that in the Sverdlovsk region, the Sverdlovenergo company, tired of fighting against the thieves, proposed to designate the theft of electrical equipment a form of terrorism and introduce a state of emergency. As a result of incessant thefts in this area, the power supply to a number of industrial enterprises near Nizhny Tagil is disrupted, and there is no electricity in a large number of villages. The list of settlements left without communication is even longer. And so on, throughout Russia.

There are a lot of places in the country where stolen industrial scrap can be sold without any problems. The ongoing uncontrolled purchase of non-ferrous metals from private individuals continues to provoke people to steal. In this case, the recipients of non-ferrous metals operate underground: the majority of locations are illegal, and many operate under fake licenses. At the same time the "purchase" prices are understated by up to 25 times. But the tremendous poverty of the people in a country that belongs to the elite club of the eight most developed countries in the world, and the desire to earn "easy" money, provoked by the criminal behavior of the authorities themselves, again and again pushes people to disrupt train schedules, destroy communications and steal metal containers for storing radioactive waste.

Oil and gas are being stolen directly from the pipelines. Attackers steal fuel in a rather artless way: they drill a pipeline and pump fuel into ordinary cylinders. This problem is especially urgent in the south of Russia, for example, in the Stavropol Territory, where thefts of gas condensate from trunk pipelines that come from the Stavropol oil and gas fields are becoming a regular practice. Criminals sell the stolen stuff to the population, since it can be used for ordinary cooking stoves and heating boilers.

Many craftsmen have used "bugs" to adjust household electricity meters so that they not only give out any data they want, but they can even spin the dial backwards, up to zero results. In 1998 in Volgograd Region they stole 10.5 million kilowatt-hours this way, worth 1.8 million rubles. The most striking thing is that electricity is often not stolen by poor people. Owners of mansions already built, and especially those under construction, account for a significant share of the thefts. Power engineers are forced to shut down transformer substations from time to time. Transformers designed for a certain number of consumers are heated to a dangerous limit due to overload. To avoid an explosion, electricians shut them down.

The toll overpass built in Saratov showed only great potential for theft. As soon as cars started going back and forth, the staff instantly realized that the cash does not all have to go to the cash desk, it's more convenient to put some of it in their own pockets. Two shifts of workers were fired and the boss was replaced, but it didn't make much difference.

In Volgodonsk, thousands of people suffered from the explosion of an apartment block in 1999, including the injured young children. But a significant part of the money that was transferred to the charity account to meet their urgent needs was spent on the personal instructions of the head of city administration Sergei Gorbunov. In particular, part of the funds was transferred to the Volgodonsk branch of the capital commercial bank Vozrozhdenie. Window and door frames provided for the reconstruction of the apartments were openly traded at the construction material markets in Rostov, in Salsk, and in Volgodonsk itself.

The Botanical Garden of the Siberian Branch of the Russian Academy of Sciences was stolen. Ordinary citizens stole unique plants, who sell the exhibits right at the nearest subway stop. Such thefts can also be made to order: wealthy "new Russians" ask the diggers for a more exotic plant. Sometimes they act as performers: they come to pick themselves a bunch of lilacs with half-meter-long inflorescences or junipers, driving straight into the garden in their Mercedeses. Desperate botanical garden workers tried to fight the theft by removing labels from the plants, explaining what was what. The plant thieves were confused: how do you know what to steal? The thieving citizens became so desperate about this that they loudly protested right in front of the gloating plant breeders.

Massive and illegal logging is taking place in the Leningrad Region, where entire criminal gangs have formed to make a living in this way. They are well aware of the locations of the forest rangers and police checkpoints, and they send a car ahead, which "drops off" the loggers in the forest. Coordinators in the car patrol the surrounding roads. If there is any danger, they use a walkie-talkie to warn the sawyers, and they go deep into the forest. If all is quiet, at dusk a timber lorry pulls up, loads the logs and quickly retreats.

The world's largest payment systems, Europay and Visa, are not safe in Russia. There have been dozens of cases of plastic card fraud. Groups of swindlers get the PIN-codes of credit cards and then withdraw money from the accounts of their owners in other countries, by using a scanning strip at ATMs and directly from accomplices in the processing centers. Meanwhile, Russia has "identified" those groups of cardholders who are the most dangerous to banks. According to a letter from the Moscow Branch of Sberbank, its branches should refuse to issue cards to pensioners, housewives, students, graduate students, military personnel, the temporarily unemployed and employees of small firms.

Theft is no less rampant in the cultural sector. All-round piracy is flourishing in the audio and video production market. Piracy flourishes among popular music performers as well. The melodies of almost all songs sung by

Russian pop musicians are identical to those of various foreign performers. Without the slightest hesitation Russian composers put their names under these tunes, and Russian poets write lyrics to them, often simply translating and perfecting the text. Musicians can easily name the Western source of their inspiration, that is, the performers from whom they stole the song.

Elections in Russia are extremely lucrative. Approximately 80 percent of the candidates have no chance of winning. By participating in the election race, they are simply profiting at the expense of sponsors. For example, they order leaflets in a printing house and indicate an official circulation of 5,000 copies. They explain to their sponsor that they printed 20,000, but they actually ordered 5,000 because the election committee didn't allow more. In fact, 10,000 were printed, and the difference in the cost of the underprinted 10,000 leaflets is pocketed. It is almost impossible to detect the fraud.

The army also steals. For several years officers of the central machinery of the anti-aircraft defense forces stole spare parts for anti-aircraft missile systems and sold them to commercial organizations.

Sometimes the bombs dropped by the Russian air force on Chechen fighters do not cause any harm. Here is one of the reasons: employees at the military airfield in Dyagilev near Ryazan, where the bombers are based, removed the explosives from the bombs and sold them to criminal groups. The employees explained the theft of explosives in the traditional way — they did not have enough money to live on.

As for the theft of explosives on a large scale, including hexogen, which was used to blow up apartment buildings in Russia, this is only possible with the involvement of high-ranking officials. There is no point in speculating about explosives being imported into Moscow if a large number of Moscow enterprises are already full of explosives for anti-tank and anti-aircraft missile systems. As Russian practice proves, it is quite feasible to hide a whole train-car load of hexogen at railroad marshalling yards. The image of a corrupt official who cares about nothing but money comes to mind again. The only thing he had to take care of was not getting his own house blown up.

In the late '80s and early '90s, the military, not wanting to fall behind the civilians, "privatized" property by entire squadrons, tank columns, and arsenals. The guilty were almost never found. Then came the second phase — the parts of ships and lots of firearms from warehouses were used — with the obligatory fires in the end (the empty warehouses were burned to hide the shortages). When there was nothing large left, only old equipment — they started to pull small pieces. For themselves. For their homes and families. The economic department of the General Staff of the Armed Forces of

Russia, selling the building of the former Reception House of the Ministry of Defense, hid more than $4 million from the treasury. All this was happening right before the eyes of the whole country. Every single one of the generals who worked in the Defense Ministry and was convicted of embezzling money and property spent it on the same thing: building a huge red-brick mansion an hour's drive from Moscow with a mandatory garden, a place for a greenhouse, a bathhouse and a barn, for free, using the labor of conscripts.

A group of admirals of the Russian Navy, including the head of the Naval Academy, Admiral V. Eremin, the head of the auxiliary fleet of the Russian Navy Rear Admiral Y. Klichugin, Deputy Head of the logistics and transport academy, Vice Admiral E. Serbo, is accused by the Prosecutor's Office of the Pacific Fleet of illegal use and sale of warships and auxiliary ships for personal gain. According to preliminary data, the total damage caused by them to the Navy and the state amounted to more than $600,000. The case includes such episodes as, for example, the illegal sale abroad of the practically new large naval transport of arms, the Anadyr, designed for the transportation of strategic missiles.

After the military reform was announced, the air defense garrison on Sakhalin Island, the same one from which the fighter planes that shot down the 1983 Boeing passenger jet from South Korea took off, was disbanded. Leaving the island, the pilots looted everything they could carry or take away. They were helped by civilians from surrounding settlements who finished off the remaining windows, doors, roofs, and floors. When unit No. 29728 arrived here permanently, the officers were dumbfounded. The only thing they could use was the runway! The military said it felt like the bombed-out capital of Chechnya. All around were remains of buildings with empty window frames and doorways. Even the "alley of military glory" was torn to pieces. And this is an active military unit! Officers of the aviation regiment filmed everything they saw on videotape and sent it to the military prosecutor's office along with an inquiry about the theft of property. The prosecutor's office opened a criminal case, but that was the end of the process. The explanation is very simple — Sokol is a long way from any civilization and nobody wanted to do investigative work. When they tried to add floors and ceilings to the walls, the walls collapsed and soldiers died under the rubble. After that, it was decided to demolish the rest of the infrastructure and move the equipment under the open sky. By the way, in Sakhalin's climate one winter is enough to damage the equipment.

Radioactive contraband is flourishing in Russia. In Primorye Territory, in 1999, 18 attempts of illegal trafficking of cesium-type substances were interrupted; and that is only the official number. This does not correspond to the real number of such attempts, because only a quarter of Primorye check-points have radiation detection equipment. By the way, these devices began to be installed only in October 1999, at the expense of American taxpayers — the installation is paid by the American government.

A large amount of liquid radioactive waste is accumulated in the North of Russia, which requires processing and storage. The Atomflot enterprise in Murmansk, which operates all the nuclear-powered icebreakers, has a shortage of onshore storage facilities for radioactive waste. In addition, the existing Atomflot installation for processing radioactive waste has an annual processing capacity of 1,500 tons, and it cannot meet the delivery schedule. A new plant with a capacity of 5,000 tons per year is being built. This project is financed by Norway and the United States. Commissioning of the new plant was scheduled for 1996, but has been postponed several times due to the fact that it is a convenient excuse to siphon money from Western sponsors. Norwegian officials say they may cut off economic aid for construction of the new plant if it is not completed by the end of 1999.

There was a devastating accident in Tomsk on April 6, 1993, and officials misused 900 million rubles allocated for the clean-up. The promissory notes received by the Tomsk State Inspectorate for Small Watercrafts (whose functions also include control of the environmental condition of water bodies) were cashed in and used for personal purposes. The money to compensate for the consequences of the explosion of a tank containing uranium at the last stage of enrichment, which contaminated an area of 1,500 square kilometers with uranium and plutonium isotopes, was stolen.

What is called misappropriation of budget money is in fact theft. Here is an example. In Chelyabinsk in 1997, the management of the crew which built the subway appealed to the deputy mayor, Vasily Granin, for a regulation giving bonuses to metro builders. The list of those awarded, besides construction officials, included a certain resident of Moscow (judging by the amount of bonus, he is the main metro builder of Chelyabinsk). The list also includes the head of the city himself, Vasily Granin. The money spent on the bonus would have been enough to pay off subway construction workers' wage arrears.

One of the schemes for embezzling budgetary money went like this. The Ministry of Finance of Russia had a fictitious debt to the administration of some region. With the help of fake documents, a fictitious debt appeared from the regional administration to the oil company Yukos in the same amount. The regional administration received funds from the federal budget and give them to Yukos, while Yukos paid its debts to the budget with budget money. Yukos received real money from the budget through the region, while the budget received only conditional units. And, of course, no penalties for tax arrears. The administrations got their share. Personally. For this purpose, in fact, a front company "Emitent" was created for the theft of budget money by the Yukos oil company.

With all of these regions and businesses, the Issuer LLP was going to make mutual settlements with all the indicated regions and enterprises. All or almost all of them received packages of contracts for the supply of fake petroleum products. In total, these contracts amounted to 1 trillion 869 billion 51 million rubles in 1997 prices. All the above is, by the way, also known to the Prosecutor General's Office of Russia.

The illegal diamond trade is flourishing in Russia. Diamonds are illegally exported to Israel, Belgium and the Netherlands, and a description of the structural schemes of these operations, the names of firms and participants can be found in the book *The Diamond War*, which made a lot of noise in "narrow professional circles," and not only among diamondaires but also in the intelligence services.

According to the Russian Federal Service for Foreign Exchange and Export Control, in the first half of 1999, the illegal supply of seafood to Japan by Russian fishermen amounted to approximately $320 million. Sixty percent of seafood shipments from Russia to Japan are illegal. In Primorsky Krai, the fish industry's production accounts for 38 percent of the total volume of industrial production, while its share of federal budget revenues is only a little over one percent. The same situation is observed in the Russian North. Russian ships prefer to offload cod to Norwegian ports rather than deliver it to Murmansk or Arkhangelsk.

Cyprus, the Czech Republic and Finland are considered the most favorable areas for "money laundering." Cyprus legalizes funds transferred to the accounts of newly registered firms, received for stolen oil, timber, nickel and other natural resources from the state. It also transfers the hidden difference between the purchase price and sale price of consumer goods imports, as well as purely criminal money (drugs, prostitution, smuggling). The Czech Republic serves as a permanent channel for supplying counterfeit dollars to Russia, as well as a place to invest criminal and tax evaded money in real estate and services. The presence of a large number of Russian spies in Czech representations only confirms that official authorities are aware of this fact. This is nothing but an attempt to control the hidden financial flows from Russia.

Recently there has been an outflow of money from Moscow to St. Petersburg, closer to the Finnish border, which in Russia is considered "translucent" in terms of capital export. It is precisely the proximity of St. Petersburg to Finland that forces Moscow to lock up financial flows here, pumping "dirty" money in transit through the accounts of local firms under production and trade orders to Finland. This is done through the purchase of clothing and food, building materials and much of the printed matter. Many trea-surers and "holders" of criminal "pools" buy real estate in Finland, live there, and participate in the activities of their structures in Moscow, Murmansk, Karelia, St. Petersburg and other regions.

6. Cities and Housing

If you have ever been to Russia, then you must have been deeply impressed by Red Square or the palace complexes in the suburbs of St. Petersburg. But have you paid attention to what surrounds these attractions? Have you traveled by public transport or trains rather than shiny new tourist buses? Have you stepped inside the ordinary entrances of ordinary apartment houses?

In Russia the housing provided for people even with an average income is not up to any standards. Now in Russia, 6.3 million families are on the waiting list for housing but no more than 400 families receive it each year. The wait list for new apartments is 15 years, and there is plenty of social discontent.

The quality of housing in Russia is appalling. These are certainly not huts like those in Africa or some Asian countries. But in those places, no one even thought to inspire people with the illusion that they are living with dignity and in decent homes, have decent jobs, and have great ideas. In those places, whatever it is, it is. And whatever it is not, it is not. In Russia, the opposite is true. A gray nine-story building with paint-spattered and pissed-on front stoops, with broken windows and doors, is considered a good dwelling for an ordinary person. Iron security doors to apartments, broken railings, broken chutes with garbage falling out of them, torn off doors to basements where drug addicts and criminals congregate, the elevator buttons always burned out, dog droppings from the incessant packs of stray dogs (and around the front doors, from domestic dogs), and cockroaches, of course. It's good if the landings are cleaned at least once a week.

But even this is better than "Khrushchevka" — whole neighborhoods of hastily constructed post-war housing from the 1950s and 60s. Blocks of cheap public housing projects can be seen on the edges of US cities as well, but not like this: dilapidated five-story building with holes as big as a finger in the ceilings between apartments. And this is not in the slum areas, just standard neighborhoods, standard houses, new buildings, which the city halls are so proud of. The last word in the parliamentary promises was to repair the doors in the entrances, to ensure the operation of elevators, to patch up garbage chutes. Just promises.

In the 1980s it was safe to walk home alone at midnight, and even "Beatnik" types were likely to hold their cigarette butts or candy wrappers until they reached the next urn rather than toss them on the sidewalk. Now, city sanitary and epidemiological services, as well as AIDS centers, issue constant warnings to public utilities about the need to clean up the entrances to apartment buildings. In many cities, syringes used by drug addicts are scattered in stairwells and often children play with them; they can become infected with AIDS. Residents are forced to install steel doors with combination locks at the entrances, since wooden doors with the same locks are broken open almost the next day. There are also fewer burglaries in entrances with armored doors. The windows of the first floor, regardless of whether we are talking about institutions or residential apartments, are everywhere covered with steel bars. This is the only way not to attract robbers or just hooligans. Despite the significantly increased demand for metal doors with combination locks, the authorities are asking producers not to increase prices. "We won't be able to call residential buildings safe until an iron door with a coded lock is installed in every entrance," said V. Bibikov, head of the coordination council for ensuring security in the Komi Republic.

In short, in the best case a multi-story building has steel doors at the entrance, steel doors to each apartment, steel control panels for elevators, steel nets over light bulbs, and steel doors to the basement with large padlocks so the shanks cannot be sawn through. In the worst case, the entrance is in a condition beyond description. It's clear that the public is silently protesting against the surrounding reality. Garbage-clogged trash chutes are set on fire on a regular basis, forcing everyone living in the house to prepare as if for a gas attack, lining the front doors with old clothes and opening the windows wide. For this and other reasons, mainly from despair and low class, people throw quite a lot of trash out the windows and off the balconies. Therefore, the spaces around residential buildings are a natural trash heap where you can find everything: from a gnawed chicken leg to a TV box.

Garbage has been accumulating on the streets in recent years. Hundreds of unauthorized landfills are being formed within the city. In fact, this is a continuous zone of environmental disaster. There is no fundamental distinction between rich and poor areas; all are equally polluted. The authorities prefer to build luxury homes in poor areas, hoping that people with money and social status will begin to improve the environment themselves. Vain hopes, especially in Russia, where the principal goal for a rich man (by Russian standards) is to slip through the filthy entrance into his big four-room apartment, renovated and furnished according to the latest fashion trends.

The cultural level of people in provincial towns can be even more impressive than that seen in bigger cities: piles of cigarette butts, glass, and plastic bottles are everywhere in the streets. No one condemns this and no one is fined. People are used to walking through piles of garbage and are only looking for sturdier shoes. This sight made such an impression o, the Belgian scientist Jean Blankoff, professor of history at Brussels University, that he paid for a clean-up of part of the town of Kargopol in the Arkhangelsk region. In the town of Zapadnaya Litsa in the Murmansk region, garbage has not been cleared from the streets for four years. It is so dense that sometimes it is impossible to walk through without stepping in rotten fruit or vegetable. In the winter, the snow hides it, the stench disappears, and the garbage won't stick to your shoes. But in the spring, the absurdity of the notion that urban services are operating becomes apparent again, as the stench and visual mayhem return. It's a good thing that summer doesn't last long in the Arctic Circle. One of Russia's cities with a population of over a million, Kazan, faces an environmental disaster. The city simply has nowhere to dump its garbage. There is only one official landfill and it was already overflowing years ago.

Thus most cities are reduced to burning their trash, and the acrid smoke hangs in clouds over the landfills. The consequence is severe air pollution, primarily from dioxins, which are dangerous for nature and for people. They impact the reproductive functions, they destroy the hormonal system — which leads to immune deficiency, they provoke the appearance of cancer... the number of female illnesses, miscarriages, birth defects, and children born with disabilities are growing.

According to a study conducted by the consulting agency William M. Mercer, of the forty cities in the world with the lowest quality of life, six are in the former Soviet Union: two in Russia — Novosibirsk and Kazan, and four more in the Commonwealth of Independent States — Minsk, Alma-Ata, Baku and Tashkent. This is based on political and socio-economic factors, climate, crime rate, quality of education and health care, environment, public transportation, housing infrastructure, the degree of personal freedom of the population, inter-ethnic relations, etc.

Russian cities are also perhaps the most boring in the world. While the Soviet system provided children's clubs, sports training, and youth organizations as well as summer camps out in the woods, now the only recreation opportunities for young people are "taverns" and "gangster" clubs. There is no policy regarding youth recreation anymore. They receive no support; and creative groups of any orientation are squeezed into poverty. Young people have a hard time finding work, and the city's job exchanges are being closed down. Drug use is on the rise, but the authorities aren't doing anything about it except to try to crack down. The infrastructure of a Western city with a population of 5,000 is often equal to or better than that of a Russian city with a population of 500,000. Therefore, it is not surprising that when a reporter asked a 15-year-old girl in the million-strong Rostov-on-Don what she wanted to be, she answered that in Rostov, she didn't want to be anyone at all.

In order to keep busy, people will resort to anything. Schoolchildren like to break fluorescent lights, but they contain mercury vapor. Hooligans thus spread mercury in the hallways and stairwells. And the residents come out in their housecoats to clean it up with whatever they have at hand — rags and buckets with soda. Every month, tons of mercury are spilled all over the country. Mercury vapor has no odor or color, and has no immediate irritant effect, but it is no less dangerous than radiation, but Russians seem to be oblivious.

Abandoned cars pile up behind residential buildings. Besides the obvious problems this causes, this becomes a safety issue. Almost every day there are cases of teenagers throwing firecrackers into the gas tanks of trucks; the trucks catch fire and burn the giddy children.

Telephone coverage in Russia still lags far behind more-developed countries. Home telephones are still considered something of a luxury. People in socialist times waited for 15–20 years for telephone installation. This is no exception today. In rural areas, the level of telephone coverage is two or more times lower than in urban areas.

In one Irkutsk neighborhood, there are ten heroin outlets known not only to drug addicts and locals in general, but also to the police. Most of them are registered by local police as drug houses. Two, by the way, are right next door to the police station. Everyone knows the addresses of the dealers, but no one is in a hurry to shut them down. There is indeed no limit to the corruption of the relevant authorities. They just explain away the spread of drugs as a result of the inaction and corruption of the police as a plan by Islamic extremists to destroy Russia from within by spreading drugs. Meanwhile, the entire Irkutsk police rushed into the "fight against terrorism" when they got the chance. The Department of Internal Affairs created a temporary headquarters, each unit has a special group, the number of guards was increased by 20%, holidays were canceled, and a 12-hour workday was introduced. Almost all security agencies are involved and there is active cooperation with the military. Cadets and students of the Higher School of Police check basements and attics all over town. The thermal power station, the dam and the water canal are placed under special protection. Citizens' reports are checked. And heroin outlets in the Solnechny district go on operating.

Travel in Russia has become a chaotic undertaking. The Federal Air Transport Service has a difficult equipment shortage. There is no money to buy new equipment or to repair or upgrade the airfields. Even in Moscow the equipment at the air traffic control center is extremely worn out. It would be cheaper to throw it out than to repair it. In a number of regions, the Federal Air Transport Service radars are shot, and nothing has been automated in most of the country. In addition, you may find yourself flying at the wrong time and in the wrong direction. On May 24, 1999, the Saint-Petersburg–Arkhangelsk flight took an unscheduled stop in Moscow to pick up more passengers. It is not known why the two flights were combined.

About a hundred passengers on the Novosibirsk–Sochi flight operated by Siberia Airlines were delayed one day due to the loss of a life jacket from the cabin. After landing, everyone was loaded into a bus and taken to the airport terminal building for inspection. The situation was resolved without a scandal: On the way, the "kidnapper" inconspicuously planted the vest in the bus, where it was located. Nevertheless, the passengers' indignation was boundless. Ironically, on the same day the company's management was holding a meeting on improving passenger service.

The train service is no better. If the train is late, no information or updates are given. Moreover, railroad officials are free to suddenly cancel any train altogether. Too bad for the passengers. Trains are canceled every day, in every direction. And if you buy a ticket ahead of time, it will cost more than if you waited until just before the train leaves.

7. Russia's Main City and Its Mayor

Russia's main city is familiar to foreigners mainly for St. Basil's Cathedral, and to Russians for the (in)famous Moscow residency registration requirements and the rampages of the Moscow police. Although one cannot say that these outrages are worse than, for example, in Novosibirsk or anywhere else. In Moscow, anyone can be stopped on the street and taken to the police station at any time of the day or night without any substantive reason. The Moscow police force actively uses its power to make money, and they don't shrink from emptying the pockets of citizens, which — in legal language — is called robbery. There's no point in complaining about the police: they don't turn in "their own" people.

And if you don't have a Moscow resident's registration, they will send you to the immigration office, as if Moscow were a separate country. This practice goes back to the time of the famine of the 1930s, when all the food-stuffs were taken away from the peasants in order to feed the workers in the cities, who produced weapons. Hungry peasants went to the cities in droves to get at least some food. Then the towns were surrounded by barrier troops who opened fire without warning on anything that approached. It is difficult to establish how many people died of hunger and how many died under the bullets of those troops. At least now they don't shoot you for coming to the capital from the provinces. But still, the rich capital does not want to feed the "freeloaders" — that is, the rest of the country, having previously taken from them up to 70% of the money in the form of taxes and other deductions. This constitutes Moscow's wealth. Everything is just like in the legendary 1930s. Some 80–85% of all financial opportunities are concentrated in Moscow. The President is there, all the legislative structures and the government are there, and the mayor's policy all contribute to this over-concentration. Moscow does not want to share any of its powers with other cities or regions.

The Moscow authorities don't give a damn about people's opinions. No one wants to listen to them, they don't even try to pretend that they are listening. Most people are extremely dissatisfied with the bureaucratic arbitrariness of the city. A person coming to Moscow from outside will have great difficulty to start working normally; everything is built on bribes and is reduced to idiocy. The main problem, as elsewhere in Russia, is the complete centralization of decision-making. The mechanism of personal control by a manager replaces the effective work of his subordinates. The capital's authorities create unfavorable conditions for business development in the city.

Moscow's economic miracle is struggling for breath. The city is no longer able to get by without help from the federal government and the Central Bank. The mayor of the capital can declare anything he wants about Moscow's readiness to pay its debts, and about the inadmissibility of price increases in the city; but the ruble exchange rate is not subject to his orders, so he has limited room for maneuver. Moscow officials have no choice but to assert that it's just a false rumor that Moscow is in considerable financial difficulty. The capital is issuing its own bonds to repay its foreign loans. The Moscow authorities claim that they borrow money to implement important city projects — commercially profitable ones that will pay off, and the money will be paid back. Moscow, at times and not without difficulty, did pay its debts. But so far it was a question of paying interest on loans. The main payments are to come in 2000–2001, when it would have to pay $700 million a year on foreign debts alone. This cannot be done without borrowing more money. Behind a façade of prosperity, the same problems are hiding in Moscow that are characteristic of all of Russia. There are serious concerns that if the current mayor (Yuri Luzhkov) becomes President of Russia, he will bankrupt the whole country in an effort to close the books on his Moscow problems.

Moscow is actually a state within a state. The city's declared population is supposedly 8 million people. In fact, if you also take into account the residents of the suburbs and nearby regions who live and work in the capital for weeks on end, if not more, as well as a significant number of illegal residents from outside of Russia, near (Azerbaijan, Georgia, etc.) and far (Vietnam, Afghanistan, Syria, etc.), the city population could surely be one and a half to two times greater, i.e. 12–15 million. This is almost as many as live in the Netherlands.

The significance of the capital for the Russian economy is such that in the century ahead, Moscow mayors will be running for president. Mayor

Luzhkov has a donor region the size of an average European state, significant paramilitary forces and fairly powerful financial and information resources. Given the capital's role in the country's life as the political, financial and economic center, which has an important influence on the subjects of the Russian Federation, long ago we should actually have been introducing the post of Minister of Moscow Affairs into the government instead of the mayor.

Yeltsin put Yuri Luzhkov in charge of the Russian capital in 1992. Since then, he has never for a moment forgotten to look after his own enrichment but has become a desperate opponent of the reformers appointed to the government by the president. Luzhkov stubbornly builds his image as the mouthpiece of Great Russia, for example, by regularly demanding that Crimea be returned to Russia. (In 1783, the Russian Empire annexed Crimea; it then became part of the Russian Soviet Federative Socialist Republic, and was gifted to the Ukraine in 1954 by Soviet Premier Khrushchev, himself a Ukrainian.) Luzhkov exploits populist and nationalist sentiments to the fullest extent. His statements about diasporas, "Africans" and the like are well known. Luzhkov's famous cap, which he always crumples in his hand, is a symbol of his ideological closeness to the people, and should also bring back memories of the founder of the Soviet state, Lenin, who is depicted in dozens of paintings with the same cap. Without blatant sycophancy to Mayor Luzhkov, it is impossible to exist in the capital. Politicians, businessmen and smart cultural figures ‑ —poets, writers, sculptors, musicians — do this. Other times, incorrigible freethinkers, speaking in public, must insert some obligatory phrase about "dear Yury Mikhailovich," about "how great and wonderful" he is.

Luzhkov himself likes to fly in a helicopter to the nearby fields and talk about bringing vegetables into the capital. He even created teams to provide Muscovites with watermelons and tomatoes. After this, large piles of watermelons appear in the capital on every corner. That's due to the work of people from the Caucasus, not Muscovites. Only once did Luzhkov have to go to the Moscow suburbs by car. He was going to take over the fields of agricultural associations in Kolomna and Serpukhov districts, but he was already in disgrace with the President. In order to annoy Luzhkov, the power structures — which were supposed to give permission for departure — by order from the Presidential Administration forbade him to do this. By the way, the Moscow region ranks second in Russia in economic potential after the city of Moscow, but in terms of standard of living it ranks 57th among other regions and republics of Russia. In this region there are state employees with miserable salaries, a deplorable state of social security, retirees eking out a miserable existence, and a high level of unemployment. But the region ranks first in the country for the number of robberies, murders and robberies.

Luzhkov has been patiently, masterfully creating the preconditions for his rise to power, assembling an impressive team of businessmen, journalists and politicians for his election campaign. Unlike President Yeltsin, who had a bad habit of changing his entourage every two or three months, Moscow Mayor Yuri Luzhkov is known for the cohesion of his team. He has known many of his colleagues, if not since diapers, then at least since college. While working with others, he has created his own "family" as opposed to the "family" of the president. However, Luzhkov's "family" lived together while they were building houses and sweeping up streets. The appearance of the Fatherland movement and the prospect of presidential elections fundamentally changed the situation. Now Luzhkov's entourage is engaged in a struggle, the consequences of which can only be guessed. Day by day, animosity among those who are close to the mayor of Moscow is becoming more and more provocative. In "Fatherland" there is a growing number of structures with the same functions, which, in fact, are doing nothing but creating intrigues against each other. At the same time, everyone defiantly declares: our goal is Luzhkov's victory in all elections. Everyone is trying to secure a place for himself closer to the "body," not caring too much about the other members of the team. Loyal associates of the Moscow mayor, just in case, are trying to get their hands on the most liquid assets of the city, while they are still within their reach.

Luzhkov's financial empire is the Sistema Company, the Bank of Moscow, Mosbusinessbank, the Ogni Moskvi Bank, Mosvodokanalbank, Moseximbank, Guta Bank and Promradtekhbank. The president of the joint-stock financial company Sistema is Vladimir Yevtushenkov, Luzhkov's right-hand man, a man rumored to be in charge of $4 billion in capital, state-level coal speculation and relations with the Solntsevo criminal gang. Yevtushenkov has always been the leading sponsor of Luzhkov's election campaign and his Fatherland movement. In recent years, Yevtushenkov has managed to take over all mobile communications in Moscow, except Bee Line. Sistema also controls virtually all of Zelenograd's electricity plants. Analysts claim that virtually every sector of the capital's market has been divided between commercial entities close to the mayor's office. The capital's gasoline business is also controlled by Yuri Luzhkov's people.

Moscow is by far the richest, most populous and influential region in Russia, and its strength lies in the constant siphoning of funds from the provinces. Hence there is one problem, a very significant one: the traditional distrust of the provinces for the capital. In order to overcome this obstacle,

Luzhkov as a contender for the presidency has made an alliance with regional leaders. The price he would have to pay would be high. To gain their support, he has to contribute to the further expansion of the sovereignty of such republics as Tatarstan, Bashkortostan, and Ingushetia. It is on these terms that the presidents of the ethnic republics are ready to support the mayor of Moscow in his role as head of Fatherland, which calls into question the state unity of the Russian Federation.

By holding Fatherland congresses outside Moscow, Luzhkov is trying to show that he is not indifferent to the problems out there. However, in fact, the congresses are held in cities no more than a few hours away from Moscow. This is given the size of the Russian territory. Moreover, Luzhkov meets informally with the Communists, claiming that his aim is to help stabilize the Russian political scene. "Tough economic bosses" like Moscow's mayor remain no less of a threat to Russia's freedom than the Communists. In fact, Luzhkov has remained a devotee of centralized power. No one really knows where the tax money collected in Moscow goes. Luzhkov is so influential that he is capable of imposing an economic blockade on a whole region, which is exactly what he did in Nizhniy Novgorod after criticisms by former Prime Minister Sergei Kiriyenko. One can only guess what would have happened to freedom of speech if Luzhkov had been head of state.

The Moscow elite would not take well to Luzhkov's resignation as mayor. The fact is that business is structured in such a way that only Luzhkov can keep the various clans apart. No one else has sufficient authority. This means that a serious fight can break out. The mayor of Moscow has a large security force and about 100,000 well-armed guards at private business structures under his command. Thus, there are more paramilitary associations and organizations under the control of the mayor of Moscow than there are under the control of the President and the Government of the Russian Federation. The situation in which there are several armed forces of approximately equal strength in one state was deliberately created by the current political authorities within the framework of the "reforms," who were afraid to let one of the power components get the upper hand.

But Luzhkov also has opponents. More and more evidence is emerging every day of secret Kremlin plans to destabilize the situation in Moscow. They include various kinds of provocations designed to complicate the socio-psychological situation. The developers call it "Storm in Moscow" among themselves. A document confirming the existence of such a plan was handed to *Novaya Gazeta* back on July 2, 1999 (about two months before the deadly explosions in Moscow that started on August 31 and went on for two months). According to this plan, major upheavals were to take place in the city. Thus, it was planned to carry out terrorist attacks on several government institutions: the FSB building, the Interior Ministry, the Federation Council, the city court, the Moscow Arbitration Court, and several newspaper and magazine editorial offices. A number of famous people and ordinary citizens were kidnapped. A separate chapter was devoted to "criminal and violent actions" against businesses and businessmen who supported Luzhkov. A command was issued to gather additional "operational" material on Luzhkov's friends: the famous singer Kobzon, the banker and owner of a large TV channel Gusinsky, the sports magnate Tarpishchev, a descendant of the famous revolutionary Ordzhonikidze, Luzhkov's wife Madam Baturina, the president of the joint-stock financial company "Sistema" Yevtushenkov, Gusev, editor-in-chief of the newspaper *Moskovsky Komsomolets*, General Gromov and other persons. The businesses of Luzhkov's supporters would have to be destroyed, and the security of like-minded people would not be guaranteed. A separate program was developed to pit organized crime groups operating in Moscow against each other. These "activities" have several objectives: to create in Moscow an atmosphere of fear and the illusion of criminal mayhem, and to plant the impression that Luzhkov has lost control over the situation in the city. Blowing up apartment buildings in Moscow fits perfectly into the strategy and tactics of the struggle for parliamentary seats and the presidency.

What are the military options for declaring a state of emergency in Moscow? Interior troops could be involved, with the police brigade, and the Ministry of Internal Affairs has a special police detachment, some 17,000 men in total; various rapid response teams could add 1,000 more. And, of course, there is the army, with two armored units quartered near Moscow. As the experience of '93 shows, there will be plenty of people eager to shoot at the hated banks and government institutions.

Looking into this money laundering, FSB officers noticed that an obscure, unremarkable bank in the Vladimir region, just east of Moscow, handled payments one day in April 1999 that amounted to one and a half times more than the annual budget of Vladimir overall. It turned out that the company Inteko, owned by Elena Baturina, wife of the Moscow mayor, was behind it. Tracing this money, FSB officers came upon the Russian Land Bank; however, no sooner had they obtained access to the documents than scandalous articles complaining about a criminal case against Luzhkov's wife appeared in all the Moscow newspapers at once, as if following a direct order. Luzhkov stated in his speech about this case that Inteko did not have any financial or economic relations with the Vladimir companies which were being investigated, and that this was the beginning of "a new stage in the use of security services in the campaign against the mayor of Moscow." Luzhkov claimed the Kremlin was behind the criminal case "who want to destabilize the country." According to him, the authorities were harassing his wife instead of going after the real criminals. However, during the reconstruction of the Luzhniki soccer stadium, the progress of which Luzhkov personally supervised, Luzhkov's wife won the contract to supply 80,000 plastic seats. In Moscow and in all of Russia, no other firm engaged in the manufacture of plastic products could be found. What is this situation called in world political practice?

As far as the city itself, almost every Russian dreams of moving to Moscow. Moscow is the only place where you can live more or less decently, get a quality education, get a good job. But to buy or rent an apartment in this city is not an easy task. Even if the whole family works at a government job, and doesn't eat or buy anything, they may not be able to pay the monthly rent for a decent place (which doesn't compare to a decent apartment in any European country).

Moscow officials say that the capital's mortgage lending program is good for citizens and offers the following: A person deposits 50% of the annual cost of the apartment, becomes the owner after construction is completed, and then in the course of 8–10 years he pays the remaining 50% at 8% per annum in foreign currency. But there are other fees that officials fail to mention. For an apartment in a building facing the street, where you can try to get a mortgage, the program offers participants $800 per square meter. The construction cost is not more than $170. And by contributing 50% of the cost up front, the participants end up both paying the cost of construction and providing the organizers of the experiment with additional funds. In other words, the mortgage lending program in Moscow is nothing more than a way of replenishing the city budget, it's not a scheme for lending to the population. Naturally, once the first 150 mortgage certificates were issued, interest in the program dropped. Nobody was in a hurry to sign such contracts. But city officials like the schemes quite a lot and are constantly expanding them and transferring them to other types of construction.

Construction in Moscow is an amazing combination of poor taste and thirst for money. The implementation of the Master Plan will not only fail to improve the living conditions of Muscovites and make it difficult to attract investment, it will also drastically reduce public space in the city. With this kind of construction going on, you have to either jam high-rise apartments and offices into the small yards behind existing residential buildings or build up the remaining open space in Moscow, including parks and protected areas. The General Plan foresees eradicating almost all the public squares and green areas. Today there are only 20 sq. m. of green spaces for every Moscow resident (by comparison — about 400 sq. m. in Washington). [Wrong: Here, the author seems to have misread something, somewhere. As of 2019, Washington showed just 55 m. sq. (592 ft sq.), and New York — a far more appropriate comparison — 14 m. sq. (146 ft sq.), per resident.[1] But if he thought this was reality, it must have outraged him, for sure.] The city builds residential buildings of reinforced concrete, which has long been rejected by world practice. The construction of huge underground shopping centers in Moscow is like a symbol of the entire Russian economy going underground, into "black money," criminalization and lack of transparency. In the course of the privatization of the construction sector, over two thousand companies from various industries have been sold "for free." Corruption and patronage in all spheres of urban planning is rampant. Moscow architect Tsereteli has decorated half of Moscow with his works and there are almost no works by other artists. Is there really only one talented sculptor living here? Or were other sculptors somehow unworthy of having at least one major work in the center of Moscow?

The metropolitan roads built during socialism were not prepared for the arrival of capitalism. Back then, the car was a luxury, not a means of transportation. People were encouraged to ride in crowded buses, trolley-buses and streetcars, and in the subway. The only people who proudly rode the streets were public and official state transport, and some lucky people who, after saving up for a dozen years, bought a knock-off of the legendary Italian Fiat of the '60s, called the Zhiguli and manufactured in Togliatti. After perestroika, everything changed. Personal cars flooded the roads. In the coming millennium, transport collapse in the capital is inevitable. The center of Moscow is constantly jammed with traffic for hours on end. At the intersection near the Rossiya cinema and Russia's first McDonald's, you can sit quietly for hours in your car, playing cards. Furthermore, when there are special exhibitions or state events, the entrance to Pushkin Square from Sadovoye Ring road is closed till 9 pm and the traffic jam takes hours more to dissolve. Three and a half hours is a normal time to cross the main intersections into and out of the central part of town. The limousines of high officials, businessmen, politicians and criminal bosses can cut through this chaos, as they all have flashing, blinking and honking sirens. These cars jump out into the oncoming lane, causing accidents and then quietly fleeing the scene. The

---

[1] See "The Allocation of Space in U.S. Cities," Urban Footprint, https://www.geotab.com/urban-footprint/ and "New York Ranks Last For Amount of Green Space Per Resident Among the Major US Cities," NBC New York online, by Alessandra Rizzo, July 15, 2019 at https://www.nbcnewyork.com/news/local/new-york-ranks-last-for-amount-of-green-space-per-resident-among-the-major-us-cities/1529935/.

capital's traffic is so dense that if you are in a hurry to do your business, it is easier to drive through the courtyards/parking areas of residential buildings, parallel to the road, which many drivers do, despite the protests of the residents and the large number of children playing in the yards.

The Moscow subway may stand still underground for hours, with the occasional very reassuring remark from the loudspeakers such as, "The train will not go any further. Please remain calm in the cars." Optimistic, when you consider that the cars are crammed to the roof with sweaty, cursing people. Some subway stations have simply been closed for years, despite safe subway operating rules that set a maximum distance to be traveled between boarding platforms. The engineers are not hesitant to lay subway lines through quicksand, and the rails sometimes float out of place overnight.

After the bombs went off in apartment houses and shopping malls in Moscow wide scale and gross violations of citizens' rights became more frequent under the pretext of searching for terrorists and preventing new explosions. (Authorities declared these attacks were not the work of Muscovites; the public mainly blamed Chechens, from the Caucasus region.) The Moscow tragedies only resulted in the increased rigidity of the passport regime and thorough checks on the residency permits. All temporary residents of the capital (and some other cities) had to go to the passport office at the police station and report why they were in Moscow.

As elsewhere, there is a shortage of low-skilled laborers and so migrants flock in from places near and far, including much-resented darker-skinned folks from the Caucasus Mountains and Turkic peoples from the Asian/Siberian republics. Their excuse for existing has to be backed up by a certificate from their place of study or proof of medical treatment, or by presenting work documents. Tens of thousands of people who for various reasons were unable to show such documents were expelled from Moscow. The Moscow authorities decide for themselves whether this or that person "needs to stay here or not." The police regularly fine violators of the registration rules and "encourage them to leave the capital voluntarily." If they are unwilling to return to their historic homeland within three days, they may be forcibly removed from the capital (at their own expense). It's like before, in the 30's and 40's. The echelons of citizens to be deported from Moscow are supposed to be assembled by geographic region, loaded into trains and shipped out. However, the federal law makes no provision for re-registration, let alone expulsion. The Law on Citizens' Right to Freedom of Movement, adopted in 1993, only provides for registration at the place of residence and domicile. But the main city of Russia is not governed by Russian laws.

This is nothing new to Russia, it is just one more new wave of reactions: the fabrication of criminal cases against natives of the Caucasus, their arbitrary detention, violation of the inviolability of the home, humiliation of personal dignity by largescale, blatant, unreasonable refusals to register and re-register newcomers, and constant threats to deport them outside of Moscow. Many newcomers are expelled and the rest are simply intimidated. It has become difficult to be a non-Russian in Moscow. Moscow thus ceased to be a federal center. It became a national center. Nationalist, even, if not national chauvinist.

People suffer from the arbitrariness of the police and other officials. Moscow Mayor Luzhkov declares that "the registration scheme for newcomers in Moscow does not contradict Russian law." "What we are doing is absolutely in accordance with the norms of the law and the Constitution," he stresses. However, a representative of Human Rights Watch said that in order for the Moscow government's decree "On the Special Situation in Moscow" to be legally binding, the Russian Federation must, at a minimum, withdraw from the UN, Council of Europe, and OSCE, withdraw its signature from the international declaration of human rights, and amend its own constitution. Nevertheless, regardless of what anyone says, the "special provision" is in force!

The city authorities are in a hurry to "deal with the newcomers," fearing not so much new terrorist acts but opposition from those who consider them illegitimate. At last, a convenient excuse to throw everyone out of the capital has arrived. It is not the criminals and terrorists who are suffering from this new crackdown, but the ordinary citizens. As is true anywhere, the real criminals have their ways of getting around the obstacle.

The victims of the terrorist attacks were promised direct and indirect assistance by the Ministry of Internal Affairs, the City Hall, the Federal Security Service and the government. All the newspapers carried official promises to pay 75,000 rubles to everyone who lost their apartments, large sums for burying loved ones, and several thousand for arranging new places of residence. After a while, it became clear that the government is not in any rush to help the people who have been blown up due to government actions, but it is also turning a blind eye to the fact that the police are directly abusing the victims. Tens of thousands of new apartments are empty in Moscow: it's expensive. There would be enough housing to accommodate a large number of refugees and victims. But people are forced to seek shelter with their relatives. Sometimes, in order to settle the new victims, other refugees are expelled. The 1987 refugees from Baku and Sumgait (Azerbaijan) who have nowhere to go — old people, children, women with higher education, petrochemical engineers, city dwellers who only speak Russian — are forc-ibly evicted to remote, primitive villages.

The current terrorism prevention campaign is helping the city admin-istration solve long-standing city problems, such as eliminating parking lots near apartment buildings. Officials want to use this car problem to make money. And also to show car owners who's boss. All illegally parked cars will be removed to the pound. The measure, the legality of which was much debated in "peacetime," is to be introduced without any discus-sion. In Moscow, since January 24, 1996, parking in courtyards is actually prohibited by law. The city authorities continue to force car owners into expensive multi-story garages. It is clear who controls these parking lots. Every proposal to create cheap parking lots on open land are blocked by the Moscow City Government.

Moscow authorities signed a cooperation agreement with the Federal Migration Service so that the Migration Service of Moscow could hire an additional 100 employees, whose work would be paid from the city budget. This is necessary to quickly develop a schedule for the eviction of refugees from the hotels, and then, according to the authorities, this problem "will be solved once and for all." The hunt for terrorists and the tightening of the passport regime are above all a new way for the police to make money ille-gally. The police comb the farmers' markets, throwing all the vendors in the mud; they grab people at subway exits and look for people with "too much luggage" at the train stations.

At the same time, for days on end, people have been trying with rare persistence to find at least one policeman on duty in their neighborhood. Correspondents found out that the police force that was promised to everyone after the explosions is not present in any single district of Moscow. The headquarters for the investigation of accidents and terrorist acts are closing so quickly that it seems they were only opened to avoid looking bad in comparison to the rest of the world. The city government sends all questions to the notorious headquarters. They do not know anything about this at the place where new apartments are allocated to the victims. The departments for media liaison say they are not authorized to answer ques-tions. While the government is bombing Chechnya and shouting about flows of refugees instigated by Chechen terrorists, it is fooling the whole world about the situation in Moscow. The promised calm is nothing more than a myth. Vans and trucks are still coming into Moscow, but they are not always inspected. No one knows what the vehicles are bringing, but they drive around the country, often with license plates taped over with a piece of paper where the registration area code is written in by hand. These cars with childish tricks pass all the police cordons and can quite easily end up in a huge residential neighborhood with large bags of explosives as cargo. "We already know on whose conscience these villainous acts lie," Yeltsin said of the house bombings. "The perpetrator's name is terrorism."

Continuing in this vein, we should say that the name of the ruin in Russia is Theft, and the name of the murderers of politicians and bankers is Corruption. Hooray, now the President of Russia knows who they are!

Contact is made with the press and the people only via formal procedures, written requests, bureaucratic rigmarole that really serves only to give importance to the numerous investigators, judges, and prosecutors. One office is responsible for the light bulbs, another only for the sewage system, the third is not open at all. In addition, despite the fact that houses were cordoned off immediately after the explosions, many valuables were looted, possibly by the police themselves. Properly filed requests for the return of passports and other documents, money and valuables, are met with obfuscation at best.

One hospitalized man wrote to the newspaper *Novaya Gazeta*,

> To compensate for the property my daughter was asked to fill out an inventory of what was in the apartment and forced to cross out all the jewelry and money... In response to my daughter's requests to give me and her some kind of certification that we were victims of the explosion, all the agencies that were supposedly providing assistance refused and sent us to each other, so it's a vicious circle. My words, everything is written down correctly. My daughter Elena wrote it down. September 21, 1999.

Another man wrote to *Izvestia*,

> Within 24 hours, they were supposed to check all the basements, attics, and other rooms on the first floors of buildings that had been rented out as offices and storage. So, here's the deal. I live in the South-Western district. There's a company (in the basement) in my entryway, and none of us have seen the employees, and we don't know what kind of firm it is or what it does. On the other side of the house, in the same basement, there's another firm, also not very clear. And there is also a separate entrance to the basement. Someone also sealed off the attic, in such a half-assed way that it is not actually sealed. Where are all the police, who are supposed to be taking this seriously?

> We were told a policeman would be posted by every large building. It's true, I saw one once. I went out on my balcony for a cigarette and saw a policeman. He walked in between the parking lots, pulled down his pants and did his business, then walked away.

We were told that every precinct officer will come and inspect all the houses in his area. I'm terribly sorry, but I'm not particularly familiar with him, our precinct officer. Someone came recently but did not explain what, where, and who he was. After the terrorist attacks, no one came and asked anything. Where are the precinct officers who are supposed to go into every apartment?

Everyone says that someone wants to start a civil war. I am against the war, but still: how should I treat the Armenians who live on the ground floor and never close the main front door behind them, with the combination lock? What should I do with them?

And it doesn't take a real explosive to destroy the peace. The local FSB ran an unannounced "demining exercise" that left residents as shattered as if the "charge" that was found had been real. One of the residents was called outside at 11:00PM, in her nightgown, leaving her bedridden mother behind. All the residents were gathered in the courtyard for hours, with no information. She begged the police to help her get her mother out, but they ignored her. Finally, they let her go back in, but did not tell her it was all just for training purposes. It turns out three other families had the same situation. Then people started thinking, what is this, a selective evacuation? If you can't walk, the hell with you? They were not let back in until it was time to go to work in the morning, and no explanation was ever forthcoming. Imagine the rage. None of this is provided for by law. So, citizens, do not be disheartened if you are turned into guinea pigs. The example of the "Ryazan exercise" reminded the authorities that Russia is a laboratory, the population are guinea pigs, and the authorities are gambling experimenters.

Not a single Chechen trace has yet been found in any of these explosions. And it would be strange to suppose that the Chechens themselves destroyed with their own hands the peace and financial flow into Chechnya, which was so profitable for them. As soon as the military offensive in Chechnya began, the explosions stopped immediately. The authorities explain it as a result of the measures taken. But anyone who has served in the army and knows the basics of military affairs knows very well that it would be no trouble at all to blow up another house in Moscow. You don't need a truck: you can just put a detonator in the trunk of any car. The most efficient district police officer would not able to check all the residential buildings in his area every 5 minutes. And if you follow the logic, you can draw the sad conclusion that explosions have stopped going off in Russia not because of police vigilance but because they are no longer necessary. There is widespread media speculation about the involvement of security services in the preparation and execution of terrorist acts in Russian cities. Bombings in Moscow and other Russian cities might break out again if Russian troops suffer any defeats in Chechnya. The authorities will stop at nothing to hold their ground.

According to various estimates, more than a million people from the North Caucasus live in Moscow. They follow the news from the North Caucasus with great concern. The story of General Shpigun's kidnapping in Chechnya is a graphic example of the relationship between the Moscow and central authorities and representatives of the Caucasian diaspora. Prime Minister Stepashin has vowed to get him freed immediately. The fact is that Shpigun's kidnapping is a purely commercial operation. At first the Chechens asked $10 million for him, then the price dropped to two or three million. Stepashin's challenge was to find the money. So he decided to make the toughest members of the Chechen diaspora in Moscow pay this sum — or simply lock up some of their representatives so he could exchange them for Shpigun, and he hinted at this in a television interview. That same night, all the wealthy Chechens left Moscow — some for Chechnya, some for other countries.

The Liberal Democratic Party of Russia (LDPR), which has gained about 10% of the popular vote. They hold unsanctioned rallies in Moscow under the slogan "Kill the Caucasian bandit, save Russia," calling to restore order not only in Dagestan and Chechnya, but also to the neighboring countries that provoke these conflicts. All this has consequences in the form of colossal massacres, such as what happened at the last City Day celebration, when about 50 young people came to Manezhnaya Square in the center of the city and began savagely beating indiscriminately all the Caucasians who were there. They used knives. Two people were critically wounded, twenty people beaten and thirty people arrested. Truly, as Jesus said: "Judge them not by their words, but by their deeds."

8. Crime and Corruption

Corruption in the Russian government costs the country more than education and health care. In terms of corruption, everyone in Russia is the same, whether they are former or current communists, democrats or nationalists. Every anti-corruption campaign raises a real hurricane in the corridors of power (but only there) and goes on to replicate every other campaign of this kind. All good intentions sink irrevocably into the quagmire of bureaucracy, unable to overcome the resistance of political circles. Every campaign is launched largely due to someone's vested interests, someone's desire to use such an investigation of high-ranking officials and tycoons into their political weapon. Even Otto von Bismarck, who was at one time envoy from the Prussian court to St. Petersburg and later became Chancellor of Germany, considered the fight against corruption at the top of the Russian government an absolutely insurmountable task.

The best answer to the question is, as you know, action. This was very clearly understood by Acting Prosecutor Vladimir Ustinov, who did not attend the UN's international conference "Responding to the Challenge of Corruption" held in Milan. Earlier, Russian Prosecutor General Yuri Skuratov had planned to fly to the Swiss city of Lugano to attend the annual General Assembly of the Swiss Criminal Law Society, where he had been invited to speak by Swiss Federal Prosecutor Carla Del Ponte, his foreign passport was suddenly revoked. The Ministry of Foreign Affairs said that there were some technical inaccuracies in it and that they would re-issue it shortly. In other words, he'd be able to travel abroad just as soon as the session was over.

In Russia, all corruption cases are classified. When the special commission on combating corruption was dealing with criminal cases against Prosecutor General Yury Skuratov and closest members of the presidential entourage, information on the case was available only to members of the Commission on Corruption. According to Oleg Korolev, former Federation Council deputy speaker, the commission worked in extreme secrecy. Naturally, the "very sensitive topics" modestly named by members of the commission are nothing more than evidence of systematic plundering of the country by its leaders under the guise of democratic reforms. In the end, everything is completely swept under the carpet. Maybe the judiciary goes through all this charade, a show of boisterous activity, in order to give all of the parties time to come to an agreement behind the scenes. Everyone is well aware of the names of corrupt deputies, governors, high-ranking officials, a huge number of bankers, and ministers of current and former governments who are involved in illegal economic activities. Their financial and criminal power is also well known to all. Many deputies shy away from investigating corruption cases once they get a glimpse of some of their colleagues' entanglements. The least one can lose is his appetite and the ability to sleep at night.

The most reliable pillar of organized crime is the criminal organization of all life. Everyone is fed up with extortions, but they do not want to refuse officials, because they are afraid of trouble from the tax and security services. The Russian historian Karamzin, who wrote the classic *History of the Russian State* (12 volumes, completed in 1826), was asked to describe it in one word. And two hundred years ago he summed it up, saying: "They steal." That's still true today. Any attempt to investigate what is really going on in the higher echelons of power is rudely suppressed. Yevgeny Primakov (Prime Minister 1998–99) and Prosecutor General Yuri Skuratov were promptly removed from power because they posed a real danger, primarily to President Yeltsin's family. Yuri Skuratov tried to launch an investigation into embezzlement in the highest levels of Russian power, including the "Swiss trail."

According to Swiss Federal Prosecutor Carla Del Ponte, who broke a Sicilian mafia money-laundering operation in Switzerland, more than 300 firms in Switzerland are to some extent controlled by organized criminal groups from the former Soviet Union. According to Carla Del Ponte, the influence of the Russian mafia on the Swiss economy is still growing. In 1998, only about 80 companies were reportedly caught in the sphere of influence of the "Eastern Mafia." Within a year, that number has almost quadrupled. Swiss companies, especially banks, are used for money laundering, and it is easy to assume that a large mass of the money whisked out of Russia during the mad dash to privatize state assets ended up in Switzerland. The bank accounts of prominent Russians are overflowing with "black" money. The West has until recently remained meekly silent in the face of the blatant financial irregularities occurring in a country that, on top of everything else, holds its creditors responsible for its own mistakes. But the criminals follow their wealth to the West, so there is a real danger that calm and prosperous countries (compared to Russia) could also be overwhelmed by the mass violence that accompanies Russia's internal squabbles. According to Carla Del Ponte's estimates, the Russian mafia keeps up to $40 billion in Swiss bank accounts. And this fact can already be regarded as the main external threat to the state security of Switzerland.

What had long been intolerable to Russians was finally noticed in the world outside as well — and here the scandal began. Through a collective epiphany during the summer months of 1999, the West finally caught on to what everyone living in Russia had known for years: that the corruption in the country was immeasurable, that large-scale financial fraud and scams were taking place all over the place. The only thing that Western justice has been able to do in response is to pull some legal levers. The first step was taken by the Swiss prosecutor's office, blocking some accounts of Russian origin and launching an investigation into corruption, money laundering and criminal transactions.

The Swiss prosecutor's office stumbled upon the Russian officials' accounts by accident. It was investigating the financial director of one of the divisions of the company Mabetex, Franco Fenini, 47, who in 1991–1995 worked in Russia in the office of Banco del Gottardo, where he extorted money, abused clients' trust and falsified documents. He told Carla del Ponte about a "suspiciously rich" client, a 35-year-old native of the USSR, who received Israeli citizenship and settled in Spain, Philippe Turover. And Turover, in turn, made a deal to reveal some secret Russian accounts. Turover told Del Ponte about Mabetex, a Swiss construction firm based in Lugano. Mabetex paid bribes to high-ranking Kremlin officials in exchange for a lucrative contract to restore the Kremlin and other sites in Moscow. Mabetex, owned by Kosovar Albanian Begjet Pacolli, received the contract in 1994–95. Swiss investigators have confirmed almost everything Turower said. Investigators found American Express credit card statements signed with the name of Boris Yeltsin himself and his two daughters using Euro-card. The documents show that the American Express card account amount is small, but the Eurocard account amounts were $600,000 each year in 1993 and 1994.

Investigators also learned of the existence of the Dean Bank account. According to the first documents obtained by the newspaper *Corriere della*

Sera, the Dean Bank account was in the name of three individuals: Kremlin administrator Pavel Borodin, who signed the construction contracts, his daughter Ekaterina Zilelskaya, whose husband is the owner of Mercata Ltd, which also received the Kremlin restoration contract, and Begjet Pacolli himself.

Turover had hoped that his information would be useless to the Swiss prosecutor's office, which cannot prosecute bribe-takers from another country anyway. But Carla Del Ponte shared the information with Russia's Prosecutor General Skuratov, warning him that the credit cards in question were in the name of the Russian president and his two daughters, among others. Skuratov had long been hesitant to open a criminal case, but once the videotape became known with his "private life" in the presidential administration, he went ahead

The Attorney General of Geneva began an investigation of Pavel Borodin, an all-powerful figure who was, at the time, the manager of the President's affairs and of all assets under the jurisdiction of the presidential administration. He was accused of money laundering. The investigation was to determine whether funds obtained through abuse of office and corrupt activities had been deposited in the Geneva banks in the name of Borodin and other persons under suspicion. Borodin hired Swiss lawyers to prove that he did not have Swiss bank accounts. How did the Presidential Chief of Staff pay for the services of Geneva lawyers, whose fees exceed the monthly salary of a Russian government official? And why would Borodin, who says that "every penny" of his savings is in Sberbank, hire expensive lawyers in a situation where no formal charges have been brought against him and no criminal case has been opened?

Borodin claims that his signature was in effect Photo-shopped onto the letterhead of a Swiss bank by his political opponents. But high-ranking officials of Swiss banks claim that it is extremely difficult to open an account in any Swiss bank with a forged signature. The rules are very strict, especially for Russian citizens, who are subjected to heightened control procedures. The depositor must present himself and sign all necessary documents in person. Only in very rare, special cases, can he be replaced by a notary or lawyer. Then the signature must be certified by the Swiss consular office in the relevant country.

Borodin is not the only Yeltsin associate to attract the attention of Swiss justice. Suspicion has also fallen on Tatiana Dyachenko. All the oligarchs — millionaires who made their money from the illegal sale of state property — appeared only after they started carrying suitcases full of cash to the Kremlin. The address for the money deliveries was the president's daughter

Tatiana Dyachenko and the head of the presidential administration, Yuma-shev. According to General Korzhakov, Yeltsin's former head of security, they accepted this money right inside the Kremlin, in the first building next to the president. Indirect confirmation of all this is the fact that in recent years 4.6 billion pounds sterling has passed through the accounts of President Yeltsin's daughter and personal adviser Tatiana Dyachenko, at the Bank of New York in the Cayman Islands. The companies controlling these accounts were not big enough to handle such sums. Yeltsin's son-in-law, Tatiana's husband, also has a $2.7 million account at the Bank of New York branch in the Cayman Islands.

It is simply impossible to list all the Russian thieves. If we look into the chain of money laundering from the sale of Lada cars, we see the joint-stock companies Aeroflot; Andava; Anros–Avtovaz; Avva (International); Forums Holding; and on and on. The Swiss Prosecutor's Office and the Bratislava Interpol Office in Slovakia report that the trade in cars is just a cover for illegal transactions. The amount of money transferred by these firms to various banks clearly does not correspond to the volume of car sales.

There is a constant struggle for control over the Central Bank between the Russian government and the State Duma. For the officials, the Central Bank is not primarily a means of state regulation of the economy, but a source of fabulous personal fortunes and a channel for transferring stolen money abroad. The financial activities of the past and present management of the Central Bank of Russia are shrouded in obscurity. On August 14, 1998, Chairman of the Duma Security Committee Victor Ilyukhin stated that the Russian President's family and some high-ranking government officials were involved in embezzling the $4.8 billion loan given by the IMF on August 14, 1998. The chairman of the Duma committee also sent a letter to the Prosecutor General of Russia, Yury Skuratov, which contained documented proof of the charges. According to copies of relevant financial documents, it can be assumed that the above funds did not reach Russia but were shared between President Yeltsin and a narrow circle of top-ranking officials. $2,350 million was sent to the Bank of Sydney where, according to the documents, $235 million was credited to an Australian company where the President's daughter Tatiana Dyachenko, through her authorized Luxembourg representative, has a 25% stake as the predominant voting share. The balance of $2.115 billion, converted into pounds sterling, was transferred to Westminster Bank in London, United Kingdom.

Also on August 14, 1998, $1.4 billion were transferred to the Bank of New York, $780 million was transferred to Credit Swiss on August 17, 1998, and the remaining $270 million was also transferred to the Lausanne branch of Creditanstalt-Bankverein in Switzerland on August 17 of the same year.

Viktor Ilyukhin also suggested that all the money transfers were carried out with the participation of former Chairman of the Central Bank of Russia Sergei Dubinin. The only way to bring the investigation to an end is to publicly review the above facts. Nevertheless, the Directorate for Investigation of Special Cases of the General Prosecutor's Office, after conducting a "thorough" check, found that all the expenses of the bank management were made in accordance with the "Law on the Central Bank of Russia" and did no harm to the state. The case was dropped "for lack of evidence." Russia's attitude toward the scandal involving the use of IMF money was best expressed by Deputy Finance Minister Oleg Vyugin. "Russia will definitely receive the next tranche. Just don't make a fuss and wait for the dust to settle."

So how do Russian state officials make their fabulous fortunes?

The country's chief banker, Viktor Gerashchenko, is one of the classic time-hardened Soviet cadres who do not seek glory and prefer to do big things in silence, behind closed doors. But sometimes fame comes to them unbidden and lifts the veil of secrecy around the Central Bank, which concealed and continues to conceal their truly out-of-control actions. For example, Gerashchenko's monetary reform of 1993 caused an inflow of old-style banknotes (about 1.5 trillion rubles) from the CIS countries into Russia, which provoked a 20% inflationary wave and an increased demand for new money in the neighboring countries. The resulting mess was a limitless opportunity for a financier of remarkable intelligence and imagination to take "unconventional" decisions and actions. And so it happened. Immediately after the currency exchange, the Central Bank of Russia unilaterally and without any coordination with the government and its agencies unexpectedly sent 50 billion rubles in cash to Uzbekistan. All attempts to obtain official explanations for this action were fruitless. Later, Gerashchenko orally referred to some kind of "cash deliveries to credit accounts." After the scandal broke out, Gerashchenko tried to explain his actions as the sale of Bank of Russia currency to the Central Bank of Uzbekistan. But Gerashchenko never produced any justifying documents.

Was the multibillion-dollar sale of cash to Tashkent a sham? There is also a suspicion that Gerashchenko manipulated the Soviet Union's foreign debt in 1989–1991, and lost $30 million. At about the same time, Gerashchenko's subsidiary Sovzagranbank, a subsidiary of the Russian Central Bank, pumped $6 billion into its banks, much of it disappearing without a trace. Gerashchenko supported the rebellious Committee on the State of Emergency (GKChP) in 1991. Gerashchenko was one of the main perpetrators of hyperinflation in 1992. Gerashchenko financially supported Khasbulatov's Supreme Soviet during its confrontation with Yeltsin in 1993. Gerashchenko was the author of "Black Tuesday" in 1994.

In July 1998, Sergei Dubinin, the former chairman of the Central Bank, having realized that the state treasury was depleted and the short-term government bond pyramid was about to collapse, somehow managed to "get" President Yeltsin to give him permission to export several tons of palladium. However, the banker did not have time to do it, as the crisis of August 17 was approaching. The banking system collapsed, and along with it Dubinin himself. Viktor Gerashchenko, who replaced him, having dealt with the current affairs, decided that it would be a sin not to use the paper that was already in place and had long ago taken effect. In December 1998 and January 1999, 300 tons of the precious metal was taken out of Russia. The palladium was pledged to Deutsche Bank against a $3 billion loan. And the money was sent to an account in one of the Soviet foreign banks. The money never reached Russia. According to some reports, this $3 billion was repeatedly funneled through the Sovzagranbank system, apparently bringing them considerable profit. Which, unfortunately, cannot be said about Russia.

The activities of FIMACO (Financial Management Corporation Ltd.) are evidence of a major scam, which involved the top leaders of the financial and political leadership of the country. The offshore company FIMACO was registered on the island of Jersey (Channel Islands) on November 27, 1990. From the time this company was formed to the related scandal that broke out, which cost the country billions of dollars, many events occurred: the collapse of one state, the Soviet Union, and the formation of another — the new Russia; a change of regime (or two); and the evolution of a new economic system. FIMACO survived five governments, two coup attempts and one war.

This company was created when Viktor Gerashchenko was the head of the State Bank of the USSR, then became the chairman of the Bank of Russia, was dismissed, then was again in the same position. When Evgeny Primakov extracted a loan from Kuwait (which went to FIMACO through Eurobank), he was a candidate member of the Politburo of the Central Committee of the Communist Party of the Soviet Union (CPSU), and later became prime minister of Russia. When Gennady Kulik signed a contract with the Swiss export–import company Noga (perhaps because of this company's lawsuits against the Russian government some of the Central Bank's reserves were moved to FIMACO in 1993), he was the minister of agriculture in one of the USSR republics — the RSFSR; later he became Deputy Prime Minister of Russia. The offshore company FIMACO was a tool to "mobilize nontraditional sources of financial resources" under two Presidents (Gorbachev and Yeltsin) and two regimes (Soviet and post-Soviet) for nine years. On February 9, 1999, according to Andrei Movchan, president of Eurobank, the Sovzagranbank for Northern Europe, the Central Bank's accounts with FIMACO were closed.

Over the five years since 1993, the Central Bank has transferred $37.3 billion; 9.98 billion German marks, 379.9 billion Japanese yen, 11.98 billion French francs and 862.6 million British pounds from the country's foreign exchange reserves to FIMACO. This is almost all of the country's foreign exchange reserves and loans from the IMF. The most interesting thing is that the authorized capital of the company was only a thousand dollars. The data were so sensational that the IMF Managing Director Michel Camdessus, in negotiations with the Russian leadership as a condition of granting the next loan, demanded a full audit of FIMACO. When it was discovered that a total of $50 billion in foreign currency reserves had been kept in the accounts of the offshore firm FIMACO for five years, the General Prosecutor's Office, bewildered, found nothing better to do than to initiate criminal proceedings against the Central Bank on charges of misuse of $51,000.

The founder of FIMACO is the Commercial Bank for Northern Europe (Eurobank). About 80% of Eurobank's share capital is still owned by the Central Bank of Russia. Eurobank itself and FIMACO, which it established, had an overwhelming majority of shares in the joint-stock commercial bank Eurofinance, registered in Moscow. Why the Central Bank would keep money on distant islands is easy to see. If the Central Bank received 4% per annum from the funds placed in FIMACO, then at least 2–3% over this rate could easily find its way into the pockets of those involved in the case. And that is $1–1.5 billion. But have you ever seen anybody who was satisfied with just two or three percent, while right under their noses in Moscow speculators were giving up to 150%? Eurofinance Bank was seen on the Moscow Interbank Currency Exchange (MICEX) as one of the leading players in the market of currency futures contracts. In fact, not Eurofinance, but the Central Bank through Eurobank and FIMACO was a "seller" of futures.

Although trading in currency futures is considered to be highly risky not only in Russia, but all over the world, the Central Bank was playing a virtually win–win lottery. It has always had leverage over the trading of the Moscow Interbank Currency Exchange (MICEX). Central Bank officials were always members of the exchange's Board of Directors. On paper the exchange remained an independent financial structure, but in practice the Bank determined the "rate" of the exchange. The interests of the state were taken into account last, and the exchange was simply a hostage of the

Central Bank financial policy. To understand the "know-how" of bankers, you need to imagine a man who plays cards with his own hands using state money. In his right hand he holds one part of the country's foreign currency reserves, and in his left hand he holds another part of the same reserves, but only "received" from an offshore firm. Both hands not only know perfectly well what each of them is doing, but they also exchange cards and money. At stake, respectively, is the budget, and the chips for the game and the settlements are government short-term bonds (GKOs) and other highly liquid securities. A very convenient and effective combination for professionals. The Central Bank and the Ministry of Finance were right-handedly "fighting" for the interests of the country and the ruble with "non-residents," under the name of which their own left hand acted. For the public, currency reserves "held the ruble" and "reduced the yield on government short-term bonds (GKOs)," while for a small group of officials, those same reserves put pressure on the ruble and inflated the rates on those same bonds. Of course, one hand had to "play the fool" from time to time, but the other was winning in full measure. If we take at least 80% as an average bet, the winnings amounted to $40 billion. That is how much this game was supposed to bring to its organizers and participants. Accordingly, the budget was lightened by the same amount. It is clear that without the offshore accounts, there was no way to steal such a lot of money from the budget.

But by the summer of 1998 the situation was unfavorable for the "sellers" of futures. If the futures contracts had continued to be quoted, Eurofinance Bank would have become quite uncomfortable: it accounted for about 10–15% of all futures sales on the Moscow International Currency Exchange (MICEX) and would have had to shell out about $50–70 million to futures buyers. Immediately after the Kiriyenko government announced its famous moratorium, the MICEX stopped quoting futures contracts. Domestic and foreign bidders lost a lot of money, and the exchange took a big risk to its reputation. The Central Bank was only concerned about one thing — how to save its money pumped from Russia's main bank vault through FIMACO to Eurofinance Bank in operations on the currency futures market. Mikhail Khodorkovsky, the former head of the Menatep Bank, told the New York Times that Russian authorities began selling government securities on the eve of the August 1999 crisis because they were convinced that a devaluation of the ruble was inevitable. He said they were transferring money overseas with the help of a front company and then to the Bank of New York. Anyone who sold government securities on the eve of the financial crash and ruble devaluation became incredibly rich if they knew in advance that the ruble would be devalued.

The rule of law was discarded as unnecessary. With a gross violation of the law, the state short-term bond pyramid (GKO) was destroyed. This pyramid, as well as the notorious MMM company in Russia, amounted to the robbery of depositors. One of the main positions espoused by the government was that "there is not enough money for everyone, so we have to pay off the minimum." Only 14 to 20 billion rubles could be paid to the bond holders instead of 113 billion rubles owed. In other words, you are to be robbed completely: take your 10% and declare bankruptcy. This cynicism caused an upsurge of criminality. Hundreds of banks — owners of government bonds — went bankrupt. And all of them had obligations to clients. Certain clients were not used to losing their money just because of some officials unknown to them; and they started to extort payment from the bankers by all the means available to them. The whole picture shows complete chaos. The country is simply not run by anyone.

When the West publishes information about top government officials in Russia and it turns out they have billions of dollars, this information looks absolutely implausible: there is no way officials could enrich themselves so much in such a short time. This allows Russian officials to sue the newspapers and hurl thunder and lightning over the choice of Russia as a "whipping boy." Now, however, we see how Russian statesmen get rich. And none of this could have been possible without the participation of ministers, prime ministers and the presidential administration, who most likely had a share in the game. According to the ousted Russian Prosecutor General, 780 officials from the Russian government are suspected of corruption. Among them are two former deputy prime ministers, ministers and officials of the Central Bank and the Ministry of Finance.

The Kremlin administration is also only really in the business of privatizing the country's largest financial streams. Russian power has always been a thief, and during the Yeltsin years it became shamelessly thievish. The officials and their protégés in parastatal corporations are notorious for the fact that an entire train of oil tankers leaving one point, from Ukhta, where the oil is extracted, may not reach its destination, say, Kaliningrad. But it's not just one train. Whole trains of timber, coal, rolled metal disappear.

Recently, as the new government is being formed in Russia, the main professional criterion has become the predisposition to take a cavalier attitude to the treasury. Ministers publicly admit that they have a claim on certain corporations. Those behind criminal cases can dismiss even the Attorney General. In this respect, the statement of former Prosecutor General Yury Skuratov is noteworthy, since the people who are believed to have been involved in the high-profile murders, especially those who ordered the murders, have good contacts in the presidential administration and the closest entourage of the president.

MP Galina Starovoitova and Vice-Governor of St. Petersburg Mikhail Manevich were apparently murdered because of Starovoitova's deputy investigations, which involve the interests of several high-ranking officials, including the heads of St. Petersburg law enforcement agencies, and Duma Speaker Gennady Seleznev, linked to the so-called National Security Academy. According to Starovoitova, who wrote under the pseudonyms Anna Prokhorova and Pyotr Glebov for the *Severnaya Stolitsa* newspaper, the money intended for the speaker's election campaign was pumped through this organization. St. Petersburg Vice-Governor Mikhail Manevich was murdered on August 18, 1997 — the day before he was supposed to meet with Starovoitova.

Ruslan Linkov, a former advisor to Galina Starovoitova, believes that they were to discuss the materials of the State Duma's privatization review commission in St. Petersburg, which was headed by Yuri Shutov. In February 1999, Shutov was arrested on charges of organizing four contract murders. The deputy is suspected of leading a gang, organizing the murders of prominent businessman Dmitri Filippov, former advisor to the governor of St. Petersburg lawyer Igor Dubovik, and chairman of the board of directors of the firm Istochnik Nikolai Bolotovsky, preparing to murder State Duma deputy Vyacheslav Shevchenko, and robbery and robbery attacks on apartments and offices. In addition to Shutov, twelve people involved in the activities of the group were arrested. Yuri Shutov was first convicted in 1981 of embezzlement of state property when he was first deputy head of the Leningrad statistical office. He spent 5 years in prison and was released in 1987 under an amnesty. In 1992, Shutov was prosecuted for robbery and for weapons possession. He was arrested, but times were different, and someone in high places prevented Shutov from going to prison. Almost everywhere in Russia, those in charge of privatization were considered the most dangerous and unapproachable. Dark, athletic-bodied personalities were constantly swirling around them, ready to helpfully smash the head of the first person they met at the slightest wave of their patron's hand.

It's true that corruption flourished under President Marcos in the Philippines, under Mobutu in Zaire, and under Suharto in Indonesia. But Russia stands above the crowd, because here a gigantic country of great geopolitical importance is engulfed in pervasive corruption. Even the United States faces an immense problem in avoiding foreign corruption of its workings. And this will become just as big an issue for them as opposing Marxist ideology has been.

Moscow Mayor Luzhkov has accused the entourage of Boris Yeltsin of harassing his wife, who is a big business leader. However, it is unlikely that disclosing the details of his wife's major deals will help the ambitious mayor to gain popularity. In Russia, as things stand, it is impossible to be a success in business without being a de facto criminal. If the mafia in the West is understood to controls prostitution, gambling, the sale of drugs and perhaps liquor, stolen goods, primarily illegal types of business, in Russia the mafia seeks to control the country's largest enterprises. This includes whole industries such as oil, logging, mining, metalworking and more. The people behind the Russian mafia are not street kids who grew up in the slums and have somehow matured into an understanding of the possible global outlook, but people who have higher education, strategic thinking, economic competence and agency connections. Try to guess whom we are talking about.

At the beginning of the struggle over every respectable enterprise in Russia, harsh measures (up to and including terror) are taken first by local criminal bosses, and then by the "top" of Moscow's organized crime. At the same time, in some strange way, the name of the person responsible for this never appears in any of the numerous criminal cases connected with the murders of people who have fallen in the "war" for control over the plants and factories. Later it turns out that these people's immunity from prosecution is organized by the "organs" themselves.

If you are afraid that there will be a war in Russia that will have a great impact on the rest of the world, it is too late to be afraid. There has been a war going on in Russia for a long time now. And with the use of the most modern weapons. The opponents are physically destroying each other by the dozens and hundreds. Special police and army units are involved in the ongoing conflicts, as well as armed mobile groups of numerous criminal gangs. Some criminal groups have 1–2,000 fighters. This small army is divided into mobile squads of four in a car. Everyone is armed. In addition, each car has a machine gun, a grenade launcher and a radio. At one alarm call, all "patrol" groups immediately rush to the designated location. The discipline is harsh. Their actions are much more coordinated than those of the police. The standard structure of an organized criminal group usually includes a system of protection, consisting, figuratively speaking, of two "roofs" and five main pillars. The latter are now well known: these are the profits from drug trafficking, weapons and "live goods" (prostitutes, hostages, etc.), smuggling, control over distilleries and the sale of counterfeit alcohol. Of the "roofs," one is invisible (bribe-takers from the state apparatus and law enforcement structures), and the other is quite legal, consisting of individual media representatives and highly professional lawyers hired to work for them.

One of the most criminalized sectors of the Russian economy is the oil industry. Virtually every firm operating in the market for petroleum products is, to some extent, controlled by crime bosses. Until recently, the highest authority in the oil business was considered a "thief in law" (that is, a recognized Capo, so to speak, a well-known professional crime boss) by the nickname of Cherniy ("Black"). He was promoted to the "oil kingdom" by his mentor from Khabarovsk, who was well known not only in Siberia but also in Moscow. However, The Black One" did not last long; in 1996 he died under circumstances that are still unclear. Today, several dozen crime bosses are competing for the position of "king of Russian oil." Caucasians are especially active in this area. Some of them, for instance the Georgian "thief in law" Dato and the Armenian boss Kakha have even relocated to the main oil production area — the Tyumen Region. At least 16 thieves in law reside in Tyumen today. Additionally, until recently, the local criminal gang was also actively sharing the oil pie. Among the representatives of Tyumen gangsters are the so-called groups of athletes. One was killed in Crimea in 1996, while the other went into politics; that fall, he was elected deputy of the Nizhnevartovsk City Duma.

The heads of almost all the oil companies and their local subdivisions have stable personal connections with the leaders of the criminal world. A well-known "thief in law" nicknamed Miron, for example, maintained active contacts with the leadership of LUKoil. In the mid-1990s, he traveled to Tyumen several times, where he was involved in the affairs of LUKoil. In parallel, Miron was making attempts to establish personal relations with the management of "Sidanko" and a number of smaller companies. These budding friendships were interrupted by Miron's sudden death. He was killed in Moscow in 1996.

The Director General of the joint stock company Kondpetroleum, according to police data, repeatedly brought gangsters to Tyumen to solve his problems. Avdoshin, the boss of gangsters in Omsk, has stable contacts with Pavel Satonkin, deputy of the Omsk Oblast Legislative Assembly, who represents the interests of YUKOS in Omsk. According to the police information, Deputy Satonkin deals in gasoline and works with crime bosses to carry out certain "sensitive" instructions from YUKOS management. For example, with Avdoshin's direct involvement, the company purchased 40% of the shares in the Omskshina plant.

In recent years, officials from all branches of power have become increasingly involved in professional crime. Criminal clans are particularly interested in the heads of administration of those regions of the country where there are significant reserves of natural fuel. The fight over oil and gas has intensified. The government has officially acknowledged through the mouth of Interior Minister General Rushailo the incredible criminalization of the Russian oil products market.

Victor Kalyuzhny was of interest not only to domestic law enforcement and tax authorities, but also to Interpol, which sent a corresponding request to Russia. Kalyuzhny cooperated with the firm Verdeks and its owner Mark Gelfand in oil smuggling operations. Of the 12 people whose details were requested by Interpol, three were killed and the murders were never solved. Kalyuzhny, realizing that he was under scrutiny, did what anyone in Russia would have done in his place. He got into politics. He was elected deputy of the Tomsk City Duma and received parliamentary immunity. Later he was appointed first deputy minister of fuel and energy of Russia, and on May 25, 1999, he was appointed minister.

The criminal world is also making serious inroads into the "sacred cow" of the Russian economy — the military–industrial complex. A typical example is the attempts to take control of the financial and export flows of Russia's largest aircraft manufacturer — the MAPO MIG production association. Several organized crime groups were dreaming of taking control of MAPO MIG, producer of the ultramodern fighter planes, but the Solntsev mafia was the lucky one. Their activists were called in to serve as a "roof" by creating a bank at MAPO MIG. The initiator of this idea was Alisher Usmanov, well known in criminal circles in Russia and abroad. He is considered to be the "brains" behind many dizzying projects of recent years. Thanks to Usmanov's efforts and his business partners at the time — General Director of the Foreign Economic Association E. Ananyev, editor-in-chief of Mega-polis magazine E. Bystrov, and V. Kuzmin, head of the state-owned company MAPO MIG, MAPO Bank was established in April 1993. A little later, the leader of the Solntsev group, Mikhas, was also involved in the project. Initially, the bank was conceived to service the foreign trade activities of MAPO MIG. However, later it received a serious corporate clientele represented by the Foreign Intelligence Service (SVR) and the Federal Security Service (FSB). And Oleg Soskovets, who at the time was in charge of the defense complex in the Russian government, had a hand in this. In addition to the special services, Rosvooruzhenie and a number of other firms involved in the export of oil, metals and precious stones began to accumulate money in the bank. Do we need more proof of the ties between the Russian secret services and the Russian military–industrial complex with criminal structures? Subsequently, the criminal nature of the bank became too widely known and the special services were forced to transfer their accounts to other banks. As a result, by early 1996 the main clients of MAPO Bank were the gangsters and, of course, MAPO MIG. Later, Usmanov provided the financial and industrial group AtomRudMet, which was created in order to gain full control over the export and financial flows of the Oskolsky electrometallurgical combine. In addition, Usmanov actively tried to infiltrate the structures of Gazprom and a number of large oil companies through his extensive connections. According to some sources, Usmanov maintained close friendship with P. Rodionov, deputy chairman of Gazprom and V. Ilyushin, a board member of Gazprom. Recently, Usmanov has controlled diamond deposits in the Arkhangelsk Region and gold deposits in Uzbekistan.

For example, Italian Judge Giovagnoli admitted that all Russian businessmen in Italy were forced to "share" profits from import–export operations with Russia. According to the judge, the funds thus obtained were then sent to accounts at the Bank of New York. Any connection with Russia automatically leads to contact either with the FSB and high-ranking corrupt officials or with the mafia.

9. Central Government

In Russian society, and abroad, more and more people who are interested in Russia or have Russian roots perceive themselves as spectators in the theater of the absurd. They have started asking themselves questions they have never asked before. For example, how can the Duma initiate impeachment proceedings while the government it supports, led by the prime minister, is opposed? Why is it that the President, on his own decision, can dismiss the head of the government, who had the support of parliament and enjoyed a very high trust rating? Why, after the new prime minister was voted in by a majority, is it possible for the Duma to allow itself to immediately and publicly disclaim any responsibility for the activities of the cabinet he heads? Why does the new government, which was supposed to make a breakthrough in the economy, forget all about any breakthroughs and instead declares first of all that it will continue with the previous course while betting that parliament will adopt the very bills that it rejected when the previous government introduced them? Why can't the head of the cabinet, who according to the Constitution bears full responsibility for its work, form the cabinet at his own discretion rather than having to reckon with the opinion and obey the will of other people who bear no responsibility whatsoever?

The war in Chechnya, endless angry showdowns on the eve of the elections, false anti-Western and nationalist propaganda openly and clearly demonstrate the absence of humanity and the medieval morality of the Russian political class, which they successfully impose on Russian society. The bestial egoism of Russian officials is the reason for the miserable salaries and pensions of Russians and the criminalization and devastation in the country. Woe to the Russian people. Russian politicians behave equally ruthlessly towards strangers and their own people. Various groups vie with each other for power throughout Russia, taking advantage of loopholes in federal and local laws on the division of powers, and violate the general principles of democratic control over power. This keeps being demonstrated in one region after another, in the capital, then in the country as a whole. Ultimately, it is thanks to this morality that the people of Russia are reduced to begging and the population is declining. Nobody in Russia really cares about the implementation of the law!

The war in Chechnya, the never-ending angry showdowns on the eve of elections, the lying anti-Western and nationalist propaganda openly and clearly demonstrate the lack of humanism and the medieval morality of the Russian political class, which they have successfully imposed on Russian society. It is the bestial selfishness of Russian officials that is responsible for the miserable salaries and pensions of Russians, criminalization, and devastation in the country. Woe to the Russian people. Russian politicians are equally ruthless in their treatment of outsiders and insiders. The numerous factions fighting for power all over Russia, taking advantage of loopholes in the federal and local laws on the division of powers, violate the general principles of democratic control of power. This is constantly manifested in one region after another, in the capital, and in the country as a whole. In the end, it is precisely due to such morality that the people of Russia are being impoverished and are dying out. No one in Russia is truly concerned about enforcing the law!

Total lies and hypocrisy have plagued the Russian political elite. The political movement "Our Home is Russia," created by former Prime Minister Viktor Chernomyrdin, declared that "Russian soldiers in Chechnya are not fighting, but carrying out a peacekeeping mission." During the several months this peacekeeping mission has been in operation, according to official data, the air force carried out 3,600 sorties and destroyed more than 400 different targets and bases, 314 vehicles, 24 air defense installations, 4 industrial enterprises, 4 compressor stations for pumping oil, 6 retransmission stations, 50 bridges and more. Over 200,000 people fled from the area of hostilities, fleeing, first of all, from the Russian troops. A regular army of several tens of thousands of people, heavy artillery and front-line aviation are taking part in this peacekeeping mission. Other countries also have problems with terrorists, but no country has ever used artillery or mass bombing against them.

Russia has a long tradition of politicians who are unable to walk, think, or speak. They are constantly promising something to someone, promising for example to continue negotiations with the Americans on strategic weapons, or to sign a peace treaty with the Japanese and come to some conclusion on the problem of the Southern Kuril Islands. But in reality, all these statements are attempts to solve domestic political problems. It should be clear to everyone that whoever is saying this is irreplaceable. The entire state depends on the whims of one man, his uncontrollability and irresponsibility. It is possible that the President of Russia is not fully informed by his administration about the real political situation. There is always the possibility of foul play. The office of the head of state has turned into a destructive body that, instead of consolidating society, sets one side against another and creates conflicts. The principle of "He who is not with us is against us" is constantly cultivated.

A special relationship develops between the President and the Prime Minister. Since Soviet times, people have become accustomed to the fact that the prime minister is a major economic position, that he is not just a technical figure but a very significant one. Both Stalin and Khrushchev served as prime minister for many years. And still, post-communist officials believe that the prime minister is everything. The prime minister is always charged with the task of changing the wrong impression that the world community has about the situation in Russia. But for most Russian citizens he is just one in a long line of puppets. Every prime minister is primarily concerned with avoiding being dismissed, and strengthening their position. For that, they need the political support of regional leaders, and their dream is to create their own electoral movement, based on the governors. Therefore, the President always demands the unconditional recognition of his own authority by his subordinates and keeps the chief of each new government on a short leash. From the very beginning, the prime minister's hands and feet are tied.

President Yeltsin was very strongly influenced by a small group of people headed by his daughter Tatiana and businessman Berezovsky. It is obvious that in his reshuffle, the President did not consider the interests of the country and acted in someone else's personal interests. The fact that the Kremlin was so unanimously opposed by various political forces can be explained by the real danger of the head of state's actions, which may reflect the interests of certain individuals, rather than his concern for the country and its citizens. One way or another, the government is moving towards solving political problems by force, because it is actually losing control over the country. While the government is wasting energy on endless political shake-ups, the lives of tens of millions of Russians continue to deteriorate. Citizens' property and freedoms are threatened.

Today, a statesman should not so much dream about high positions as he should think about solving the main issues of Russian statehood. Today the question is not about reforms, but purely about the preservation of the nation, about preventing chaos. Heated power struggles threaten to burn the political arena to ashes. If that happens, neither the President nor the Parliament will be needed. During a poll of leading figures in Arkhangelsk about another dismissal of the government, respondents had only foul language to offer and they requested not to have their names used.

How is the Russian leadership better than Pinochet, who is being prosecuted by the courts of many countries for murder and criminal threats? There is plenty of information suggesting that many Russian leaders personally gave orders to kill and persecute their opponents and simple dissidents. The former head of the Russian President's security service, Alexander Korzhakov, said that Boris Yeltsin had instructed him to liquidate Khasbulatov and Rutskoy in 1993, and to collect materials on the Moscow mayor "as soon as Luzhkov became mayor." The former head of the US National Security Agency has suggested that former prime minister and intelligence chief Yevgeny Primakov was involved in the assassination attempt on Eduard Shevardnadze, the President of Georgia.

Constantly changing prime ministers and members of the government is not a personnel policy conducive to improving conditions in any way. Such a government has no chance to hold on, no matter what financial flows they may concentrate in their hands. Each resignation disrupts the power relations in the regions. Important documents sent to the government for consideration lie unexamined and unsigned. Draft legislation may gather dust for an unimaginable amount of time, only to be submitted for consideration with numerous flaws still apparent and without consultations with the agencies responsible for implementing the law. The only thing that the State Duma is capable of adopting quickly and decisively is the decision to prosecute the NATO Secretary General for the genocide of the Serb people. The speakers in the Duma talk about the other urgent problems in an inarticulate, shorthand manner, and it is clear that all the basic laws, program provisions, budget, etc., will fail again.

They have been talking about a union between Russia and Belarus for several years. But previously it was a union of two states, and now they are promising one "union state." Not a single expert in the world knows what a "union state" is. There are unitary states, there are states with autonomies, there are federations and confederations. The union of two or more states is the union of independent countries for some purpose, but without the creation of a common government. Independence with another government on top is absurd. When it comes to Belarus, they talk about the enormous benefits of strategic security and the prospects for a common market of mutually complementary economies. But they forget to calculate the cost of creating a common currency and customs area. The unification of Russia and Belarus would be more like a conspiracy among the leadership. There can be no equality between two republics with such different standards of living, population and geographical size, natural resources and industrial potential. Russia and Belarus have been developing differently and at different paces for the past 10 years, so that a political union would be fraught with serious economic difficulties and increased tensions in society. Russia would actually be rescuing the collapsing economy and finances of Belarus. Russia could lose about $560 million just from the unification of financial systems. If you add the burden of the collapsing Belarusian economy to this, a new financial crisis in Russia may be imminent. This is confirmed by the fact that as soon as the customs were removed from the border with Belarus, Russia was immediately flooded with smuggled goods. The political association of Russia and Belorussia is based only on the political goals of the two presidents, and the consequences for both countries could be very severe. One way or another, the unification of Russia and Belorussia would require changes to the Russian Constitution, and those changes might be quite significant. But those who are pressing this idea are not thinking about the consequences for the country, they are focused only on one thing: the unification of Russia and Belorussia into one state can give them greater powers themselves.

Meanwhile, Belarus sets a completely different example for Russia. President Alexander Lukashenko recently signed a decree allowing judges to individually, without the participation of lay assessors, consider cases on crimes for which the maximum penalty is not more than 10 years in prison. This decree was adopted in order to "improve the efficiency of the administration of justice." What's this? A return to the Stalinist judicial "troikas" and military tribunals? Those also began with 10 years and ended with mass shootings.

No one can guarantee that the next change of power in the country will take place in a civilized manner. In the struggle for power, everything goes: from innocent rumors to serious compromising material bordering on crime. Therefore, making any forecasts in Russia is a thankless task. Especially when everything in the country and the situation is shifting, like in a children's kaleidoscope. And in conditions of constant ideological hysteria and information warfare, all the more so. The worst imaginings become possible. The members of this government flatter themselves with the idea that they can leave the country at any time and get good jobs somewhere in prosperous nations. Then they will be replaced by those who today proudly call themselves the opposition, but who, in their own turn, will not tolerate any opposition to themselves.

Russia has its own way of resolving government crises. It just smoothly flows from one crisis to the next. Ministers come and go, and it makes absolutely no difference. Political decisions are made elsewhere. None of the leaders of the electoral associations, or former or current politicians (including mayors and former prime ministers), can boast about how successful they were in their work. None of them was able to turn around the situation in the country. A significant number of leaders are still in high positions, and it's they who are responsible for the situation in the country. They make like they're in the "opposition" but that's just a way to stay in power, without changing anything for real.

The country is stuck in a transformation from totalitarianism to democracy. It lacks not only democratic traditions, but also, to a large extent, a meaningful separation of powers. The Russian elite still primarily thinks of political power in terms of tsarist or communist-like centralized power. The pseudo-democratic constitution of the presidential republic conceals an authoritarian state regime. The separation of powers in Russia is still a fiction: The president has the right to do everything, yet is not responsible for anything. The country is stuck in a transformation from totalitarianism to democracy. Both houses of parliament, the State Duma and the Federation Council, have mainly symbolic powers and hardly any real right to participate in major decisions.

In August 1991, the metallic voice of an announcer alerted the country to the transfer of power to the State Committee for the State of Emergency (GKChP). There were armored vehicles in the streets of Moscow, rallies on Manezhnaya Square and outside the Moscow City Council, flyers with proclamations by Yeltsin and the GKChP, curfews, barricades, and a human shield outside the White House. At the moment there is almost nobody left among the former allies of the president's entourage. There is no more talk about the unity of the democratic flank.

In 1991 Yeltsin was a hero who climbed onto a tank and stood up to defend Russian democracy. Today, he embodies the tragedy of Russian reform. The man who is supposed to serve as a guarantor of civil harmony is perceived as a constant generator of social danger. People who have been fired after years of service in the president's administration do not miss their past at all. Of course Yeltsin, like any other leader of the USSR and Russia, after being in office for a while adopted the image of the Tsar (in Yeltsin's case, a reformist Tsar), who understood and loved his people but, at the same time, was able to be stern. President Yeltsin solemnly proclaimed, first, a "pact of social harmony," then a "year of concord and reconciliation," and later an "agreement of all branches of power." Gradually, the old treaties and beautiful names were forgotten, and the fate of the new creations did not look promising.

In recent years, Yeltsin has won the most antipathy of Russians by a wide margin. According to public opinion polls, only 6% of Russian citizens supported President Yeltsin's policy in 1999. The President of Russia has long been hated by his people. In order to stay in power and protect himself in case he had to leave office, he was forced to bring closer to him the former Leningrad lieutenant colonel of the KGB, Vladimir Putin, who has made rapid career advances in recent years. When and why did Yeltsin trust Putin completely?

Prior to the story with Putin, Nikolai Bordyuzha, the former head of the Russian Presidential Administration, blackmailed Yuri Skuratov by making public some now well-known videotapes. He suggested that Skuratov write a letter of resignation. One of the "prostitutes" captured on the video with Skuratov had a police officer's ID.

If the reforms that President Yeltsin intended to implement had been successful, he would not have nominated Putin as prime minister and would not have declared him his successor. Yeltsin was not motivated by concern for the fate of his beloved Russia or any political consideration, but solely by the desire to secure the most painless exit possible for himself and his cronies,. If Russia had been advancing along the path of democracy, Yeltsin would have chosen some other politician who would have continued the reforms, but Yeltsin was very much afraid of sharing the fate of numerous dictators hated by his people. Yeltsin and his family had reason to worry.

If Yevgeny Primakov or Yuri Luzhkov had won the presidential election, their first act would have been to launch a large-scale corruption case. [Apparently, different factions support different mafias.] Unfortunately, it would not have been an impartial investigation of the plundering of the country's wealth and international loans, but just another redistribution of property. At the time when the State Duma was voting to impeach the president, on May 12, Yeltsin's entourage was preparing to prevent his impeachment at all costs. Despite all the assurances of the authorities, a state of emergency was to be declared in Russia on May 13, 1999. Some newspapers even printed the draft of the presidential decree. Certain places read as follows: "To appoint S.V. Stepashin the head of the Provisional Administration; A.I. Lebed to be the deputy head of the Provisional Administration." General Lebed was indeed unexpectedly summoned to Moscow on the evening of

May 11 and left the capital on the 13th. He was supposed to introduce the state of emergency on May 13, 1999.

It is no secret that the country's top officials are guilty of embezzling billions of dollars from various funds and international aid funds. Corruption in Russia is so entrenched that governments and humanitarian organizations try to conceal its extent so as not to discourage donor countries from helping. The only official response is to claim that "lies and fabrications designed to defame the government and block access to financial aid. They treat the Russian people like complete idiots, claiming that articles about financial abuses by the President's family and the violation of moral and ethical standards by his closest relatives just discredit Russian journalism and seriously violate the rights of the reader to receive objective and reliable information. The Ministry of Information constantly repeats that the Russian reader is being deliberately misinformed for unscrupulous political reasons and tries to deflect attention to straw-man "enemies" in order to direct the public anger against Russia's top statesman.

Statements by the central government are almost always irresponsible. One day the new Prime Minister, Vladimir Putin, announced that the media's allegations of Russian money laundering at the Bank of New York were not confirmed; but that very same day, the U.S. Justice Department notified the White House that a link had been found between the Swiss and New York banking scandals. The U.S. bank was indeed being used to move money around, with recipients including Pavel Borodin and Yeltsin's son-in-law, Alexei Dyachenko, husband of Yeltsin's youngest daughter, who wired $2.7 million to the Cayman Islands. At the same time as Finance Minister Mikhail Zadornov was claiming that Russia had nothing to do with the Bank of New York problem, U.S. law enforcement discovered an account where Russian organized crime was laundering money. The Russian Ministry of the Interior was forced to cooperate with the FBI on this matter.

The ITAR-TASS news agency, citing the president's press service, reported that the Russian president, his wife and children had never opened accounts in foreign banks and that their incomes were properly declared. But bank documents were discovered in Lugano, Switzerland, showing that Boris Yeltsin and his daughters Tatiana Dyachenko and Elena Okulova had been issued American Express credit cards to which funds had been transferred from an unnamed company account in Canton Ticino. The firm belongs to Sylvia F., the wife of a former banker who later worked for the famous Mabetex company and is now under investigation for abuse of power, fraud and forgery. The fact that the name of the Russian President appeared was officially confirmed by the Swiss prosecutor Jacques Ducry, who was present during the seizure of documents confirming the existence of these credit cards.

The political tradition in Russia is to deny everything, even if you are nailed to a wall. Even when newspapers published a photocopy of Pavel Borodin's Swiss bank account, he calmly denied everything and went on with his super-profitable activity of managing the assets of the presidential administration. In Russia, an official's briefcase serves many functions: in addition to being a reservoir of power, it can be an excellent bullet-proof vest.

The international criminals from Russia have built a planet-wide structure through which they can move the fruits of their plunder. The investigation of this case already spans from Moscow to New York. Russia's chief privatizer, Anatoly Chubais, has also been implicated in the scandal. Semyon Mogilevich, a Ukrainian Jew and organized crime boss, founded the firm Arbat International in the British offshore zone in the English Channel. Arbat owns 20% of shares in TEMBR Bank. Meanwhile, this bank performs settlements for the joint-stock company UES, run by Anatoly Chubais. The UES itself owns 30% of TEMBR-bank and there may be financial links between the bank and Anatoly Chubais.[1]

Dubious deals are a daily occurrence. This report of corruption at the highest levels of government was received in Russia with complete equanimity. Indeed, why should there be different rules for the Kremlin and the rest of the country? Moscow is once again trying to shift the blame abroad and, as with the corruption and bank fraud scandal, is once again painting itself as the victim being persecuted by all. There is a constant search for whoever is behind this global conspiracy against Russia. "We'll sue you!" — Russian politicians quickly have learnt from the West. Now they threaten newspapers whose reports have been meticulously corroborated with evidence and documentary proof, and confirmed by foreign and domestic investigators and international financial institutions. Their promises to take the most vigorous measures to stop any illegal money found flowing through Russia are ridiculous.

A year ago, the world press was reporting on the great achievements of Russian reforms, and suddenly, in one day, everyone had an epiphany. For

---

[1] Chubais is best known for his role in the 1990s 'loans for shares' scheme, under President Boris Yeltsin, which is today blamed for having helped to create the 'oligarch' class in Russia. It also caused millions of Russians to lose their savings and many people in the country have long held a negative view of the 66-year-old former Kremlin official. ... He has a reputation as an avowed liberal and is known as a strong proponent of integrating Moscow with the West. "Controversial 1990s figure quits Kremlin," RT, March 24, 2022, at https://www.rt.com/russia/552555-chubais-resigns-leaves-russia/

10 years, the West has been finding partners in Russia that Russia itself has always considered completely useless. In fact, it was no secret to anyone, especially to Western diplomats, that corruption at all levels flourished in Russia with impunity. Among experts and observers who follow the fate of Russia, this topic has been discussed many times. Figures of billions of dollars of capital flowing out of Russia were even mentioned. Only the names of those responsible remained secret. Since the concept of "Russian Mafia" was first introduced, it has been suspected of being an amalgam between corrupt bureaucrats, professional criminals and businessmen unclean before the law. Now the question is being asked: what is the future of a country in whose past one can only see periods of relative order, but not true legality. Historians have singled out as surprising not the fact that crime spiked after 1989, but that Russia was tried to be run as a normal, rule-of-law state. The scandal showed how, even in the tradition dating back to the days of the Communist regime, the rule of law was only an outward appearance.

Officially, three-quarters of the foreign loans were "eaten up," meaning they were used to pay off debts on salaries, as well as for departmental expenses such as business trips, consultants, and PR campaigns. Foreign currency loans were converted into rubles, and were supposedly used to pay salaries to the military and state employees, to pensions, subsidies to coal miners and agriculture, but in fact they often ended up in the accounts of private companies — companies that were set up with a bit of help from the very officials responsible for how those credits were disbursed.

Is there any occupation that is even less respected in Russia than politics? In different cultures of the world, there are professions that are considered, to put it mildly, less than prestigious. Somewhere they dislike the military, somewhere they despise lawyers. In Russia, politics is considered the dirtiest business. Nothing spoils a person's reputation in the eyes of Russian society like political activity. The centuries-long alienation of the Russian people from politics and public activity results in their social apathy. The image of the Russian politician combines all the nastiest qualities: he is deceitful, cynical, self-serving, cunning, cruel, etc. He takes advantage of the public's trust, committing crimes against his own people. Recent Russian history shows that a politician can never be trusted, no matter what ideas he advocates, communist or democratic. Since he is a politician, by definition he lies in a way that benefits him.

Indeed, in Russia you cannot rely on bureaucracy. Many current politicians over-estimate how good they look in people's eyes. Officials consider themselves a special, privileged caste. What are the common folks to them? Slaves, farmhands, who can only silently perform the work entrusted to them. Anybody who could not cheat, steal, trick, and put together a lot of money, he is just stupid, he is not fit to stand at the helm of a large country with global claims. He will not be able to stomp and trample, guided only by the "interests of the country," paying no attention to the pathetic voices of the citizens. But those who have climbed on the heads of other people to the top of Russia's political Olympus have practically no chance of falling from there. But if they do, this class doesn't hand "their own" over to the mob.

Miners, teachers, students, pensioners, those who rummage in garbage cans or stretch out their hand on the sidewalk, people who carefully divvy up their last piece of bread among their family members, those who lie in field hospitals or who weep over the graves of their sons killed in the never-ending Caucasus war — they hate the Russian authorities. They do not need material evidence of corruption and callousness in the highest echelons of power. No publication will add to this hatred or diminish it. The population does not need to read newspapers to see what is going on around them. The fact that information has appeared in the foreign press, and in such quantities, only confirms the validity of the population's suspicions.

On the other hand, many a person who hears every day on TV how dashing ministers and factory directors steal millions of dollars a month thinks he is just as good as they are (and he thinks this is the example to follow). The paradox is that while people hate the officials who steal from them, they themselves don't mind stealing anything of any value.

Russian politicians are 60 years old - the age of the highest professional flourishing: a personal place in a residence near Moscow (in form and in essence, a sanatorium) and a personal room in the Central Clinical Hospital. No one, not even the Constitutional Court, can explain what is meant by "the President's persistent inability to perform his duties for health reasons" and how, in such a case, the procedure for handing over his powers to the Prime Minister is carried out. People in Russia have long felt dissatisfaction with the authorities, insisting that all of Russia's troubles stem precisely from an endemic epidemic of Alzheimer's disease in the elite circles of society.

For Russian politicians, 60 is the age when they enjoy the highest profes-sional flourishing: private accommodations in a residence near Moscow (in form and in fact, a resort) and a private ward in the Central Clinical Hospital. No one, not even the Constitutional Court, can explain what is meant by the "persistent inability of the President to perform duties for health reasons" and how the procedure for transferring his powers to the Prime Minister should be carried out if it ever came up. People in Russia have long been dissatisfied with the authorities, insisting that all the troubles of Russia occur precisely because of the epidemic of Alzheimer's disease in elite circles of society.

It is always hard to tell whether the head of state is acting of his own free will or at the behest of others. It is also unclear whether the recent actions of Russia's leaders are simply a whim or the beginning of a coup d'état. The actions of the presidential entourage, on the contrary, can hardly be called uncalculated. Officials in Russia are all too prudent when they have to make a choice between what's good for Russia and what's good for them. The President also may well be unaware of what is happening, receiving information only in small doses. And it is unclear who determines when it's time for one of Yeltsin's so-called "routine" medical examinations and what they consist of.

10. Parliamentary Deputies and Bureaucrats

Russia is still at a crossroads. It has done away with totalitarianism, but it has not experienced true democracy. It has lost its superpower status, but it has not taken on a secondary role. Russia is getting weaker militarily, but it remains a nuclear power and is conducting experiments in space. So which way will Russia go? Russian Foreign Minister Ivanov categorically declares that "Russia was and remains a world power," but what can Moscow offer as a world power to other states and to its own society? Military security, financial aid, manufactured products, or a progressive social model? The only thing that defines Russia's world power status is that it has nuclear weapons and the ability to destroy the entire globe.

The Russian state, like the double-headed eagle on its coat of arms, is trying to look in different directions at the same time. On the one hand, market specialists are convinced that they know how to manage the market, on the other hand, regulators are convinced that they know what to do. But neither of them really knows anything. Years of reforms have shown that the methods both are using are very far from modern conditions. Clearly, in the pre-election period the economy will be a victim of politics, because it is no longer able to feed anyone or do anything. The country is still searching for miracle cures and quick and global solutions. At the same time, the idea that there is a long and difficult road ahead is pushed into the background in every possible way. At the first sign of trouble, the strategic concept is tossed aside, a new government is appointed, and so on until the next pop up. The government agencies can't let go of the elements of the old, Soviet experience which are unacceptable and even harmful in a market economy.

No one is doing anything concrete. It's as if all the issues have been resolved, there is no drought, the fires have been put out, everyone is fed, clothed, and has a job. And the country is not in a bind, on the verge of famine and civil war, and Russia is not on a course that will lead to a decline in living standards for the vast majority of the populace. In truth, the leadership has plunged the country into poverty, people are unemployed, families have not received their salaries and child allowances for months and years. Education and science are in limbo. This is a factual genocide of the people: more Russians are dying than are being born. The chronic under-nourishment as well as malnutrition of tens of millions of Russians is causing a decline in the health of the nation. And the executive branch only urges the country to stay calm. This kind of talk ignores the events looming on the political horizon.

Leaders are not being appointed or fired based the results of their work (or the lack thereof); the motivation is always to put one's own person in place, someone who will allow others to dictate their terms and, as they say in Russia, "snatch what you can in troubled waters." And now at this difficult time for Russia, politicians are not only busy saving their own hides but are trying to extract dividends from the crisis. Officials are very fond of organizing all kinds of closed briefings and meetings. However, by "closed" they mean open to a narrow circle of journalists, to whom no secrets are revealed, but their own important role in the political process is constantly emphasized.

In any civilized country, a high-ranking official found guilty of outright lying resigns. Not so in Russia. It is well known that every second person in the government could be exposed for one thing or another at any time. In the Russian high society, people with a decent reputation could soon find themselves in the Red Book. Honor and reputation, alas, are not concerns in Russian political life. What is happening suggests that for the foreseeable future there is no point in relying on any politician's internal sense of responsibility.

Russian officials may behave chaotically, but in any case they must be ruthless. First act, and then look for a rational explanation for your actions. Their concerns do not extend beyond the walls within which they sit. The trouble with Russian politics is that certain politicians constantly need something to fall on the heads of voters: they have no other way to attract attention. Populistic pronouncements, scandalous revelations, anything goes as long as it makes them memorable. Dragging a woman by her hair or cursing on TV is socially reprehensible, but such behavior by a candidate is perceived positively by some voters: he's a real man, and he can put a woman in her place. But this kind of style generally indicates a leader who will suppress any reasonably significant personalities among his subordinates, tearing them down in every possible way and turning them into a faceless mass, a backdrop against which he himself will shine. Politicians who adhere to diplomatic methods of work, masters of compromise are not in demand now that Russia is *in extremis*. The most popular official or candidate is the one who promises to save citizens from rampant democracy, restore general law and order, and establish iron discipline. There are plenty of unflattering things to say about the quality of Russian democracy. Often it looks like some kind of parody, even a mockery of the principles of people's power. No wonder in Russia the word "democrat" has become almost a swear word, a synonym for thief and embezzler. Russia is simply obsessed with "decisiveness" and a "strong hand." And although it has more than once paid dearly for this, it has not freed itself from the national delusion — once again voices are heard: "We need Stalin." The data from a poll on the 120th anniversary of Joseph Stalin's birth shows: 44% believe that Stalin's times brought good and bad to our country in equal measure, another 19% believe that they brought more good than bad, and 3% consider Stalin's times only good. This adds up to 66%. The trend is clear.

Yeltsin was also elected because he "resolutely" threw away his party ticket at the CPSU Congress. Only unlike Moses, Yeltsin led the people not to the promised land but to the ashes. This is Russia's payback for the love of "decisive" people. Things in Russia are no less bad now than they were in 1993, when Yeltsin stormed the parliament. And the same chaotic and corrupt atmosphere that now exists in the country already existed in pre-Soviet history. That was during the last years of Nicholas II's reign, on the eve of the Bolshevik revolution. In terms of the rate of change of ministerial cabinets, Yeltsin was well on his way to breaking the record set by Nicholas II. And the record set that time was not a good one, because the year 1917 came immediately afterwards.

What does it mean in Russian political slang to make elections "fair and transparent," to prevent "extremists and criminals" from coming to power? This means that based on the results of the previous elections, thousands of thieves and bandits are in office at various levels and the holding mandate of a parliamentary deputy is just a guarantee against criminal prosecution for them. Perhaps only the abolition of this immunity for State Duma deputies and governors will help prevent the criminalization of power. Although a number of serious civic initiatives have recently been launched to control the elections, the authorities are just talking to themselves. The official campaign for "honesty" is simply the most important element of the regime's political strategy, which makes a good land mine for a bad game, not wanting to admit its criminal contours. It is about more than elections — it's an attempt to ensure the survival of the existing system after a possible regime change in the country. A Russian proverb says that it's usually the thief who shouts "Catch the thief!" the loudest.

The stunning indiscretion of the majority of people's deputies, who care only about material benefits and privileges for their loved ones, naturally causes a harsh negative reaction from the public. The status of a deputy confers upon its owner not only an almost complete sinecure for the period he exercises deputy powers, but also a well-provided old age. Even members of the royal family did not have the privileges which deputies of various levels have and demand for themselves. In terms of material wealth, deputies of the State Duma are equal to federal ministers. But while there are several dozen heads of ministries and departments, there are 450 deputies (and almost 200 senators). Each one's salary is 6,000 rubles a month. In addition to the basic salary, people's deputies are given an allowance for their own parliamentary activities (amounting to five times the minimum wage). Naturally, everyone has the right to an official car and driver, to use air, rail, city transport, and all types of communication free of charge, and also has a separate room equipped with office furniture, communications and equipment. The right to free medical care in the elite Kremlin hospital is also granted (a one-day stay in such a hospital costs about $100). Before leaving for the holidays, people's deputies are given 40,000 rubles each — they get vacation, medical, all kinds of compensation. Are MPs worth the money? 21 of these elected representatives never said a word from the rostrum, 160 deputies left the party factions from which they were elected, and many in the course of 4 years only visited the State Duma meetings a few times.

An ex-deputy's pension is 75% of his ministerial salary, one and a half dozen times higher than the usual state pension. Moreover, unlike ministers who are entitled to such a privilege only in the event they retire directly after serving as a minister, parliamentarians receive their 75% salary regardless of how long ago they may have served in the Duma. And this occupation, apparently, is very harmful to one's health. Therefore, deputies are entitled to a full-fledged vacation — 48 working days, like academicians and doctors of science. Vacation pay is supplemented by a "treatment allowance" in the amount of double the deputy's salary. Vouchers to the health resorts of the former 4th Department of the Ministry of Health, which once served the highest Soviet and party nomenclature, are provided to deputies at only 10% of the cost. But few of them use this benefit: Russian parliamentarians prefer to rest and be treated abroad. For some deputies, the material benefits due to them do not seem to be of any interest at all. There are some who do not even apply to the Duma treasury for their salary for years; apparently they get enough through bribes. In addition to the material side, there are many other advantages. A deputy certificate, for example, is very useful when communicating with law enforcement representatives. In order to spare the police and the Traffic Safety Inspectorate (GIBDD) from needless worry, the parliamentarians have supplemented the law on deputy status with another useful privilege — the right to special state license plates, including on their personal cars. On trips abroad, deputies are reliably protected from the police by their diplomatic passports.

In addition, the deputies demand to be received immediately whenever they ask for a meeting at any institution, organization or business, and their demands should be responded to right away. Deputies have life and health insurance paid for by the state. A deputy cannot be fired during his entire term in office plus a year after. In addition, they expect to be able to buy entry tickets without standing in line, they get a fully-furnished office with telephone and communication equipment, and ever more assistants paid from the public budget. And at the same time, there is nothing you can do about it if a deputy fails to keep a single campaign promise and does nothing at all in the Duma. And the overwhelming majority are running for another term in the Duma. They will have a significant advantage over other candidates: the opportunity to use their reception halls and Duma offices as election headquarters, free travel, free communications, and a large staff. Each time there is a vote to increase parliamentary benefits and privileges, two-thirds of the lower house vote in favor. Factions such as the Communist Party of the Russian Federation (KPRF), the Liberal Democratic Party of Russia (LDPR), Our Home is Russia (NDR) ardently support the amendments to the new law — although they rant more and louder than others about the plight of the people.

And the people are in desperate straits, indeed. According to the State Statistics Committee, 55 million Russians live below the poverty line. Ten million citizens were starving during the first quarter of 1999(the latest statistics available at the time of this writing); their average per capita income was less than 400 rubles a month (8–13 rubles a day). Another twenty million, who had 400–600 rubles per person, are persistently malnourished. The next group — 22 million people — also live in poverty (incomes from 600 to 800 rubles a month, when a subsistence wage would be a minimum of 824 rubles).

In May 1999, the wage accrued (but by no means always paid) was on average 1,465 rubles nationwide. In terms of purchasing power, that was 35 percent less than in May 1998. Many sectors were paid even less: light industry, 731 rubles (April data); agriculture, 480; education, 812; public health, 872; culture and arts, 785.

The mindset of deputies and heads of local governments has not changed since communist times. Voters lose every time. They are "skinned alive" by taxes, and they never know how that money is spent. The budget revenue may come in at 90 percent, but in reality one can scarcely see any sign of it. There is no effect on health care, education, or simply the cleanliness of the streets. But the administration receives a quarterly bonus equal to its salary. Despite the general collapse of the country and the overall poverty, officials are entitled to bonuses at the expense of taxes collected from the poor and hungry people. As you know, bonuses are rewards for some kind of success. But what do deputies excel at? If there is any talk about the absurdly high privileges of officials, it is just talk. And the financial activities of such offices are never seriously checked. Firstly, no one dares to touch their tangle of financial and political intrigue, and secondly, the very people who should be supervising them share in their gains.

And so it is all over the country. In Russia, if something happens in one end of the country, the same thing happens in the other. Social scientists, brought up on the principles of mythical socialist political economy and equally mythical scientific communism, can argue as much as they want that one single nation was not formed in the common Soviet space (this contra-dicts the communist view that nations have the right to self-determination); nevertheless the actions of deputies in St. Petersburg, for example, are no different from the actions of deputies in Vladivostok. Their language, the way they think, their attitude to others, their desire for personal social well-being at the expense of others — these things do not differ. The same prob-lems are present everywhere.

Valery Vybornov, a government official in St. Petersburg, was charged with illegal acquisition, storage and transportation of firearms and ammu-nition; Alexander Morozov, a former regional deputy in Chelyabinsk, at the entrance to Siberia, was accused of illegal possession of weapons and resistance to police officers, as well as the creation of a criminal gang. One can only guess how many deputies and bureaucrats across the country are carrying illegal guns, violating state laws and calling in the services of crim-inal groups. A Parliamentary Deputy of the Komi Republic, V. Sorvachev, is accused of embezzling funds through dubious deals in coal. The Russian Minister of Fuel and Energy, Viktor Kalyuzhny, is mentioned in Interpol certificates on organized international crime and his name appears in several criminal cases related to murders simultaneously.

The laws that have been passed so far show the astonishing incompetence of the deputies and enthusiasts from various committees, who prepare various drafts. The bill passed by the State Duma "On Restriction of Smoking and Consumption of Tobacco Products" is so progressive that it would be the envy of citizens in most countries where legal restrictions on smokers have already been introduced. The authors are so radical in their approach to the idea of improving the health of the nation, that the nation simply may not stand for it. Under the law, the retail price of tobacco products cannot be set below 200% of the production cost plus excise taxes, which cannot be less than 80% of the selling price. This means that most smokers will have to switch to cheaper and harmful varieties of cigarettes. But even here it is not so simple: "The manufacture, sale and importation of cigarettes and cigarettes containing more than 1.1 mg of nicotine and more than 12 mg of tar in a single cigarette are prohibited. The poor smokers are amicably switching to homemade cigarettes.

Deputies are hampered not only by ideology, social demagoguery and incompetence, but also by outright bribery. For example, an amendment to the law costs $20,000 and up. This practice is flourishing in the Duma, and the corresponding law on lobbying was defeated by it. The mechanism of "black lobbying" corrupts the State Duma, turning it into a malleable political body. Regardless of who wins the Duma elections, ideology and theft will flourish under the current circumstances.

Laws are still passed in Russia this way. On Friday morning, an electronic scoreboard showed that 30 elected persons were present in the Legislative Assembly of St. Petersburg. But a number of deputies had signed a statement the day before refusing to participate in meetings due to numerous breaches of regulations, and some are on vacation, and one is in a detention center, so that in reality no more than 26 deputies could be present. Why this obviously exaggerated number appeared on the scoreboard became clear at the press-conference held by deputies who did not take part in the voting and did not give their keys to vote to anyone. They showed their keys to the journalists. This confirmed the assumption that the Legislative Assembly has duplicate keys, which are used "as needed." Curiously, the deputy who is in police custody "took part" in the voting. Absolutely the same thing happens in the Russian State Duma.

The deputy corps sometimes resorts to simple measures to combine making money on the voting results, avoiding the slightest responsibility, and ensuring that sitting idle is a profitable and safe occupation. When solving important issues, dozens and sometimes hundreds of deputies (up to

25 percent) ail to show up at meetings, while dozens of others simply spoil the ballots, making them invalid.

When deputies' votes are being bought, everyone knows who is being bought and for how much. For example, although rumors said that Vladimir Zhirinovsky had been promised control over one of the oil companies in exchange for is loyalty during the impeachment of the President, more pragmatic sources indicated that Zhirinovsky had valiantly fought impeachment for a very modest reward — the equivalent of about two acres of living space in the center of Moscow. Some Duma members became very alarmed about the harm that impeachment would cause only after hearing an amount with a very good number of zeros ($15,000–30,000), which the grateful Motherland is ready to share with them. Deputies were offered $5,000–10,000 for approving Prime Minister Sergei Kiriyenko. The deputies are only concerned about retaining their seats after the next elections, and they consider that to lose a comfortable springboard for the Duma election campaign just because of one whim or another on the part of the President is too high a cost. Therefore, they will eventually approve any candidate at all for the post of prime minister.

They are trying to deprive Sergey Belyaev, the former chairman of the State Property Committee of the Russian Federation, of parliamentary immunity. He is accused of abuse of power and apartment fraud. When Belyaev was appointed Director General of the Federal Office for Insolvency (Bankruptcy) in December 1993, under the State Property Committee of Russia, he received ownership of a 3-room apartment in Moscow on Selsko-khozyaistvennaya Street. Belyaev already had a privatized 5-room living space in St. Petersburg. According to the investigation, in order to take possession of the Moscow apartments for free Belyaev concluded a fictitious purchase-and-sale agreement, and as a result, the State Property Committee paid for the apartment. Having become Chairman of the State Property Committee in February 1995, Belyaev repeatedly appealed to the Office of the President of the Russian Federation and to the Chairman of the Government of the Russian Federation with a request to allocate a 4-room apartment for his family of 4 people. He did not report that he already had housing in Moscow. As a result, Belyaev was allocated an apartment on Udaltsov Street. Later, as a deputy of the State Duma, Belyaev exchanged both Moscow apartments for 6-room apartments. Belyaev agreed in writing to appear at the prosecutor's office upon her first request, but he has been hiding from the investigation for several months. It got to the point that Moscow Prosecutor Sergey Gerasimov sent a request to the Prosecutor General's Office to bring Belyaev in forcibly.

When communicating with deputies, you should never forget what kind of people you are communicating with. According to the members of the election commissions, many deputies are illiterate and make about five spelling mistakes just in the application for approval to run. Candidates and the movements they represent are often totally unfamiliar with even the elementary requirements of the law.

It should also be remembered how they got where they are. The overwhelming majority prefers to bribe voters, use criminal services, and hide their property and foreign passports. Eleven of the deputy candidates have foreign citizenship, including Azerbaijani, Moldovan and Turkmen. Bykov, a businessman who has been charged with two murders, "forgot" to note that he owns a Jeep Cherokee, two VAZ-2109 cars and a house in the USA, and he also distorted the size of his residences in Russia. In addition, his documents omit to mention that Bykov has a Greek ID card. Another candidate, Musatov, hid his three Mercedes cars; and Zhirinovsky hid his two cars. In total, according to the Central Election Commission, 86 candidates from the Liberal Democratic Party of Russia (LDPR) committed such violations. Things are no "worse" in other political parties. Many of the candidates under-counted the number of cars they have; others indicated cars that area used by other persons. This includes   former Prime Minister Primakov, Moscow Mayor Luzhkov and others. Others have amassed real estate in Moscow and the United States, as well as stables full of luxury cars.

"If our country is criminal, ... then the Duma should be criminal, too... Maybe it will be good." That's how General Korzhakov, the former head of the presidential guard, and now a deputy of the State Duma, began his Duma candidacy. In turn, General Viktor Rozhkov, the head of the Tula militia, a rival of General Korzhakov in the Tula electoral district, published a dictionary of criminal jargon in one of his pre-election publications — to make it easier for the voter to find a common language with the future government. The country knows many of the candidates for deputies not by their surnames, but by nicknames. The list of primary candidates for the Liberal Democratic Party of Russia (LDPR) included Anatoly Bykov, chairman of the Krasnoyarsk Aluminum Plant board of directors, who is wanted by law enforcement agencies, and President of National Information Company Ashot Yeghiazarian, one of the defendants in the "Yuri Skuratov case." Then came the leader of a criminal gang, Sergei Mikhailov (aka Mikhas), followed by criminal mastermind Viktor Averin (aka Avera). The party's list for the Far Eastern region includes Dmitry Yakubovsky, who has a criminal record under articles 164 ("Theft of items of special value") and 113 ("Torture") of the Criminal Code of Russia.

It is not at all surprising that in St. Petersburg, for example, campaigners collecting signatures for competitors were beaten, their clothes were torn, women were lowered upside down from the stairs. Nikolai Demidov, the confidant and de facto head of the campaign headquarters of the Father-land–All Russia bloc, was brutally murdered in a hotel in the city of Irtil, Voronezh region. Six thugs beat Nikolai Demidov, his driver and assistant with barstools with impunity. Then they stabbed them with knives. In Ulyanovsk, Boris Kasatkin, the press secretary of one of candidates for the State Duma was beaten up. In the village of Borisovka, Belgorod region, the coordinator of the Liberal Democratic Party of Russia (LDPR), E. Oleinik, was killed in the courtyard of her house. Uralmash, a well-known and very influential criminal group in the Urals, has simply transformed into the Uralmash socio-political union and is now openly fielding candidates for the State Duma and regional authorities.

In Russia, there is no mechanism for punishing state officials for crimes, so at the moment no socio-economic programs can be implemented in the country. No new loans will bring tangible benefits. Like all the previous loans, they will either be mindlessly squandered or stolen. Here are some ideas of how they do it.

The Small Business made the news with a financial scandal reported by the newspaper *Moskovsky Komsomolets* and journalist Alexander Khinshtein. The money from the fund ended up with the financial company Troika Dialog. Irina Khakamada (at that time Chairman of the State Committee for the Support of Small Business), her husband, businessman Vladimir Sirotinsky, as well as the acting General Director of the same Fund for the Support for Small Business Svetlana Palamarchuk are suspected of involvement in the scam. The fund suffered losses of more than a million dollars. Nevertheless, Hakamada confidently entered the top three on the federal electoral list of the Union of Right Forces along with Sergei Kiriyenko and Boris Nemtsov, former prime ministers of the Russian government.

In the city of Togliatti in 1997, 180 billion rubles disappeared from the city budget. The same company accused of embezzling the money sued the mayor's office, demanding compensation for costs in the amount of 108 million rubles that it incurred in the course of joint financial transactions with the municipality. The announcement that the very businessmen who failed to return 180 million rubles to the budget were now demanding another 108 million had an effect. But the fact is that the three founders of the company, who were directly related to the non-return of funds, are deputies of the city Duma and are responsible for the formation of the budget of Togliatti.

As has happened in the US as well, former wrestlers or boxers can win high offices. Even rumors of a candidate's criminal past do not hurt his chances of winning. This is in part the echo of the cult of power. If you look closely at the faces and behaviors of those responsible, and listen to what they say, there will be no doubt that the country has been invaded by barbarians who are prepared to destroy anything that gets in the way even slightly with their policy of divide and conquer. Moreover, unlike the nobility of any country, the Soviet political elite is a product of the civil war, with their hands drenched in blood. The tradition goes on — the politicians, who saw great career prospects open up in the year 2000, are also eager to show their determination and toughness. Not for a single day do the "raids" on powerful corporate groups by the president's entourage cease. The bet is never on the principle of democracy, but only on the repressive apparatus.

Russian citizens pin their hopes for changes in Russian society on the results of future elections, as a result of which more worthy people should be elected. Such aspirations are apparently not destined to come true. It's not about people. The system of state power with all its vices inscribed in the current Constitution will reproduce itself again. There is absolutely no guarantee that the new President will not succumb to the temptation to enjoy all the fruits of unlimited power. Meanwhile the elected officials behave worse than unhinged hooligans. In July 1999, two high-ranking officials of the Kazan mayor's office staged a drunken brawl in one of the city cafes. They molested the employees and visitors, and broke furniture. The policemen who arrived at the scene were beaten, and police authorities who arrived later were scolded. Only the head of the local Department of Internal Affairs was able to take away the brawlers. The next day, no evidence of the incident could be found. Police officers and café workers deny everything, and even a video recording made by television journalists has disappeared.

Another case. This time the hero is Anatoly Matveev, a member of the Supreme Court. At the end of May 1999, an eleven-year-old activated the alarm system on the judge's big Pontiac by kicking the wheel and drawing the letter "L" on the door with his finger. The judge caught the schoolboy, took him to the trash and put him in the garbage can. After the trial, during which the judge explained his act solely based on pedagogical reasons, the board decided to retain his judicial powers and only warned about the inadmissibility of such actions.

Another example. A group of deputies to the Voronezh city council decided they had to remove the head of the city administration, Alexander

Tsapin, from his post at any cost. So the opposition, meeting separately, made amendments to the city charter and the regulations of the council itself. In accordance with these amendments, they relieved Tsapin of his duties and elected Vasily Kochergin as the new mayor. The justice system unequivo-cally called the election illegal. However, something resembling a military coup took place in the city. At 8:15 a.m., a Fiat minibus with Moscow license plates, carrying men in black berets and carrying assault rifles, pulled up to the mayor's office. Kochergin, the "newly elected mayor," was in charge of them. Having crushed the policemen guarding the mayor's office on their way, the attackers rushed to Tsapin's office. Kochergin broke the locks and climbed into the cherished executive chair. The security guards, once they came to, had to call the police commander for help, as well as investigators from the Department of Internal Affairs and the deputy regional prosecutor. Only upon their arrival on the scene were the guys in black berets disarmed. According to preliminary information, they are all members of the Special Police Rapid Response Unit from Moscow.

In the city of Rybinsk, north of Moscow, members of the city council, elected from the Communist Party, use their position to prevent the most important issues of district life from being put on the agenda if they are not beneficial to the Communist majority. Other deputies are deprived of offices and access to office equipment. There is trouble just as well on the far end of the country, in Primorsky Krai, near the southeast tip of Siberia. The local Duma refuses to provide the Auditing Department of the RF Ministry of Finance with accounting and financial documents related to the expenditure of funds from the federal budget. This is due to the excessive appetites of the people's elected representatives. In 1998, their needs cost the treasury six million rubles, but in 1999 the appropriations more than tripled, to almost twenty million rubles. The sums are mainly spent on foreign business trips: to study international experience. For this purpose delegations from Vladi-vostok have already gone as far as Ireland. In Vladivostok, a certain Kopylov appointed himself (!) acting mayor at the suggestion of the Governor of the region, Nazdratenko. Court decisions which coincide with the interests of certain persons are issued in Primorsky Krai even on weekends.

The methods of political struggle in Russia are purely economic. For example, a large number of fuses disappeared all at once from high-voltage substations in Barnaul in 1996 and Tomsk in 1999 (among others), much to the amazement of local power engineers. The criminals are highly profes-sional. The reasons for the theft were not immediately clear: the copper content is insignificant, and it is almost impossible to sell them. It turned out that candidate deputies were behind the escapade (and some of them won election). They thought that mass blackouts would help create a favorable environment for their campaign slogans.

Deputies of the Ekaterinburg City Duma lost their access to the Internet due to spending too much time "surfing" on pornographic sites. It cost them eight thousand rubles. The provider was forced to disconnect the debtors from the network.

A group of Arkhangelsk residents is attempting to legally initiate the recall of the city mayor. Deputies state in response that they (the citizens) are simply taking advantage of the difficult socio-economic situation in Arkhangelsk and that today it is all too easy to accuse the city government. The problems of fuel supply are difficult to solve, there are disruptions of gas and electricity supplies, and delays in salary payments, but it should be noted that the majority of Russian cities are in the same situation. And why do they (the citizens) single us out us? There are many regions with the same problems. No one wants to take responsibility. As a rule, demagogic methods are used to avoid responsibility. $$

The police department, in fact, is a special caste that shares harsh anti-Western views, in the spirit of communist opposition to the rest of the world. Every police chief aims to have his own "rapid response forces" (special troops, municipal police, patrol service, etc.), which sometimes perform actions that are not quite characteristic of them. For example, totally plastered, they may stop cars on the road and demand fines for non-existent infractions while shaking a machine gun with live ammunition in the nose of the driver. Sometimes they threaten to shoot the drivers if "they try to escape." It is no longer a question of whether such units are even legal, or whether they are permitted under the Constitution or other laws. Drunken policemen harass people just like bandits do: until they get what they want. Before going to the police, some Russians stop to think whether the criminal gangs will solve a given issue faster and more painlessly. Even some of the pre-election activities of the Communist Party of the Russian Federation (CPRF) are financed by the owners of a very dubious company called "Mikom" — the Zhivilo brothers. This company is associated with the fact that the Kuznetsk Metallurgical Combine is actually on the verge of bankruptcy. Also, this particular company is associated with rumors that the governor of the Kemerovo region, Aman Tuleyev, has adopted Christianity and betrayed Islam. The leadership of the communists actually use "dirty money" to finance their activities.

In polls that the Russian people, despite their outward angry condemnation, show a great desire to be in a criminal gang — because, if neither the state nor the government is able to protect them, perhaps organized crime can. It's no secret that the latter have their representatives almost everywhere. Another reason is the need for psychological and material protection in a country where corruption and arbitrariness reign. A criminal gang is not the worst way out, young people also believe; at least they offer some support in a society in which everyone is ready to send everyone else to hell. People who go around in the US with "If you need help, contact me" badges are perceived here as complete idiots.

11. THE REGIONS

Russia's sense of self is slowly being lost. Its's hard to say what century she lives in today. Life in the provinces is certainly hard. Child benefit payments are delayed by up to 27 months. At the same time, the largest enterprises that form the backbone of the defense complex are already producing fourth-generation anti-tank missiles and the famous Igla portable anti-aircraft missile systems, and space technology samples are being developed. Russia is gradually embracing the process of Balkanization, and this is especially dangerous because the country has nuclear weapons. A wide range of social movements inclining toward separatism are being created. Separatist sentiments in the various ethnic regions of Russia create opportunities for political extremists to galvanize the voters.

State authorities and local self-government structures do nothing to counteract the appearance of political extremism. Extremists are finding their ways into all levels of government and social organizations, law enforcement, and the armed forces. No legal basis exists for countering extremism. Regional pre-election blocs are going to fight more for the political independence of the regions, and not for stability in the country. In fact, the leaders of these blocs threaten the territorial integrity of Russia.

The main problem is that so far, in some parts of the Federation, the contradictions between local legislation and the Constitution of Russia have not been eliminated. In other words, the regions go ahead and adopt laws that directly contradict the state ones. Therefore, it is very difficult to talk about what forms the pre-election struggle will take, out in the regions.

Almost all the regional leaders could be removed for violating federal laws. What is happening today in Kalmykia is convincing evidence in favor of a very sad fact: totalitarianism, with all its attributes and consequences, can triumph again with amazing ease in the vast expanses of Russia. Leaders of the Russian republics, such as Tatarstan President Mintimer Shaimiev and Bashkortostan President Murtaza Rakhimov, openly declare that federal law does not apply in these republics. The mood of the Russian Tatars is quite different from that of the Russian Russians. In Tatarstan, voices are increasingly heard saying that the republic "cannot and should not blindly repeat the criminal policy of the Russian leadership, which for continually tries to draw the peoples of Russia into war in order to solve their problems and unite the nation." Tatarstan suspended conscription into the Russian army. The current governors of Primorsky Krai, and the Moscow, Orenburg, Tambov, Tver and Yaroslavl oblasts, and Tatarstan, are openly ignoring the law "On Basic Guarantees of Electoral Rights and the Right to Participate in Referendums of the Citizens of the Russian Federation." The governors arbitrarily eliminate the electoral pledge clause, the two-round voting system, and other important provisions.

There is complete chaos in the Russian government system. Newspapers are screaming about embezzlement on a huge scale, and the prosecutor's office and "organs" have just been studying all this for a very long time. And all this time, the patterns of distribution remain unchanged, only the "shares" change hands. The Federation Council stubbornly rejects one draft after another of the anti-corruption law, both at the presidential level and the Duma. They've been "working" on this bill for seven years. What could that mean? It could only mean that the governors haven't yet gotten their hands on everything they could. In the regions one can "manage" with impunity, and the governors do not want to pass a law that would allow them to be brought to justice. It would be commendable if the political and financial elite of Russia really wanted to eradicate corruption. But behind all this is a war of the clans and a struggle for power. Regional leaders are actually stealing from their republics and regions.

Economically strong regions benefit the country as a whole. The better the regions live, the more taxes will go to the center, and the stronger Russia will be. It would seem that governors should pursue exactly the same policy towards municipalities. After all, the better people live in cities and villages, the fewer problems the governor has. But the reality is different. Year after year, the regional authorities reduce the standard deductions from federal taxes to regional centers and other municipalities. In some municipalities, the share of income tax they receive over the past three years has decreased from 100% to almost zero, income tax from 12% to 1–5%, and excise taxes from 50% to 1%. In addition, instead of local taxes, a centralized sales tax has been introduced, which significantly reduces the income of regional centers.

Unlike the Russian capital, which sucks juices from the regions, the regions live at the expense of their capitals. The Sverdlovsk region lives at the expense of Yekaterinburg, depleting its economy. The Leningrad Region — at the expense of St. Petersburg, and so on. City budgets have turned into the cash cows of the regions, which are their chronic debtors. The confrontation between the mayors of capital cities and governors has become a widespread phenomenon. If the mayor of the city wins the gubernatorial election, then he can make his former post no longer a matter for election. In this way, he can get rid of a possible competitor within the region in advance. The team of the mayor, who has bought everything and everything, is so confident of victory that it does not consider it necessary to hide how exactly it will use its power.

Members of communist and nationalist parties make harsh political statements publicly in the regions, use belligerent rhetoric, make insulting statements that denigrate the government of the Russian state, and degrade the honor and dignity of the President. It does not matter that this is happening now to Yeltsin. It will happen in any speech. This is a well-established feature of regional psychology, a traditional tactic of "hit-and-run" against anyone who gets in the way of "divide and rule" in any given region.

The West is not familiar with life in the Russian provinces. The struggle for power there is not exactly what one would call a fair fight. For example, the chairman of the regional legislative assembly, a candidate for the regional council from the mining town of Leninsk-Kuznetsk, Mr. A. Filatov, delivered his "election platform" to voters on television: "If I had a gun," he declared, "I would shoot Governor Tuleev. And I would crush the head of the regional election commission chairman Razigrayev." During a live TV debate, Vasili Shandybin, candidate for State Duma in Bryansk's electoral district #64, threatened another candidate, Lyudmila Narusova, that when his party came to power, she and her husband Anatoly Sobchak[1] would be sent to "clean up the Belomorkanal."[2] On January 13, 1998, Alexander Shokhin, head of the inter-departmental commission for economic security of the Russian Security Council, said on television in reference to a journalist: "Now everybody will see what caliber weapons we will use to shoot Kislinskaya." Deputy of Liberal-Democratic Party of Russia (LDPR) A. Mitrofanov pounded on the

---

[1] Mayor of Saint Petersburg from 1991 to 1996, Sobchak was accused of corruption involving his family's real estate, but by 1999 Vladimir Putin rehabilitated him. Nonetheless, he died under suspicious circumstances the next year.

[2] Sending convicts to work on "the [local] canal" was in many countries a sentence to forced labor leading to death.

Duma rostrum and threatened the Communists: "You are coming to power step by step. But in response, we'll flail you, we'll flail you! We will rip you to hell!" It is not surprising that such people win elections in a country that is permeated with the spirit of violence.

In terms of criminal danger, tiny provincial towns are not much better than large metropolitan ones. Take, for example, the 60,000-strong city of Volzhsk in the Mari El Republic, where one board member at the paper mill recently found a coffin and a funeral wreath near his apartment door after a shareholders' meeting. Small towns have seen everything that big cities are seeing: the redistribution of property with the special forces lending a hand, kidnappings, and the shooting of cars on the streets. People are so used to the killings that the local newspaper condenses information about them into two lines: "Citizen A. was killed on Zelenaya Street with a Makarov pistol." That's it. They write more than that about stealing a piglet from a barn.

The desperate and drunken people of the Russian provinces commit a lot of crimes, one more horrible than the other. In 60 cases out of 100, they murder their own relatives — over dividing a piece of property, for a refrigerator or a television set. Or for not letting them sit quietly and have a drink. In most cities (never mind rural villages), total chaos reigns, often lacking basic communication with other localities. The "eternal flame" to communards and monuments to Lenin in central squares are juxtaposed with Orthodox chapels and Plaques of Honor to foremost workers of market reforms.

Moscow groups dominate regional businesses, and every month millions of dollars in profits are pumped into their accounts located outside the regions. Regional budgets lose huge amounts by local standards. At the same time, local combines, having no way to accumulate funds for investment in fixed assets, are rapidly aging and in a few years may close their doors altogether as production facilities. This destroys the livelihood of the local inhabitants.

In Russia, the idea of establishing regional provincial banks is in the air. According to their proponents (which include members of regional administrations and representatives of credit institutions), the financial business in Russia is threatened by foreign expansion, and the aggressive policy of foreign capital is aimed at suppressing the Russian credit and financial system. This can be countered only with the help of powerful provincial banks. The creation of such banks will also remove regional and regional administrations from the control of the federal center.

What's different in the new stage of the power struggle in Russia is the active participation of the regional elite. Regional politicians are protesting against lack of respect for the rights of the regions, as well as the dominance of Moscow figures in all constituencies and the lists of candidates for every party. Muscovites are elected even from the peninsulas of Chukotka and Taimyr, which lie beyond the Arctic Circle. At the same time, in Moscow itself, a person may be denied registration as a candidate on the grounds that he does not have a capital residence permit. That is, de facto, a person does not have the right to run and be elected in his own country. In the past year, regional politicians have had problems consolidating their power. Unable to find statesmen among their own numbers, the regional elite was forced to form an alliance with someone who would help them stay in power, no matter what color his stripes. Russia runs the risk of becoming an oligarchic, semi-criminal, bureaucratic state in which society will have no control over the institutions of power, a state torn apart by conflicts between regional and oligarchic elites. The situation in the border regions is such that their inhabitants may vote for extremists or nationalists. People have given up on trusting the authorities and are ready to trust anyone who promises to fix everything. Russia is tired of radical reforms that have lowered living standards and the people are looking for a defender who speaks of the need for a social adjustment in the course of reforms.

In Primorsky Krai, there was a Committee for Forecasting Regional Policy, whose official purpose was to shape public opinion on regional social and political issues. With expenses paid from the regional budget, their activities included making recommendations for disrupting city referendums, finding ways to discredit the Vladivostok City Hall and the mayor of Vladivostok himself, recommendations for monitoring what the local deputies of the State Duma were up to (including via covert surveillance) and so forth. It's gotten to the point that the mayor and the governor, who are rivals, have resorted to psychotronic weapons in their battle against each other.

The mayor can easily get rid of the city TV and radio company if it criticizes him, especially after it has been energetically discussing the mayor's remarkable salary increase for several months. Reveling in his power, the mayor reads out the resolution to the TV crew in person. He is confident in his victory, because he won his last war — against an opposition newspaper.

Say the inhabitants of a city overwhelmingly vote against having something harmful installed on their territory. For example, the people of the Udmurt city of Votkinsk voted against plans for a waste disposal site for solid rocket engines. This type of issue, too, is easily solved by Russian officials; the results of the referendum are simply declared illegal through a biased court. And the mayor simply redraws the boundaries of the city and creates a new municipality, includes villages located near the proposed waste site. No referendum is needed anymore.

In some districts (the Khanty–Mansiysk Autonomous Area, for one), laws are being adopted that essentially say that civil servants can be corporate board members. It is no longer rare to find officials joining the boards of joint-stock companies, but until now it was considered a crime. By eliminating this restriction on public servants, the deputies of the regional Dumas have directly violated one of the main principles of public service — the separation of business and government. Meanwhile, despite all the efficiencies provided by modern means of communication, the heads of cities and districts travel large distances to meet monthly in person, to exchange information in the regional centers: the top officials meet with the governor, and the heads of representative bodies meet in the Legislative Assembly. On different days, wasting expensive gasoline in official cars, they come for half a day to hear speakers at the podium give background information that they could better have received by courier or by electronic communications.

Regional politicians protect the interests of their region only; they do not care about the country as a whole. The Minister of Internal Affairs of Mari El did not consider it necessary to interrupt his vacation even after the terrorist attacks in Moscow and Volgodonsk, and another vacationer, the head of the republic's FSB,[1] was so uninformed that he only learned about these explosions from the President of Mari El, Kislitsyn, when he was called to his office in the morning. So far, restrictions on *propiska* (residency permits for specific locations) have only been introduced in Moscow authorities and the North Caucasian regions, but since the summer of 1999, other regions have also started to put this process in place. Compulsory registration and a special regime for visiting citizens have been introduced in the Rostov Region and the Krasnodar Territory (north of the Caucasus Mountains) where migrants from many Russian regions and CIS countries seek to resettle. They have no friend or relatives to go to, there, and there is no one to receive this influx of outsiders, especially immigrants from the North. This migration process appears to be uncontrolled and it threatens stability in the region. Migrants provide serious competition to local residents — for work, housing, and simply for the available food. Whereas in previous years the resettlement of migrants was financed from the federal treasury, plans for 2000 imply that funding for refugees and migrants will have to come from the regional budget. This means that large-scale migration flows will begin to hurt the local budget. In the Astrakhan *oblast* (region), they have stopped registering nonresident citizens altogether, except for relatives of citizens who are already residents, and military personnel. In 2000, they plan

---

[1] Russia's Federal Security Service responsibilities include internal surveillance and security, counter-terrorism, and border security.

to limit new permanent registrations to just 200 people. And the governor of the Altai Territory announced that non-residents will not only have to be registered, they will also be videotaped and fingerprinted.

The leaders of the Nizhny Novgorod region are now charging fees for "services" allegedly provided to the population by the passport and visa service. At the same time, citizens are obliged to register at their place of residence. To call this process a "service" on the part of the state is strange, to say the least. As it turned out, the appearance of the document is a forced measure. It's no secret that internal passports have not been issued in the country for a long time. With an annual demand of 130,000, the Nizhny Novgorod region had only 1,500 blank passports, and their last delivery from the central office was a year and a half ago. And they hit a new record for the cost of a Russian passport. The police asked a pupil for 150 rubles. The discouraged boy wrote a letter to the newspaper saying he wanted to have an identity card from the state authorities, but not buy it. The local passport and visa service in Novosibirsk did not receive any new blank passports for more than a year. When they did receive them, there were only 17,000 "books" — 1/20 of the demand already accrued. These will be used only for those in dire need: retirees who will not receive pension benefits without a passport, school graduates going to study in other cities and demobilized military personnel applying for a housing loan. In June 1999, the price of new forms went up — from 2.5 rubles to 42 rubles — almost 17 times.

Supplying the northern regions is a special issue in Russia; they are constantly suffering from an energy crisis. To change this would require rethinking the very concept of fuel supply to make it independent of external sources. While the Russian authorities are talking about this, some Russian northern and Far Eastern regions such as Magadan, Vladivostok and Khabarovsk, survive only because of the proximity of countries such as China or Japan. Almost all goods are delivered from there. No one here places their hopes on the central government. Entire cities in the Russian north exist only because an enterprise is located there that produces oil or gas, coal or fish. But tying the entire social infrastructure to the economic structure of one enterprise is nonsense. No economic system can sustain the entire life support system. No economic system can sustain the entire life support system. A draft "Concept for state support for the Russian North under the new economic conditions" has already been prepared. These bills, which as a rule are prepared in far-off Moscow, actually provide for northerners to be deported en masse to the central and southern regions of the country.

The Northern Territories, although sparsely populated, are overpopulated even so. With a population of 250,000 in the Norilsk industrial region, the surplus is 100,000 people. The presence of these people here, to put it mildly, is not dictated by economic expediency. The Government says that by 2010 it wants to remove pensioners, the disabled and the unemployed from the North at public expense. It is not yet clear how about one and a half million people should be removed to the south. Many settlements were physically liquidated. There was even a proposal to make the northern cities "closed cities,"[1] but Moscow did not support it. Instead, they plan to make the region less attractive by abolishing the "Northern" cash allowances as being incompatible with the turn to a market economy, thus reversing the program that had been used to attract labor to these parts. A countervailing concern is that the high northern prices in markets and shops cannot be canceled by any decrees.

Russia has a horrendous policy towards the indigenous peoples inhabiting the North. While the governor of the Chukotka Autonomous Okrug is giving expensive presentations in Moscow, the Chukchi are dying like flies. The cessation of tin mining in the mid-90s forced hundreds of people to move from this remote peninsula on the Bering Strait, the northeasternmost portion of Russia, to the mainland. Now the current collapse of gold mining will mean tens of thousands of migrants, or, more precisely, refugees. On the mainland, no one is ready to receive them. We're talking about some hundred thousand people. Half the population of the Chukotka Peninsula. Indeed, from the census of 1989 to 2002, the population of the main population centers of Chukotka dropped from roughly 65,000 to about 34,000.[2]

In the southwest of Buryatia, between Lake Baikal and the Eastern Sayan Mountains, live a people who are probably not mentioned in any reference book or dictionary. These people, who call themselves Soyots, have long and hopelessly tried to prove their existence. Back in 1929 the tribe's elders appealed to the All-Russian Central Executive Committee (VTsIK) of the USSR for social and ethnographic support. The Bolsheviks responded only with increased taxation. Worse still, some of the "petitioners" ended up in camps, where many perished. But the Soyots have not quit, and right up to the present, "democratic" time, they write to the Moscow authorities: we exist, we are not extinct. They are not calling for benefits nor help. They only want recognition. The State Statistics Committee responded as follows: "According to the last census, there are no such people." No people — no problem.

---

[1] Generally, high-security government-run production sites where nobody could leave or enter without a special permit.

[2] https://citypopulation.de/en/russia/cukotskijavtonomnyjokrug/

Then something changed. The Soyots seem to have been included in census statistics since 2002 (a whopping 2,700, increased to 3,680 by 2010),[1] and at about the same time efforts were begun to reconstruct and revive their distinctive branch of the Tuvan-Turkic language.

The military term "partial loss of control" is now firmly embedded in the political life of the country. And we are not talking about Chechnya, which is an openly rebellious area, but about both large and small legal, social, political and national conflicts that have engulfed dozens of Russia's 89 regions. Nine out of ten criminals wanted for terrorist attacks in Moscow and Volgodonsk are from Karachay-Cherkessia. Recruiting systems in this mountainous Caucasian republic have been receiving international terrorists for about five years. Something similar is going on in neighboring Balkaria. Apparently there are rest camps for terrorists in Adygea. Several basic federal laws are being ignored in Ingushetia. In the Sverdlovsk region, contrary to international agreements signed by the federal government, attempts are being made to introduce the death penalty. The list is so long that it one can no longer call the federal government a centralized force.

In Tatarstan, there are plans to build a madrasa where they will teach not so much the Koran as how to use a grenade launcher, and the official Tatar authorities, instead of stopping all this, are cancelling conscription into the federal army. The leaders of Bashkortostan and Tatarstan have already stated that they will fight for their sovereignty in case of Russia-Belarus union, so that they can join the new union on equal rights with their western neighbor. If that happens, Russia will inevitably get a second or third Chechnya. In Tatarstan, Tatar nationalist and Islamic religious groups are gaining strength, and the leadership is turning a blind eye. The former state dacha "Tesseli" in the Crimean town of Foros, which has been leased to Tatarstan, hosts conferences attended by religious extremists. Crimean mosques call for jihad. Posters of the Turkish ultranationalist organization "Grey Wolves" are distributed among Tatar students in Crimean universities. The Azatlyk Union of Tatar Youth advocates the complete separation of Tatarstan from Russia, the introduction of its own currency and the creation of its own army, as well as for boycotting Russian elections and creating its own legislative framework. On the territory of Tatarstan, supporters of independence have more than once blown up the main gas pipeline Urengoy–Pomary–Uzhgorod, which transports gas to Europe. The conflict around Chechnya and the entire North Caucasus, and the means by which it is being waged, destroys Russia's relations not only with other Islamic countries, but, most of all, with the Muslim republics within the Russian Federation.

---

[1] https://live.dbpedia.org/page/Soyot

In fact, it is in Russia that a general war between Christians and Muslims could be provoked.

Russia is capable of blowing up the situation in all the former Soviet republics. In fact, it has taken on all peacekeeping functions in the "hot spots" of the CIS. But often Russian peacekeepers have been drawn into direct conflicts, which tend to escalate into protracted military confrontations. The Russian army brought Rakhmonov to power in Tajikistan, separated Transnistria from Moldova, fought on the side of Abkhazia against Georgia, and armed Armenia against Azerbaijan, by the way, its ally in the Treaty. Most of the former Soviet republics have found the instability in Russia dangerous, especially since constant changes of government make economic and diplomatic policies unpredictable. One way or another, all the republics are still dependent on Russia. In 1998, for example, the leaders of Azerbaijan announced that the country's monetary income had increased by 26%. For the most part, this money was extracted from Russian retail shops and transferred to Azerbaijan by the three million Azerbaijanis who live in Russia and trade not only vegetables and fruits from their homeland, but also vegetables grown on Russian territory. These three million "Russian" Azerbaijanis support their families at home with the money earned in Russia. And this is about 90% of the residents of Azerbaijan. There are already constant disputes over energy supplies, and none of the former Soviet republics wants to become even more dependent on Russia. In Ukraine, ethnic Russians voted for independence from Moscow in 1991, and they are almost half of the population.

Russia is unilaterally ignoring agreements signed in the framework of the CIS meetings. According to the Bishkek agreements, any CIS country that decides to change its entry–exit regime is obliged to notify its partners at least 90 days in advance. But Russia, taking advantage of the "emergency situation" can in fact introduce a new visa regime on an emergency basis and without warning anybody. If that happens, a question arises about the citizens of those countries which are subject to the visa regime. There are millions of visitors in Moscow alone, and all of them would automatically become illegal immigrants, whom the Moscow police should catch and send back home. Including those who have recently paid to re-register. But that is nobody's business. The trick is that the interests of the political forces in Russia, which are on the rise, are such that they have no interest in Ukraine, Azerbaijan, or even Chechnya. Their main goal is to take advantage of people's disgust with "capitalism" as it was built here in the last several years and the growing anti-Western sentiment in order to once again "restore" Russia in their own way.

12. The Caucasus and the First Chechen War

Many mainstream sources offer nearly identical narratives about the first Chechen War and conclude that it was a senseless, barbaric bloodbath caused by the Russians. The geostrategic importance of Chechnya is rarely mentioned, or the history and political implications. It's worth remembering that "Russia had to endure heavy losses over the fall of its former empire. Socialist policies had run down every institution in the country. The ex-Soviet Russian Federation had no interest in a further decline. If Chechnya had successfully seceded, who would be next? Would the federation be divided by a Muslim corridor? Furthermore, the Caucasus is rich in natural resources and a gas pipeline from the Caspian Sea to the Black Sea passed directly through Chechnya."[1]

According to the Chechen state, the aggression was committed several hundred years ago when Russian troops occupied the region, and today it is a question of liberating occupied territories. War always entails the abolition of a number of legal mechanisms in favor of law enforcement mechanisms. But the Russian Army, which is committing all sorts of abuses, is rapidly decaying and becoming incapacitated. There is a loss of control over the military leadership, a lack of discipline, a habit of protecting each other's back. By corrupting the army, society is losing too much. A rejection of democratic institutions of the state — civilian rule, freedom of speech, and constitutionalism — is developing along extreme lines.

The West is quite unfamiliar with the long-running hatred and confrontation between Chechens and Russians. The Russians have tried to exter-

---

[1] "The First Chechen War," CaesariusStudios, by Caesarius, undated, at https://caesariusstudios.com/the-first-chechen-war/

minate the Chechens three times. The very first attempt was made by the Tsarist government, pursuing a deliberate policy of ousting the Chechens, Abkhazians, Adyghe and other peoples close to them from the state during the Caucasus War. This led to the fact that three-quarters of the ethnic Abkhazians lived outside of Russia and the USSR. During Stalin's collectivization, almost all of these peoples were subjected to repression, and the Chechens as a whole were exiled to the starving steppes of Kazakhstan. Those who didn't want to leave were shot on the spot.

The brutality on both sides has been unusually shocking, with reports of looting and burning Chechen houses, and cutting the ears off prisoners on the one hand and the impaling, beheading and crucifying of captured Russians on the other. Even in countries that are accustomed to mass extremism, apartment buildings where dozens of people are sleeping are not blown up. During World War II, no German terrorist blew up a single residential building in Moscow or another Soviet city in the rear, and no Soviet terrorist blew up a single residential building in the German rear.

During this part of the war, more than 100,000 people were killed, most of them innocent civilians. At least 50 settlements on the territory of the republic were razed to the ground. The norms of international law do not allow a state to bomb civilians even in the fight against terrorism.

The most devastating shock of the war came in late 1996, after most of the fighting was already winding down. Russian military units were already leaving Grozny when the Chechens assaulted the town. There was plenty of evidence that a major Chechens attack was imminent, but the city was left lightly guarded and warning signs were oddly ignored.

Efim Sandler points to many telling details:

- "Information about the probable operation and grouping of Chechen rebels [had] been available long before August. Several groups of Chechens were captured trying to gather information about Russian forces. In addition, [they were trying to] help the families of the leaders to escape the city."

- "[Nonetheless,] most of the units were packed and ready to leave to their bases outside Chechnya. Despite the relatively high number of Russian troops, the city itself remained literally unprotected."

- There was a quite obvious "dislike" of army leaders by police generals and vice versa, not to mention the FSB officers.

- The day before the assault, the street dogs were killed.

- On 5 am August 6, the first Chechen detachments began to enter the city bypassing Russian outposts...at exactly the same time a 1500 Russian police withdrew).[1]

---

[1] "First Chechen War, 1994-96," by Efim Sandler, for *Rebellion Research*, November 17, 2021, at https://www.rebellionresearch.com/first-chechen-war-1994-96

There were some bloody battles but principally, "the Chechens just entered the city and pushed towards government buildings in the center trying to persuade Russians to leave the buildings — according to the participants it looked like they just had to show the gains but not actually fight."[1]

However, "the memories of 1994/95 were still fresh and many officers were keen for revenge." Some 6,000–7,000 Chechen fighters were in the city by mid-August. With 50,000–200,000 civilians still in the city, both Chechen and Russian, as well as thousands of federal servicemen in Grozny, on August 19 General Konstantin Pulikovsky gave an ultimatum for Chechen fighters to leave the city in 48 hours "or it would be leveled in a massive aerial and ground bombardment. This was followed by a chaotic of scenes of panic as civilians tried to flee before the army carried out its threat, with parts of the city ablaze and falling shells scattering refugee columns."[2] The bombardment was halted by a ceasefire brokered by Yeltsin's national security adviser Alexander Lebed on August 22 with Aslan Maskhadov.[3]

Sandler puts it somewhat differently: "On August 22, Alexander Lebed (Boris Yeltsin's emissary) arrived in Chechnya....halting all Russian military activities. Lebed, accompanied by Russian businessman [Jewish oligarch] Boris Berezovsky, personally managed the negotiations with Chechens. In addition, they signed the agreement literally backing off all Russian forces." What was Berezovsky doing there?

Hostilities wound down to a simmer after that, until 1999, when "a few of Maskhadov's former comrades-in-arms, led by field commander Shamil Basayev and Ibn al-Khattab, launched an incursion into Dagestan in the summer of 1999, and soon Russia invaded Chechnya again, starting the Second Chechen War."[4]

Our author Sidorov offers his perspective from Moscow.

The increasing influence of Muslim fundamentalists in Russian society is clearly growing as social and economic conditions worsen and more and more citizens are financially stressed, particularly in regions with a predominantly Muslim population. The local police continue to harass the people. Wahhabism is gaining popularity largely as a protest against police brutality. If the fight against corruption doesn't start to show results soon, the population will turn away from all authority and go over to the Wahhabis. Russian

---

[1] Ibid.
[2] Aslan Maskhadov, 1999, Interview. *Small Wars Journal*, 6.
[3] "First Chechen War," *New World Encyclopedia*, at https://www.newworldencyclopedia.org/entry/First_Chechen_War#cite_ref-30
[4] Ibid.

law enforcement agencies have been talking about the danger of the spread of Wahhabism for at least two years, and even more about the "outlaw commanders" Basayev and Khattab. But, nevertheless, the militants regularly make successful sorties; they are superbly armed and, apparently, have more complete strategic information than the special services. Then, who can be surprised that the first day of the armed conflict in Dagestan, 1999, was marked by a victorious strike by the Russian military against Dagestani militiamen who were fighting on the side of the federal forces? Four people were killed and several injured as a result of a helicopter attack by a police car.

The future of the Caucasus is gloomy. It is an extremely poor and ethnically fragmented region consisting largely of isolated valleys carved apart by rugged mountains. The general background of the situation in the Caucasus is the same as in the whole of Russia, only several times worse: total corruption of the authorities, 85% of the national wealth is concentrated in the hands of two hundred families, 85% of the basic population lives below the poverty line — three or four times worse than the average Russian. And we know how the average Russian is living — it doesn't matter. Until now, Caucasian traditions — respect for elders, respect for authority, the authority of Muslim leaders and elders — have held people back. But as corruption grows, all restraints are loosened, and the current religious leaders are seen as being in the service of the Russians. Thus, the Russian government itself is fueling a hotbed of hatred here.

When it joined the Council of Europe in 1996, Russia pledged to end the war in Chechnya. Fencing off Chechnya with checkpoints and guard posts, Russia has de facto recognized the independence of the rebellious republic. Several strongholds have been equipped on the 400-kilometer administrative border with Chechnya, a 60-kilometer trench is being built by engineering units to hinder the movement of armed formations, and internal troops are being equipped with new military equipment. The Council of the Federation did not even have any representatives of this Federal unit; after the deafening explosions of housing blocks in Moscow, this began to be discussed.

Russia's annual budget, which is being debated in the Duma, is only $30 billion. And the war has practically drained it all. As a result, the costs of the "quarantine zone" being created around the rebellious Chechnya will come not only from the Ministry of Defense, but also from the budget for internal security troops, the police, border guards and other law enforcement agencies. Almost all of Russia's most capable ground forces, internal troops, special operations police units (OMON) and militia are now in the Northern Caucasus, stretched to the limit.

According to General Andrei Nikolaev, who created a "fortified area" on the Tajik–Afghan border, "it will take 4 to 6 months and 60–65,000 military personnel [to construct the 650-kilometer border with Chechnya], and the cost of the border will range from 1 to 8 million rubles per kilometer." But given the general corruption of the guards, this very "cordon sanitaire" actually loses its meaning. It will always be permeable or available to buy. It's just pointless, besides being costly. Of course, you can limit the traffic, but if someone really wants to get through, then he will get through. He'll just pay to get across.

The total cost of the current military operation in the North Caucasus is considered "classified." But it is known that the Caucasus consumes almost a quarter of all funds allocated in Russia for national defense. After what happened in Dagestan, the budget limit for the Defense Ministry for September 1999 was increased from 8.3 to 10.8 billion rubles. This money would have to cover fuel, ammunition, and salaries. But every calculation showed that the cost of maintaining several thousand federal troops in full combat readiness on the border with Chechnya for a prolonged period would be impossible to support. From this standpoint, it would be better to take offensive action (as was confirmed by subsequent events).

At the end of 1999, the federal forces had officially lost 741, with 2,233 wounded. However, in an interview the head of the rear of the Armed Forces, Colonel-General Vladimir Isakov cited a much larger figure for the Ministry of Defense, announcing losses (injured and wounded) of 3,656 people. Meanwhile, only about 4,000 people passed through Mozdok Hospital No. 1458. By the way, these numbers are growing: on January 6, a Scalpel military medical aircraft arrived in Mozdok; these aircraft have always been a sign of heavy losses. During the first week of the new year 2000, Yekaterinburg received two batches of wounded — more than 70 people who were taken to the Ural District Hospital for Internal Troops. The wounded are not yet being lined up in the hallways, but the wards are quite packed. Rostov District Hospital is now accepting new wounded from Chechnya. The exact number of soldiers undergoing treatment in Rostov-on-Don, of course, has not been announced, but television cameramen gave away the approximate figure by showing close-ups of the hallway — it was crowded and showed no fewer than 100 people. Moreover, these were only military personnel who were able to move without assistance. The chief of the hospital, Colonel Chuiko, admitted that in the autumn of 1999, his institution regularly received planes with wounded from Chechnya — up to 10 soldiers and officers per day. The Union of Committees of Soldiers' Mothers of Russia has its own data on losses among Russian servicemen — about 3,000 men killed and about 6,000 wounded. Thus, the soldiers' mothers believe that official data on Russian losses are underestimated by at least seven times. How many civilians have died? Statistics are not even kept. During the Chechen campaign of 1994–1996, the total losses of all Russian combat units amounted to 3962 people killed and 17,892 wounded. It is clear that soldiers and junior officers are by no means burning with fighting spirit and, in fact, are waiting for the politicians to actively take steps to stop the turmoil in the Caucasus.

Sidorov observes that having survived the humiliation in Yugoslavia, Russia cannot afford a second failure in the North Caucasus. Russia feels like a great power again, fighting the people of little Chechnya. There is a risk the war may spread to Georgia, which found itself at the center of a conflict of interests between Russia and NATO, which continues expanding to the east. Georgian president Shevardnadze publicly declared that he would like to see Georgia as part of the North Atlantic Bloc. The economic and military security of Russia would be crucially undermined by such a step, nor can the Kremlin afford to accept Shevardnadze's plan to lead his country out of chaos by allowing Western projects to pump Caspian oil, bypassing Russia. Thus Georgia and Chechnya find themselves on the same side. Shevardnadze has very warm relations with the leaders of Chechnya and did not even bother to formally express his condolences to the victims of terrorist acts in Russia. In response, Russia lifted the economic blockade on the rebellious Georgian Republic of Abkhazia, where a new outbreak of violence could occur. An explosive situation is also developing in Karachay-Cherkessia. According to Georgian press reports, militants are already crossing from Abkhazia to Karachay-Cherkessia. The Circassians, Abazins, Kabardins and Adyghes living in Karachay-Cherkessia and neighboring Kabardino-Balkaria and Adyghea are related to the Abkhazians (unlike the Karachays, who belong to the Turkic group).

During the war in Abkhazia, Circassia was a training center for fighters who fought against the Georgian government forces. If armed clashes break out in Karachay-Cherkessia, Abkhazian units will try to "thank" their Circassian and Abaza brethren for their assistance during the war against Georgia. Accordingly, any new flare-up of the Georgian–Abkhazian conflict will force the Circassian and Abaza volunteers to go to the aid of their Abkhaz brothers. The route has been known since the Abkhazian war: mountain trails through the Caucasus Range, through the territory inhabited by the Karachais. Then, in 1992, the Karachais remained neutral. This time, volunteers from one side or the other (Abkhaz or Circassians) are unlikely to be able to cross the mountains unimpeded.

The Stavropol Cossacks, recently included in the Terek Cossack Host and already included in the state register, demand they be allowed to return to the Stavropol Territory of the Naursky and Shelkovskaya regions, once inhabited exclusively by Cossacks, that were transferred to the Checheno-Ingushetia in 1957. If this happens, Chechnya may demand that Aukh be returned to it — most of the Novolaksky and part of the Khasavyurt regions of Dagestan, which were torn away from Chechnya in 1957 as "compensation" for the Naur and Shelkovsky regions. Even worse is the situation around the Prigorodny district of North Ossetia, which Ingushetia claims under the same "compensation" scheme. This dispute already led to a bloody conflict in the fall of 1992, and to this day the situation around the Prigorodny region remains one of the most explosive in the North Caucasus (except for Chechnya). There is reason to believe that in the Russian regions, which lie hundreds of kilometers from the Caucasian theater of operations, the preconditions are being created for enrolling the population in new cycles of Caucasian feuding. Such regions include the Volgograd region, where several such conditions have already been established: first, there are several cohesive and influential Caucasian diasporas; secondly, the position of "Caucasians" in the criminal hierarchy of the region has been strengthened; thirdly, there are Wahhabi strongholds in the region.

The utility of a small victorious war in influencing domestic politics cannot be underestimated. The Kremlin chose its timing when it unleashed the Chechen conflict. The federal authorities are absolutely not interested in decisive and effective actions to stabilize the situation in one of the most explosive regions of Russia. The words of former Prime Minister Sergei Stepashin, who declared that the Chechen situation of 1994–1995 would not be repeated again, do not correspond to reality and are only the good wishes of a private person. Russian security agencies are interested in ensuring that the conflict in the Caucasus continues to smolder and tensions constantly exist. By conducting military operations, the army hopes to regain the credibility it lost during the previous war in Chechnya. A weakened army pretends to be capable of great feats. The generals avenge their defeat in Chechnya in 1996, when after a two-year war in which about 100,000 people died (of which almost a quarter were killed — ethnic Russians who were living in Chechnya). Russian troops were forced to withdraw from Chechnya in disgrace. Victory over the Chechen militants was not just the goal of the military operation but also an obsession for Russian generals humiliated by that defeat.

The public demands revenge, society is hungry for blood: political points and percentage points in the ratings of the executive power and law enforcement agencies are earned on the Chechen campaign. Communist leader Gennady Zyuganov is holding a solemn reception for family members of the deceased members of the internal affairs bodies in the State Duma building. Many sources, including in law enforcement, believe that events in the Caucasus are directly linked to the future parliamentary and presidential elections in Russia. The political crisis is developing in parallel with the "Islamic" insurgency in the Caucasus. Back in the summer of 1999, it was being said in Dagestan that in the near future hostilities would be transferred to the territory of Chechnya.

In addition, war is a good pretext for theft at the state level. War can be ordered, paid for and received. Based on the well-known facts from the past Chechen war and post-war reconstruction, we can confidently say that under the guise of the war, the budget money allocated for Chechnya is being embezzled. Bombers bomb those places where restored houses and businesses are supposed to be, but they were never built. The army has to eat rotten food and walk around in tattered uniforms, although the budget spends a lot of money on this (a quarter of the budget). Corrupt officials and generals have an excellent reason to sell uniforms and products stolen from army warehouses. Moreover, there is a place to sell all this, in a hungry country that has been stripped of all necessities. Fighters in Chechnya and Dagestan are fed rotten stew. Take, for example, the Lipetsk Special Purpose Militia Unit (OMON), deployed in the Kazbekovsky region of Dagestan, bordering Chechnya. "We never stop having gastrointestinal infections," says the squad leader. "We are fighting for someone's political ambitions. For 22 rubles a day. Men who are fighting in impossible circumstances and show courage in battle are treated like useless stray dogs." At one point, in order to put some heat into the war in Dagestan, Acting Minister of Finance Mikhail Kasyanov promised solid money to those who were going to fight there. He stated that the Russian servicemen would be see a raise in salaries to the same level as Russian peacekeepers in Kosovo and Bosnia. Soldiers were to receive $1,000 a month, and officers even more. This statement was made by Kasyanov, after a meeting with Prime Minister Putin. They even promised not to even withhold alimony. Now the leaders are trying to solve the problem in the old Soviet way: collecting supplies and money from the population for the war. There are calls to send warm clothes, canned food, disposable razors, toothpaste and brushes, envelopes, and lighters to the army in the Caucasus. Farms and private owners in the Stavropol Territory have to give ten rams from their sheep yards to feed the army on a voluntary-compulsory basis.

Many events in Chechnya can only be explained by the corruption of the Russian command. During the Botlikh operation in Dagestan, trucks full of militants drove right in front of the reconnaissance groups, waving banners. In response to requests to open fire, the command was silent. The coordinates were reported, but no combat helicopters showed up, either. Colonel-General Arkady Baskayev, commander of the internal troops of the Moscow District, said that he could have had the well-known terrorist Basayev killed. However, according to him, Oleg Lobov, the plenipotentiary representative of the President of Russia in Chechnya, forbade it. The next day, intelligence reported that, in addition to Basayev, every single one of the Chechen frontline commanders had been in one of the small villages. "And we were forbidden to destroy them. This is in a war!?" Baskaev said.

More than two months before the start of hostilities, the Minister of the Interior reported personally to the President of Russia about a possible aggression in Dagestan and suggested taking preventive measures. But he never received permission. And then someone gave the order to regroup the forces, which greatly weakened the position of the federal troops. As a result, thousands of militants easily infiltrated Dagestan. How was the territory cleared of militants in Dagestan? Russian troops fired at empty trenches for several days, while helicopters fired at empty mountain slopes, and militants, in a civilized convoy, led by jeeps, left without hindrance for Chechnya. A plot worthy of a Hollywood action movie.

In the Chechen war, almost everything is being bought and sold, the only questions are who and for how much. For example, to keep the artillery from firing at the city of Katyr-Yurt, local residents collected $500 and a large TV set, and the shelling stopped. A similar price was paid to protect the city of Achkhoy-Martan. The famous capitulations of entire cities in exchange for not carrying out an ethnic cleansing are like a commercial conspiracy.

The militants have excellent communications systems, so that even the smallest groups are well-equipped. They have not only radio stations with scramblers, but also satellite communication. In principle, it's simple — to buy a satellite station, you just need to make regular payments for its use. Shamil Basayev has one, Khattab even has two. The well-known Russian millionaire Boris Berezovsky pays for Basayev's and Udugov's satellite stations. They are officially registered with him. Berezovsky also pays for their television and Internet pages. It has already become commonplace to assert that the militants, when things got critical, called their Moscow patrons for help, and they immediately responded.

According to Jaromir Shtetina, editor-in-chief of the Czech agency Epicenter, who was directly in the besieged Grozny, there are fixed prices for everything at Russian military posts. If a grandmother wants to go to some village to buy something to eat, then she has to pay 60 rubles at the checkpoint. If there is a car of refugees, they pay 300 rubles. If you pay $500, you can even drive a truck full of armed guerrillas. Jaromir Shtetina himself left Chechnya disguised as an old Chechen man. He simply took out $20 at each checkpoint, gave it to the soldier, and the soldier did not check the van. So Stettin drove to the neighboring republic of Ingushetia. This happened at many posts and was 100% successful.

Back in November 1995, Novaya Gazeta published a photograph of a secret civilian burial ground in Grozny on the Karpinsky mound near the outskirts of the city. This grave was found by correspondents from the newspaper together with the film crew of the TV program "Vzglyad" and human rights activist Viktor Popkov. There were twenty-five bodies — young men, women, old people wrapped in scraps of peaceful colored clothes and with their hands twisted together with barbed wire. According to forensic experts, they were shot, and then there was an attempt to destroy the bodies by crushing them in a concrete mixer and dousing them with acid. The Prosecutor General's Office did not react in any way to the photographs, or to the video filming, or even to the remains of the bodies. It's like it doesn't exist for them.

In Ingushetia, filtration centers are once again being built, in effect concentration camps, "with all the ensuing consequences," as the Russian Interior Minister Vladimir Rushailo said. No one knows what is being done in those centers, who is being held there, and under what conditions. From 1994 to 1996, 1,500 detainees have disappeared into such camps without a trace, and many of them were mutilated by beastly torture. Since the beginning of the conflict in Chechnya, the federal government has acted as if this were a foreign war and not an internal conflict with its own citizens, doing everything possible to operate outside out of the context of humanitarian law and, accordingly, beyond international control. Soldiers from special units were sent against the refugees from Chechnya to suppress riots in the camp. At the same time, some of these riot control specialists were appointed commandants of the liberated settlements. Rumor has it that "criminal" units are fighting in Chechnya, violent prisoners who were given an amnesty on that condition. Stalin used the same tactics during World War II. Nothing has changed in Russia. Needless to say, this fuels distrust towards the federal center in all the Caucasian republics. Political circles in

Dagestan are outraged to see extremist leaders who opposed the Russian troops were able to go back and forth to Chechnya freely and with impunity. And the saddest thing is that they didn't have to fight their way out of the encirclement, they simply went back and forth like tourists.

Despite claims that there are no civilians in Chechnya, the army is actually blocking the exodus of refugees. Even members of the puppet Chechen State Council, created as a counterweight to the pro-independence movement, cannot tolerate this. One of them, 35-year-old Malik Saidullayev, stated that he could "no longer turn a blind eye" to "the mayhem going on at the checkpoints" for Chechen refugees.

After three months of war, there were about 200,000 Chechen refugees on the border of Chechnya with Ingushetia. That was already more than the number of officially registered refugees overall. Obviously, not all of them were registered, and many left Chechnya bypassing the checkpoints. Another 500,000 Chechens dispersed over the CIS in the previous years. With a flow of over 200,000 refugees, and only some 100 to 200 people a day being let through the checkpoints, the back-up was terrible. Elderly people and even infants were being killed on the outskirts of the checkpoints where thousands of people were stranded. The military even isolated the members of the Chechen State Council who were trying to help the refugees. One can only imagine what was going on there. Finnish Foreign Minister Tarja Halonen, who visited the Chechen refugee camps in Ingushetia, was horrified by what she saw. Kim Trovik, head of the OSCE monitoring mission, was shocked by what he saw in Ingushetia. "We are talking about a very serious humanitarian disaster," he said. The refugees told the Norwegian diplomat that they had not fled from terrorists and bandits but from Russian soldiers, and they openly expressed their hatred of Russians. Lord David Russell-Johnston, President of the Parliamentary Assembly of the Council of Europe, and other participants of the visit to the North Caucasus, were firmly convinced that the Russian side was flagrantly violating human rights in the refugee camps. Russian Prime Minister Vladimir Putin said at a meeting with a special representative of the UN Secretary-General that "...those people who left Chechnya and are now in Ingushetia cannot be called refugees, because they are not going to another country, but are seeking protection from the Russian government and on Russian territory." Meanwhile, 200,000 Chechen refugees are actually living outdoors, with no winter clothes or food.

The federal authorities have established what is essentially an occupation system within the republic. They have set up government offices in the controlled areas of Chechnya with minimal involvement of the Chechens themselves. Russians are appointed as heads of regional and village government offices, as well as Russian federal offices. The military do not ask the Chechens in the liberated districts about anything — they are told the name of their commandant, and that is all.

In 1996, there were 230 people working for the Chechen Attorney General; many of them had to leave Grozny under threat of reprisals. All of them were essentially betrayed after the first Chechen war, as were members of the Chechen Ministry of Justice and the judicial system. Since the head of the supervisory department, Igor Kiselyov, and 18 prosecutors under him, will perform their duties while sitting in Mozdok, North Ossetia, it would be rare for a Chechen to get his hands on them, even if he really wanted to.

Despite talk about not declaring a state of emergency in Russia, in fact it has already been introduced. Troops have been brought into the major cities of Russia, Caucasians are being stopped for document checks, house committees are being created in apartment blocks, and army veterans are being enrolled to help keep order. In Moscow, crowded public places are thoroughly checked, residential premises are being inspected, and foreigners as well as residents of other regions of Russia visiting or staying in Moscow are under closer control. All this, to put it mildly, puts a damper on what should be a healthy political climate in the country on the eve of the parliamentary and presidential elections. In addition, somehow liberal values have imperceptibly been thrown into the trash. There was a whiff of the communist past: it was ordered that the value of the ruble be kept fixed, prices were not allowed to rise, or merchants to profit, or businessmen to pay debts.

Under these circumstances, nostalgia for the Soviet Union and its all-powerful KGB is likely to crop up. In those days the borders were secure, bandits did not walk the streets, and terrorist acts occurred "only" in other countries. True, this security was paid for at the expense of personal freedom, but no one thinks about that now. In such chaotic conditions, it is very difficult to put things in order, and unfettered democracy in this case takes too long to work. At times like this, sadly, only a firm hand and more centralized control can get things done.

What is happening in the Caucasus is primarily a reflection of what is happening in Moscow. The President and Prime Minister of Russia are pursuing the same type of policy followed by well-protected leaders in Moscow as in the United States. From their heavily guarded offices, they send soldiers to certain death and brush aside any possibility of negotiations. The Caucasus wars are the kind that, once started, can go on for decades. All of Russia is in suspense, and its politicians can constantly threaten each other and the people with a state of emergency. And this constantly wears on the small gains of democracy. If things go badly in the country, grassroots political activities will be banned, the military will take charge of the government, the populace will suffer from various mobilization measures. And the economy will be geared as usual toward supplying the military.

13. FINANCE AND ENTREPRENEURSHIP

Russia should not expect rapid normalization and good times. The prosperity of the United States and the rapid recovery from economies crises by countries like South Korea, is primarily due to a significant increase in personal consumption and large-scale investment activities of enterprises.

In Russia, there was never much development of the "consumer economy." Under communism, most economic activity was actually carried out via cash-free transfers. Vacations were organized and provided by one's workplace. Housing was allocated by the government, whereas home ownership or rent is the greatest expense for most American families. This is a particularly tricky part of the transition to capitalism and it hits households hard.

Since 30% of the Russian population still has incomes below the subsistence level, a sharp increase in prices leads to a severe reduction in sales. Even if the Russian economy shows any real growth, it will inevitably run into virtually non-existent domestic demand. The people have no money. They cannot spend in amounts that support production, and loans are stolen. Meanwhile, any figures showing growth of the national product are based only on the short-term effect of the devaluation of the ruble. Furthermore, given that the structure of the economy and the fact that the ruble is not accepted internationally, any comparative financial data are meaningless unless measured by PPP (purchasing power parity).

Today the government cannot answer the main question: does it want to earn money or does it just want to govern? If we knew that, then everything would become clear. In the field of management, we can see that state property has been looted. Private companies steal much less. Every time a state bank for reconstruction and development is opened (there have already been about five), it takes money from the budget, distributes it, and goes bankrupt. There was no system for repaying those loans, just as there is none now. The state still has not created a tool, a bank, with the financial instruments through which it can not only invest money and support companies, but also be paid back.

Taxes in Russia are based not on income but on turnover. Because of this, today it is difficult even to pay people their salaries. Each political crisis costs the country an amount roughly equal to an IMF loan. The post of Special Presidential Representative for Cooperation with International Financial Institutions is traditionally introduced in Russia only in emergency situations, when the country needs money at any cost. The Ministry of Finance is mostly misused. There are plenty of bureaucratic tricks that are used by political factions fighting within the state to stall or temporarily delay the passage of a document through the Ministry. The country's economic goals are always pushed to the sidelines. At this point, we cannot seriously call Russia a market economy.

All transactions are divided into "cash" and "cashless." "Cashless" refers to non-cash transactions mainly between governmental offices. For Russia, this is a more or less mythical category, especially since most of the payments are made by barter. "Cash" is another thing. At least 40% of all Russian cash transactions are "under the table," in the grey market (if not the black market), and the profits remain there, underground. No one knows the exact volume of Russia's shadow economy. However, even according to the Russian State Statistics Committee, whose forecasts are much more optimistic than those of other researchers, about 25% of business activity in the country is in this hidden economy. And given the fact that data on the shadow sector are included in calculations of the gross domestic product (GDP), the shadow sector makes up at least 25% of Russia's GDP. The highest level of hidden income is in agriculture, where almost half of the transactions are unofficial. If the shadow sector could be brought to light and it could be taxed, the country could receive more than $3 billion much needed funding. This "black" money does not remain under the mattress. It is spread throughout the national economy, bringing everyone illegal income. Cash, which is used by shops, restaurants, air and cargo carriers, attracts like a magnet various shady and criminal operators. When they bump into each other, as a rule it ends in tragedy.

The West continues to regard Russia as a great power in political and military terms. Russia was officially recognized as a full-fledged member of the club of the richest and most economically developed powers of the planet. Paradoxically, Russia was given membership in the club of the leading industrial countries just at the moment when the country was experiencing a deep economic crisis. Of course, everyone deliberately pretended that the Russia economy was doing fine. But in fact, under Yeltsin the country has slipped to the level of a third-rate developing country and it does not inspire confidence among creditors. No sane investor will remain in Russia just because it has been dubbed a full member of the Group of Eight (G8).[1] Foreign investors are powerless against Russian corruption and the machinations of officials and oligarchs. Many investors have learned this from their own experience. Bankers complain that the Russian judiciary serves the interests of criminal elements.

Who and what does Russia represent in the Group of Eight? Besides its own debts. The fact is that a country experiencing a severe economic and financial crisis also affects all its neighbors, to a large extent. In fact, Russia should be classified among the poorest countries in the world and its debts should be forgiven. But it is one thing to write off debts to a poor country and quite another for a member of a cohort of elite powers. Moreover, Russia itself, under the terms of membership in the Paris Club, participates in writing off the debts of underdeveloped countries like Nicaragua. And more. And writing off part of Russia's external debt would not necessarily lead to the country strictly fulfilling its debt obligations. It will simply mean reconciling the world's financial institutions to the fact that the country is constantly violating financial and political discipline. That would not be all bad, if there were a well-established tax and with-holding management system in Russia; then we could count state revenues increasing and the debt would be paid down. But, based on the state of affairs today, there is little hope of that happening.

The true consequences of the "liberal" reforms in Russia are that after seven years of privatization, thousands of enterprises have practically closed shop or have already gone bankrupt. A World Bank report published in April 1999 admits that privatization in Russia has been a failure, while in Poland and China it has led to success. "Privatization" as conducted under Yeltsin, in the most cynical way, has only deceived the public. The interests of the country and its people were not taken into account. This begs the question of why it is so much harder for Russian businesses to adapt to working in a market economy than, say, Polish and Chinese businesses. One of the reasons for Russia's lagging behind China and Poland is that Russian officials and the creators of its privatization regimes have rejected democratic forms of ownership, for example, ownership by the workers, as well as the undivided dominance of state monopolies in the market economy.

---

[1] from 1997 until 2014.

The Russian economy is increasingly taking on features of the Soviet national economy, with its fraud, inflated reports and whitewashing of data. All that's missing is to complete the process of fully subordinating the major sectors of the economy to the executive branch. The national income will be redistributed by the forces of the bureaucracy rather than by supply and demand. People's savings will be concentrated in several government-owned banks that will guarantee the complete safety of deposits. True, they won't offer more than 2% interest per annum, and, in addition, the authorities will be free to apply confiscatory monetary reforms from time to time.

When the International Monetary Fund's board of directors decides whether or not to lend to Russia, it is deciding a much more fundamental question: whether or not Russia should be part of the global economy. In Russia, they see it differently. The Prime Minister actually presented a sensational thesis at a government meeting, which literally came down to this: if we do not receive the next tranche of IMF loans, we will completely lose our economic independence. What?! Think about it! If the country's sovereignty is directly dependent upon the receipt of a half-billion dollar tranche, then the country is completely dependent on credit injections from outside. Russia was already bankrupt long ago, it just hasn't been officially announced yet. But does one wait until the bankrupt country, with its powerful diplomatic services and the corresponding ideology, announces this itself?!... The leaders of the country are eager to borrow whenever possible. Candidates for government posts are evaluated in terms of their ability to "get loans." If there was any chance of deferring at least a minimal portion of repayments or mitigation of the conditions for the provision of the next tranche, this was presented as a major success for the Russian delegation, whose leader was all but carried aloft on the shoulders of his colleagues. Because all this new money can then be stolen, and from this the well-being of the "new Russian" leader flows.

The goals of the G7, the seven most developed countries, remain the same as they were a decade ago: to get a handle on Russia by integrating it into the orbit of the world economy and to weaken it, by undermining its strong patriotism and national identity by supporting liberal forces, on the grounds that they are seeking cooperation rather than confrontation with the West. But since the current crop of "nationalist-minded" politicians are also thieves, the Western model of development is extremely discredited in the eyes of public opinion.

In the last ten years, the people's standard of living has dropped significantly both from an economic point of view and from a political point of view. The Group of Eight automatically reverts to the "G7+1" formula as soon as they start talking about the problems of the Russian economy. Fraud and corruption in the Kremlin is not the worst thing. Worse still, a political, military, and mafia network has entangled the state and society as a whole. Dozens of Russian banks specialize exclusively in servicing capital flight. Most of the money taken out will never return to Russia. It is already invested and working in other countries, and no one has any desire to destroy an established business. Any money that is returned, as a rule, was from the Central Bank, with which it played a win–win game at the Moscow Interbank Currency Exchange (MICEX). Of the funds transferred abroad, less than half are returned to Russia to service import operations under special schemes. Billions of dollars in under-reporting or non-payment of import duties and tax evasion must also be added. The money illegally transferred abroad by Russian functionaries is also related to IMF loans, food aid to Russia, the U.S.-sponsored programs for the destruction of nuclear weapons, and demilitarization of the post-Soviet space. Only a small part of the scammed money belonged to criminals, while the largest transactions were carried out by the big Russian corporations — exporters of raw materials, as well as commercial banks interested in placing funds in a politically safe zone and at the same time evading debt payment.

Russia needs laws and a cabinet that will enable it to make money on its own and rebuild its industry. The problem goes beyond corruption, which is an almost organic component of Russian power. The current "suspended" situation cannot last long. The country's finances are like a scrap of cloth worn thin and about to shred. Russia has neither a market economy nor state regulation. The Chairman of the Central Bank, Gerashchenko, has created a mechanism to keep the ruble down, which only functions properly when it siphons off foreign currency from the population. Any unexpected event or careless action in the financial sphere or in the economy generates a sharp, uncontrollable drop in the exchange rate of the national currency. The occasional strengthening of the Russian ruble can never be explained by a sudden burst of global confidence. The foreign exchange market in the country is largely a fiction. There are several exchange rates, the market is completely regulated, and decisions are made by just a few people — often by one person. The exchange rate will be whatever the Central Bank sees fit and acceptable. If it were not for financial and administrative measures, the dollar would always be almost twice as high. This policy is generally characteristic of the entire history of the Russian state. Even in the 19th century, the famous Russian writer and satirist Saltykov-Shchedrin said that in exchange for a ruble, smart people will let you have about half (50 kopecks) ... but soon they'll just "let you have it" in the face.

If state investments are most often lost or plundered, that leaves private investments. But no legal basis has been created to administer and protect such. Budget investments in Russia are always meaningless, inefficient and end up being plundered. That leaves the option of private investments. But they are impossible due to the fact that no legal basis has been created for them. Whenever any administrative barrier in the foreign exchange market is lifted, the demand for dollars shoots up. Non-residents create a strong demand for the currency, as many of them have not yet lost hope of taking out the frozen funds and are ready to take advantage of any indulgence from the Russian state to do this. When non-residents purchase currency for repatriation, with a pre-announced trading volume of, say, $50 million, demand from investors could be more than $500 million. If this money somehow ends up in the auction, it is difficult to keep the ruble. In any event, the reserves of the Central Bank in this case do not last long.

In order to cover its costs, the country constantly dumps a commodity on the global market at such low prices and in such quantities that they bring down prices and destroy the established chains of intermediaries that are needed to tie together all the moving parts in foreign trade transactions. So it was in 1988, when Techsnabexport "dumped" about 11,000 tons of uranium on the market. This was also the case when Severonickel offered an unthinkable amount of nickel on the market in the mid-90s in order to cover the costs of maintaining the artificial infrastructure of Norilsk, the huge city beyond the Arctic Circle. Then there was the gold sold by the Central Bank in 1998. And it's not always so obvious that the Russian government and banks are behind these events. Cunning networks of holding companies and shell companies, and firms like FIMACO, a financial management company founded in Jersey),[1] allow legal officials to evade responsibility and pretend that they are hearing about it for the first time.

The IMF rightly believes that the Russians are being too lax with banks that do not fulfill their obligations — contrary to the joint statement issued by the government and the Central Bank, which quite definitely said that licenses would be revoked from insolvent banks and temporary administrations would be introduced in those banks that still showed signs of life. One of the central characters in this story is the SBS-Agro Bank, which the Central Bank has been supporting until recently. The Central Bank management has appropriated to itself the exclusive right, at its own discretion, however subjective that may be, to decide the fate of not only individual

---

[1] See "FIMACO, the Russian Central Bank, and money laundering at the highest level," by Marshall I. Goldman, in the book

The Piratization of Russia.

bankrupt banks but also hundreds of clients standing behind them. In the first half of 1999, a new profitable business, bankruptcy, grew and strengthened. The story of the famous Imperial Bank is an example of how they are trying to legalize a business that is in bankruptcy. There is no other way to explain why the license was returned to this bank only 10 days after it was finally declared bankrupt by the arbitration court. As a result of the generous pardon, the bulk of Imperial's creditors and depositors are likely to be left with nothing: there is no bankruptcy — there are no assets.

In Russia, the government owns about 13,700 so-called unitary enterprises, which have become the legal successors of former state-owned enterprises. (The government owns the assets, which may not be divided up among "shareholders.") In another 6,500 enterprises and concerns, the state's share is up to 50%. The situation in these state-owned enterprises is depressing. The state scarcely manages its property; the managers are primarily looking after their own interests, and often the state receives false or misleading information about the financial and economic condition of the company. When privatization came along, the old directors and government officials were at the right place at the right time, and they derived any benefit that may have accrued during the transition.

The management of almost all Russian joint-stock companies rob the owners, especially small shareholders, holders of small blocks of shares. Most of them are employees of the enterprises. Imperfection laws allow the shareholders to be deceived with impunity. Executives run their businesses stealthily; they do not generate taxes and dividends, and they do not invest in the development of business. Russian entrepreneurs are left high and dry, and foreign investors are discouraged. The military-industrial complex still dominates Russian industry and blocks the implementation of structural reforms. By artificially lowering energy prices and providing tax incentives, the state keeps long-unprofitable enterprises afloat, thereby hindering the development of new industries oriented towards the market of the future. IMF loans keep a gang of corrupt politicians and bureaucrats in power. This is criminal not only in relation to the people of Russia, but also in relation to the citizens of Western countries, whose taxes are the source of funding for the IMF. Russia already owes too much to the International Monetary Fund, and it does not have sufficient funds to maintain its peacekeepers in Kosovo, much less to provide significant assistance to Yugoslavia, to restore Dagestan and wind down the war in Chechnya. Nevertheless, the world cannot disregard Russia, mired as it may be in political squabbles and economic insanity, which is spread over two continents and occupies 17 million square kilometers.

"Natural monopoly is the basis of the economy," they say in Russia. Russian monopolies, created by the communists, have swallowed up the entire domestic market and jealously guard it, even trying to put pressure on the state so that it lays off the when it comes to collecting taxes. The struggle between the two giants in the country — the state and the monopolies — is tearing all small businesses to shreds. There is no hint of free competition.

Gas giant Gazprom enjoys high-level patronage and can withhold much of the tax it is expected to pay. The government and the presidential administration are interested in strengthening state leverage over this company, hinting that it is not providing all the revenues that it should. The company replies that it is ready to pay, if the debtors accordingly return to it the money for fuel already received. At Gazprom's annual meetings, it is noted that even though adverse circumstances and lower energy prices may slow it down but will not stop Gazprom's further growth. The trump card is that during its entire 30 years of supplying gas to Western Europe, there has not been a single case of Gazprom violating any contractual obligations. The company's guarantees are the most reliable.

But *Kommersant*, an influential mouthpiece of Russian businessmen, claims that Gazprom is the country's most unprofitable enterprise. "It turns out," the paper says, "that Gazprom ended 1998 with a net loss of 42.5 billion rubles ($1.8 billion). The colossal losses were not even incurred by the crisis, which cut exports in half, but simply due to peculiarities of the Soviet accounting system. Pyotr Rodionov, first deputy chairman of Gazprom's management board, explained the situation this way: throughout all the previous years, Gazprom took out $11 billion in long-term foreign loans. Before August 1 they were included in the company's balance sheet at 6 rubles to the dollar. After the devaluation, the dollar loans were recalculated according to the accounting rules at the current exchange rate of the Central Bank, i.e., approximately 24 rubles per dollar. The result was that Gazprom had borrowed four times as much money in rubles as it had planned, and so it lost money. The exchange rate difference resulted in a loss due to these loans in the amount of 198 billion rubles. The company's leaders blame the officials who made the decisions on August 17 for the incident. As Rodionov put it, "assets and liabilities were summed up on recalculation, profit was taken into account, and an operating loss of 22 billion rubles was obtained." And after deducting taxes, the balance sheet loss was 44.5 billion rubles. Gazprom, as one of the main backbones of the country, is going through a very difficult period together with everyone else. The severe financial crisis in August 1998, the chronic non-payments by "domestic" gas consumers, the sharply reduced opportunities for borrowing — all these continuous negative effects added to the endless borrowings abroad. It seems someone thinks that German or American currency reserves are scooped from bottomless vessels.

The Ministry of Railways is the largest of Russia's natural monopolies in terms of the value of fixed assets. Their fixed assets are estimated at 755 billion rubles, while the joint-stock company UES of Russia at a little over 700 billion rubles, and Gazprom 250 billion rubles. Workers at the Railway Ministry work under strict, almost military subordination and every step they take is scrupulously regulated. The labor law on the railroads is very limited. The state Labor Code is not the main law but the Disciplinary Regulations of the Ministry. Failure to obey an order of a superior in the Ministry of Railways is practically tantamount to dismissal, and strikes and other forms of collective protest are prohibited altogether.

The leaders of this monopoly are outstanding: for their snoring — even compared to other tough government officials. In addition, they've built their own commercial networks around this parastatal enterprise, through which public and investment money easily flows into their pockets or the pockets of their relatives. For example, Nikolai Aksenenko, as Minister of Railways in 1997 and the first half of 1998, created a whole network of inter-related businesses around the Ministry of Railways, including some offshore, registered in the Virgin Islands, using the department's money to make profits in dubious ways. The basis of these commercial structures are the joint-stock company "Eurosib," which is headed by the nephew of the Minister Sergey Aksenenko, and the Swiss-registered Eastern Fertiliger Trading, whose representative in Russia is the minister's son.

These companies specialize in cargo transportation. The activity of Eurosib began at Oktyabrskaya Railways in 1994 with metal sales, sales of Japanese cars, and the operation of gas stations. At that time Nikolai Aksenenko was the first deputy head of Oktyabrskaya Railways. Until recently, Eurosib's debts were in the tens of thousands of dollars. The minister's nephew was bailed out by his former companion. After that Nikolay Nikitin — the name of his partner — apparently was killed in order to avoid paying debts. Nikolai Aksenenko's son works in Switzerland, transporting phosphates. The activities of Trans Rail, run by the minister's son, resulted in a $25 million loss to the Russian chemical industry. Trans Rail is an authorized agent of the Ministry of Railways, registered in Switzerland. Its turnover is $1 billion. At the same time, according to Alexander Vengerovsky, chairman of the Foreign Intelligence Subcommittee of the Duma International Committee, "the fixed percentage of deductions for Russia is 5 percent." At a time when Aksenenko is officially being declared a model of a state-regulated market, Russia is slowly turning into the firm "Aksenenko & Son & Nephew".

The Hermes Concern, which in the mid-1990s was known in Russia as a big oil refinery, was one of the strongholds of national-chauvinist and esoteric messianic ideas. The name of the concern was not only meant to remind us of the trade, but also of the special kind of secret knowledge that they claimed to collect. "Hermes published an esoteric newspaper of the same name, and cooperated with psychologists and psychics. The main thrust of the company's work was illustrated in the company's advertisements broadcast on the Russia's major television channels in 1995–96. In one of the commercials, it was X hour and the forex brokers, who are keenly watching the ticker, see that the dollar is down to just a penny. They throw the cash dollars on the floor. The cleaning lady piles them up with a dirty mop and scolds them for making such a pile of garbage. The inspiring message was that the time would come when America, that colossus on clay feet, would fall under the feet of a renewed and enlightened Russia. Instead of focusing on such objective factors as marketing, increasing the capacity of the domestic consumer market, effective management of industries and enterprises, Hermes was devoted to ideas with a distinctly messianic character. They went bankrupt. However, this mindset is characteristic of a large part of Russia's financial and political elite. It is easy to find such people on the board of Gazprom, Elbee Bank, and many other parastatal enterprises.

If you search the Moscow Registration database for information on all the firms registered in the name of one high-ranking official or another, and his relatives, the results will reveal a huge scheme to move money from account to account. Such data show clearly how ordinary civil servants become millionaire oligarchs and subjugate the rest.

How do they change the chairman of the board in large Russian companies? The government solves corporate and financial policy issues in the center of Moscow with the help of special-purpose squads. Early in the morning (taking Transneft as an good example), a company is declared strategically important to Russian security, 300 Special Purpose Police (OMON), armed with automatic weapons, occupy the company's central office and break down the doors of the CEO's office with tire irons. Naturally, the entrances and doors of the employees' offices were also broken into. Behind the special units proudly marched the Deputy Minister of Fuel and Energy Vladimir Stanev, who was there in order to appoint a new company manager. All this is, in fact, done in violation of the law and the charter of the organization, as well as in violation of Russian labor law, the Civil Code, the Law on Joint-Stock Companies, and the Constitution of the country. The new bosses openly state that since the Russian Prime Minister instructed them to build an oil pipeline bypassing Chechnya, anything goes. At part of this maneuver, Dmitry Savelyev, the former president of Transneft, was deprived of his temporary Moscow residence permit without any explanation, saying that they had special instructions for this.

In addition to mining and storming offices, company directors and bureaucrats personally delete unwanted shareholders from the register, shareholder registers are stolen, union leaders are brutally beaten and killed on the streets. Attempts to declare factories bankrupt often lack any serious justification. There is no evidence that the plant has debts to budgets of various levels. They shake out mythical debts as if the plant got its money from a gangster cash register, not from state sources. These bankruptcy attempts are not so much economically motivated as politically motivated.

Attempts to create super-monopolies are also politically motivated. Fuel and Energy Minister Viktor Kalyuzhny announced a plan according merge the Gas Ministry, the Electricity Ministry, the Coal Ministry, and the Oil Ministry into one and form a super-ministry to take over all those ministries. There will be no Gazprom, no joint-stock company UES of Russia. The Bolsheviks would have envied such ideas. Mr. Minister is either unaware or feigns ignorance of the economic reforms that have been going on in Russia for a decade. He needs to be reminded that Gazprom and UES, just like oil companies, are not ministries at all, but joint stock companies with a mixed ownership. To carry out such a consolidation plan would mean not only redistributing property but making a revolution comparable in scale to the great socialist revolution. Implementing such an idea would create a huge shock to the country's gas supply, and if Kamchatka and the Far East are routinely immersed in the dark and cold already, those conditions would spread to the whole country. The Minister of Fuel and Energy does not care, yet. But then the current financial and economic crisis could turn into a fuel and energy crisis. This is not the first initiative of this kind proposed by the Minister. In order to make repairs at the Ministry of Fuel and Energy, he tried to solve the issue the way post-Soviet managers are used to: he ordered all major oil companies to chip in $1 million.

Financially, the Russian stock market has stagnated, there is a shortage of available domestic resources, distrust of private Russian investors, and lack of information transparency. Therefore, while Russia has a high scientific and technical potential and a huge number of innovative developments, it is almost impossible to implement them.

The small business sector is in a critical situation. Business owners found themselves in tough conditions when state regulation of the economy and the tax burden increased. The state has no funds to support and develop small business and entrepreneurship. At the same time the main problems remain: inadequate legislation, little financial support for small business development programs, increasing bureaucracy, extremely high taxes. Thus, even if the same number of small businesses are operating, their turnover has gone down.

How can you honestly conduct business in Russia, if by law you have to give the government more than you earned? Why do you have to steal in order to live honestly? The unbearable tax burden forces entrepreneurs to go underground, hiding almost all of their income. So, entrepreneurs do not pay taxes either. This creates a very conducive environment for rackets that do take away that part of the businessman's money that would have been paid as taxes. In other words, businesses still have to pay taxes, or rather a tribute to criminal gangs. The mafia uses this money to buy guns and bribe officials, but the government does not receive anything. Therefore, it has no choice but to create its own repressive structures, which function very much like gangsters. The government is squeezing money out of entrepreneurs while offering absolutely nothing in return. Under such conditions, the development and even the existence of a small business is simply impossible. The "real" small business in Russia is the "enterprises" run by relatives of mayors or governors, the police elite, generals. All these people receive "preferential" illegal loans from their relatives' banks, bypassing regulations intended to protect the interests of the banks themselves. And these people do not produce or trade anything, they just take money out of the state budget and deposit it into banks at interest. They disrupt the commodity–credit chains. They prevent the state from fulfilling its obligations to the citizens. They take unwanted competitors out of their way with the help of the police, the tax police and the FSB, which are increasingly becoming a means to destroy free competition. The bureaucrats, by imposing so much tax and customs duties that any business activity becomes meaningless, keep everyone on their toes. The most energetic part of the population — entrepreneurs, from the small merchant to the director of a large company — is made into part of a semi-criminal community. At the same time, the officials "legally" get their share by handing out various privileges — tax breaks, reduced customs duties, reduced tariffs, quotas, non-refundable loans, etc. The criminal and police extortions are constant.

The "taxes" set by the Russian government can ruin any production facility. Here, as an example, are some figures from an average business that has a profitability of 25% and has paid all its taxes (calculations by Alexander Panikin, an entrepreneur):

COSTS:

Cost of fixed assets: 25 million rubles
Employees: 500 (average monthly salary of 2,100 rubles)
Product sales: 5.75 million rubles/month
Production costs — raw materials: 2.8 million rubles
Overhead costs: 750,000 rubles
Payroll: 1.05 million rubles.

TOTAL:

Expenses: 4.6 million rubles
Profit: 5.75 – 4.6 = 1.15 million rubles
Profitability: 25%

REQUIRED PAYMENTS:

Turnover tax on maintenance of housing and roads (4%): 230,000 rubles.
VAT (value added tax): (958,000 rubles – 467,000 rubles) = 491,000 rubles (20% of sales minus 20% paid for raw materials)
Payroll accruals: 415,000 rubles. (39.5% of the salary fund)
Property tax: 42,000 rubles/month (2% per year)

NET PROFIT

1.15 million rubles – (230,000 rubles – 491,000 rubles – 415,000 rubles – 42,000 rubles) = ¯28,000 rubles

In addition, there are licensing costs, advertising, equipment purchases, etc. While the pre-tax profit of this highly profitable enterprise was 35%, there is nothing due as a "net profit tax" because the company is actually operating at a loss. These simple figures speak more about the government's attitude to production than all the government's statements about supporting the economy.

Almost none of the funds allocated for expansion and modernization (from buying a machine tool to a calculator) are tax deductible, but rather the contrary — by law, the necessary equipment can only be purchased after all taxes are paid. The cost of an imported technology line and raw materials, badly needed by the industry, goes up by almost 50% once all customs duties and VAT are paid. The interest rates on loans always exceed the production profitability. As a result, companies can neither borrow nor invest their own money in the development of production. The further attempt to introduce a 5% sales tax to all retail prices is just another form of theft. And any increase in sales price means fewer people can buy the product, anyway.

For many entrepreneurs, their business is almost the only thing that gives their life meaning. They see any serious upheaval, political or economic, as a threat not only to the integrity of the company and the possibility of significant financial losses, but also as a threat to the heart of their life. Thus this type of policy toward small business causes depression and despair, damaging corporate culture and adding stress to every organization. At the same time, any entrepreneurs who dare to raise their voices against the violations are charged with crimes. Businessmen in Chuvashia, one of Russia's federal republics, have tried to propose a law imposing some responsibility on officials by providing punishment for callousness. However, it is not quite clear where the borderline lies between callousness and stupidity. The relationship between business and the government in Russia shows that firms are interested in maximizing profits at any cost and exporting them abroad, so that their interests are sharply at odds with those of the state, which seeks by any and all means to rob entrepreneurs and take their money for its ideological experiments. Small business cannot withstand the constantly increasing tax pressure and legal impunity of the bureaucrats. And most entrepreneurs are in no position to fight for their rights.

Private traders selling at street markets complain that they are inspected every day by several different commissions, and often have to pay fines to who knows who and who knows what for. All the efforts of the authorities to restore order have had no result. It has come to the point that a Book of Inspections is being introduced at the Kazan market, which will be available at each outlet and with each manager of the enterprise. It is an official document for registering all inspections, i.e., it is an inspection of the inspections.

Driving a long-haul truck in Russia is almost as dangerous as fighting in the Caucasus. At truck stops within a kilometer of the Moscow Ring Road, bandits are constantly raiding drivers: turn over your goods for half the price, or you won't get to Moscow at all. They can confiscate the entire cargo, and the vehicle, and even kill the driver if he is uncooperative.

The vodka business is particularly criminalized and it is impossible to participate in it honestly. The heads of the vodka distilleries, almost all of whom could be prosecuted for one thing or another, are usually officials, deputies or appointees of the local government. Kursk Prime Minister Boris Khokhlov is known in business circles as the sole owner of a distillery in the town of Lgov in the Kursk region and several medium-sized enterprises, including one in Novgorod.

Just the way differing taxes and age-limits are used to distort the market for gas or cigarettes in neighboring states in the US, Russian producers of the equivalent products face unequal economic conditions simply due to their being located in different places. For example, chocolate produced at the Ulyanovsk factory "Volzhanka" is still considered a commodity in daily demand and is not subject to sales tax. However chocolate produced in neighboring Samara is considered a delicacy and is taxed. This creates unfair competition, encouraged by the local authorities.

Venture capital investment in Russia faces many legislative, bureaucratic and legal obstacles. Potential venture capital investors are suspicious of this form of financing, but also, oddly enough, businesses in which risky funds might be invested have worries about it, too.

Russia has already tried creating free economic zones, but this has actually failed. Today they prefer not to talk about it. Auditors from the Accounts Chamber of Russia, checking how federal funds were allocated for the development of just one free economic zone, "Nakhodka," found major financial violations. More than 90 million rubles of state money were misspent. In addition, in violation of the law, 11.5 million rubles were deposited (not without government help), in accounts in local commercial banks.

The Tax Inspectorate wants to introduce a new license for banks to make tax payments to customers. That system could be worse than the recent crisis. Super-authorized banks will appear in the market, and their competitors will start to lose clients and go bankrupt. A new banking licensing system would become a headache not only for bankers but also for regional authorities. It could cause the complete destruction of the banking system in the regions. It is no secret that only two or three solvent banks are left in many places, and they have fewer and fewer clients. Local authorities are besieging tax inspections with requests to help transfer the accounts of big companies to the regional departments of the Central Bank, explaining that otherwise they will not be able to guarantee timely transfer of taxes. Where budget flows are transferred, that bank is the winner and dictates the terms to the others. Thus, the authorities have the power to punish and pardon, to create and destroy, and to overthrow banks, not as a result of the financial crisis but as a result of a little signature on a piece of paper. Such is the power of the virtual economy. An entrepreneur's success depends not only on media coverage and financial adroitness, but his or her ability to influence various government officials.

Honest entrepreneurs, focused on investing their money in the country's economy, know it's a losing proposition. A handful of people are enriching themselves by cheating the state at a time when the population is impoverished. There is no support for the national producer. The nation's cultural values and intellectual achievements are being forgotten. The amount of money flowing out of the country is greater even than the amount Russia seeks to obtain in loans from the West.

Meanwhile, the families of those who are engaged in business (or politics) in Russia usually live in other countries, from Poland to Costa Rica, because it is not possible to guarantee them at least some immunity. The police and the KGB, which are supposed to protect citizens, are themselves involved in political intrigues, and it is they who take punitive actions against undesirables in Russia. This includes psychological pressure, constant threats and provocations, rape and murder, and exhausting prosecutions based on far-fetched motives. Even the largest Russian bankers are ready to ask for political asylum in other countries. For example, Alexander Smolensky, the head of SBS-Agro Bank, said in an interview with the Austrian magazine *Profile* that he could be arrested on charges of money laundering and embezzling a large amount of currency. His family has been living in Austria for 10 years, and Smolensky himself expressed confidence that Vienna would not refuse to grant him political asylum. Orders for the arrest of prominent entrepreneurs and politicians are most often issued when they are outside of Russia and are unable to take full measures to protect themselves.

Russia's is the only economy in the world where domestic economic growth has failed to reverse capital outflow and to attract capital to return, according to the IMF. As John Helmer notes, "Privatization in Russia has also been unique because it has accelerated the rate of outflow of domestic funds, enlarging the gap between domestic outflow and foreign inflow. Predictably, this has led to the accumulation of a bigger Russian capital economy offshore than the domestic capital economy (except for housing); and a level of inequality of incomes which is today [in 2022, never mind what it was in 2000!] worse for Russians than it was during the last decade of tsarist rule ending in the world war and the revolution of 1917... [M]ore than one trillion dollars, [t]hat's the sum of Russian capital outflow which started in 1992 and accelerated since 2000."[1]

All the authorities' assurances about Russia's great future fall on deaf ears among real businessmen. They know the economic realities all too well from the inside. Money is flooding out of Russia. People who are still able

[1] "The Russian Revolution of 2022 – Capitalism In One Country," Dances with Bears, by John Helmer, April 10, 2022, at http://johnhelmer.net/2022/04/10/

to soberly assess the reality are quick to withdraw their money and take it anywhere else they can, as long as it is out of reach of the stupid bureaucrats. Realizing that they can't brainwash such people, the authorities can only issue prohibitions and restrictions, and use of repressive measures. In fact, a state racket is flourishing in Russia. They are not even seriously considering any possibility of economic reconciliation with real business, an amnesty on capital flight, or changes in the economic conditions. And what kind of normal economic policy can we talk about, if all the new laws are effective retroactively. For example, if you registered a company two years ago, and then a decree on new taxes was issued. For example, you registered an enterprise two years ago, and then a decree on new taxes and new payments was issued. You haven't heard of them before, but you'll still pay for them. For both prior years. Or another example. Everything that is imported from abroad has just been hit with a new, high tax. This means that a ship coming in from the sea must pay not only for the cars that the crew members bought in other countries, but also for fish caught in neutral waters, and for the remaining fuel on board, even if it is left over after refueling in the home port. Otherwise, it will not be allowed to unload.

Well, the state really needs money for various social and ideological experiments. Perhaps you think that this money will be used to pay pensions, salaries, and benefits to young mothers? The evidence shows that you are wrong. In some places in Russia, families take turns going to lunch in the workplace canteen of one of the parents: the mother has breakfast, the son goes for lunch (he gets the best nutrition), and the father goes to dinner. At the same time, semi-secret government organizations engaged in all sorts of strategic research enjoy budgets in the millions of dollars. (No one measures anything by rubles in Russia. Except for the sake of appearances.)

14. Industry and Agriculture

The plight of Russia is obvious, and the causes of these troubles are numerous. At the beginning of perestroika, it was discovered that, with rare exceptions, the USSR had no theoretical specialists in modern macroeconomics, capital and labor markets, international finance, or the theory of industrial organizations. There were no professionals who had the proper knowledge base to work fully in the World Bank or the International Monetary Fund. Russian leaders of previous eras didn't know how to build socialism any more than the current leaders knew about how to build Russian capitalism. It's meaningless to repeat the standard phrase that "the process will take some time, but by working together we will be able eliminate the current difficulties in the near future." There are huge difficulties, and no one knows how to solve them. The main reason why the economy is weak is that the government has not been looking for economics specialists. How could they go on stealing if someone is going to start keeping tabs?

Forcing this sudden transition was a desperate, adventurous decision, and it seems that few politicians in Russia calculated the political and economic consequences. In Russia, economic and political crises are mythological and occur at absolutely fixed times of the year. The first comes in the spring, when the crops are being planted; the second in the fall, during the harvest; the third — on New Year's Eve as a Christmas present to everyone. According to former Minister of Finance Livshits, this Russian cycle is well known: hot in summer, cold in winter, reforms in spring, and crisis in fall. And so far, Russia has never been able to break the cycle. Russian history is cyclical, and the society is incapable of grasping its rhythm and learning the lessons of history. Politicians blame everyone but themselves (from "the people" to "the Yeltsin regime") for the failure of the perestroika-era hopes,. The reforms have failed, while their precursors — Gaidar, Aven, Koch and Nemtsov — loudly called their brainchild "criminal, thieving capitalism," criticizing the result and questioning the country's ability to reform. Such statements, coupled with the crisis of August 1999, indicate the beginning of the end of what has not even begun to happen — reform. All the activities of liberal reformers heretofore have been aimed only at destruction — the destruction of communism — rather than at positive changes that could be called reforms. Russian statistics disorient the public and government leadership in the crucial area that determines the future of the country — the dynamics of fixed assets. According to official statistics, the main production assets of the economy have remained unchanged throughout the 1990s, which is very surprising since production capital investments, according to the same statistics, decreased by about 4 times during this period.

According to Valentina Fedotova, head of the Center at the Institute of Philosophy of the Russian Academy of Sciences, "It is a sign that a certain stage of Russia's development is over, that the bipolar model of Russian society — of reformers and anti-reformers — which was forec-fed as the real explanation on Russian citizens and on Western experts alike, who largely accepted it, is not seen as convincing today either in Russia or in the West. If it was taboo to offer alternative explanations, especially in the U.S., that is no longer the case. That simplified scheme was the basis for understanding Russian changes at the governmental level. The general public is not really aware of the differences between capitalism and socialism, between authoritarianism and democracy. They simply want to live better, and as life gets worse, they find themselves in inarticulate opposition to the regime. But the people also keep quiet because they blame themselves for their naïve belief that "things cannot get any worse," for their political inexperience, for their historically rooted anti-government sentiment and readiness to smash the old system, for their uncritical acceptance of demagoguery.

What is most disturbing is the excessive cynicism of the political elite. Everyone understands everything, but no one bothers to explain to the people why the economy has collapsed and something close to martial law is in place, — without any declaration of war, without any explanation. If chaos can be called politics, that is what we have here. One can only hope, with Shakespeare: "There is a method in the madness." Russia's economy exists in conditions that look rather alarming. All actions in this direction are taken in occasional moments of intellectual weakness. It would be more accurate to say that in Russia there is no "economy" as it is usually understood in the civilized world. Many Russian economists think that the arms race and the pumping of money into the military--industrial complex will lead to an increase in effective demand, and then to a recovery of the economy as a whole. In addition, economic ties with the West will be undermined, and Russian citizens will have to buy domestic goods whether they like it or not. However, no one mentions that the price for this kind of economic growth will be the militarization of the country and, as a consequence, the destruction of democratic freedoms.

Military equipment plants in the Urals are already expecting multi-million dollar orders from the Ministry of Defense since the government has allocated an additional 2 billion rubles for the purchase of weapons (tanks, self-propelled guns, shells) for the continuing military operations in the North Caucasus. The design bureaus of the leading vehicle manufacturers KAMAZ, ZIL, and GAZ, have created new models especially for those combat operations. Gradually, people from the military-industrial complex are coming to occupy leading positions in the Ministry of Trade. Grigory Rapota, former head of Rosvooruzhenie, was appointed First Deputy Minister of Trade, where he will supervise Russia's military-technical cooperation with foreign countries. This is very important for stepping up the sale of weapons to future possible allies. Rapota will directly supervise the enterprises Rosvooruzhenie, Promexport, and Russian Technologies, which are state arms trade intermediaries. Naturally, when people from the military-industrial complex join the Ministry of Trade, the stature of this agency will be significantly strengthened.

Russian factories producing nonmilitary products are now in such poor shape that, despite all efforts, they cannot produce decent, competitive goods. Many industrial sites are still using machine tools that were inherited by the USSR after World War II. At the same time, the managers are still relying on state orders, not seeking to make truly competitive products. It is easier to just get a huge order, somehow, including from the Ministry of Defense, or for supplies to the isolated northern regions.

The Russian space industry is collapsing. The Baikonur spaceport has become a bargaining chip in relations between Kazakhstan and Russia. When the USSR was divided up, the famous spaceport ended up in a country where there is not a single enterprise devoted to rocket or space equipment. At the same time three-fourths of the entire space industry in Russia and Ukraine depends on Baikonur, with launch pads designed for rockets assembled in Moscow and Krasnoyarsk, Dnepropetrovsk and Korolev. Kazakhstan claims its rights to the Baikonur Cosmodrome. At one time it was a loss-maker, but now that commercial launches are taking place from it, the cosmodrome is generating a considerable income in hard currency. The Proton incident served as a convenient pretext for the Kazakh government to effectively veto all Russian space launches. Russia, in fact, does not currently have a second cosmodrome at Plesetsk, since all the launchers there have recently been dismantled.[1] The rocket launcher in Yakutia near Tiksi, with its launch pad and associated equipment, is also having a hard time. The Russian space program is experiencing almost insurmountable difficulties.

At the same time, machinations are going on around the Mir orbital station, which is expected to cease operations in the near future. It seems there is no way to get $60 million to continue the Mir space research program.

However, Russian and foreign experts unanimously agree that interrupting the Mir mission is nonsense and Russian officials were merely negligent regarding the critically important space industry, where Russia is the leader. The station could continue to function and it would recoup expenses many times over and then generate profits. Some people are very eager to sink the space station and with it the story of the embezzlement of $30 million. In connection with that, the names of former deputy prime ministers Boris Nemtsov and Yuri Maslyukov, the first deputy chairman of the State Committee on Telecommunications Naum Marder, and the general director of VimpelCom Dmitry Zimin are often mentioned.

While the space showdown is going on, Russian and sometimes foreign cosmonauts are continue to be held "hostage" on this very "Mir" station (Mir means both "Peace" and "World"). The station is not generally provided with a large inventory of extra goods, except for emergency supplies, but the Progress transport ship with vitally needed supplies cannot set off until the politicians decide on whether to continue launching rockets.

A demonstration and public activities were organized in Nizhny Novgorod by Russian scientists, cosmonauts, writers and journalists in favor of saving the Mir orbital station. There was a motor rally, caricatures of Russian political figures and Bill Clinton were exhibited, there was a poetry reading, and patriotic publications were sold.

The economy is totally subordinated to the oil and gas sector. Russia's rich mineral reserves, not only the harsh political system, have helped create a complex of permanently entrenched officials. Why bother to set up a smoothly operating economy when all you need to do is to ensure government control over oil exports and feel like a king, in a favorable price environment? Oil exports are used as evidence that the modern Russian economy is operating in accordance with the concept of the "market." The more liberal the export rules are, the more "market" there is in the economy. The rest is not affected. However, oil has not brought wealth to Russia. Only those offi-

---

[1] Plesetsk became active again since the 2000s.

cials who are responsible for transporting oil abroad have gotten very rich. The short-term mindset has its negative side for those thieves in government positions. All 22,000 kilometers of oil pipelines in Russia are already due for replacement, and if they keep on ignoring this problem, those officials may soon be bereft of their illicit income.

Redirecting gas supply plants to the export market has made it even more difficult to provide liquefied gas for the populace of all the northern regions of the European part of Russia. About 14 million Russian apartments are heated by gas, which means that the gas crisis will directly affect about a third of the country's citizens. One way or another, a serious energy crisis has hit Russia, and the gas shortage is just one aspect. The federal policy is damaging because no clear strategy has been chosen. The rules of the game are constantly changing, as the power that establishes the changes. The situation with fuel oil is equally catastrophic. Only half the fuel oil needed for furnaces is pumped. The reason is dead simple: if you bring Russian fuel oil to the border, you can easily sell it for $53.4, that is, about 1,300 rubles per ton. But the cartel agreement signed by the largest enterprises and monopolies calls for the price not to exceed 780 rubles per ton. No one is fool enough to sell his products twice as cheap, especially since it is difficult to get real money inside the country. Obviously, power outages have begun in different regions throughout the country.

Because of the lack of fuel, the energy sector cannot meet even the country's minimum needs for heat and electricity. In every city, residential and administrative buildings suffer from a lack of hot water. In more than 10 regions the critical situation is constant, due to the lack of fuel for the winter period. Stocks of coal and heating oil are about half of what would be required. The temperature in apartments, but even in children's institutions, rarely gets above 3–4°C (about 38°F). Residents of these areas cannot heat their food or take a warm bath, since most people in Russia use gas stoves in the kitchen and gas heaters in the bathroom to heat water.

For example, in Chelyabinsk 5,764 houses were disconnected from the heating system. Tver only managed to provide hot water to residents by burning the reserve fuel. Tver has only 50% of the gas it needs, so clearly they cannot supply hot water to the whole city. The municipal hot water system supplies each district in turn, and the residents are already used to such shutdowns. Some boil water in pots, while others make do with cold water alone. Those who can often buy electrical water heaters and thus are vulnerable only to blackouts. In order to wash, a person can go to the old-fashioned public baths, though only one out of three of them works. The residents of the northern regions face the most desperate situation, as the winter frosts reach 40° below zero.

In many districts of the Kamchatka peninsula, electricity is cut off entirely. There is no light even in hospitals, kindergartens and schools. Kamchatka has suffered from fuel shortages for more than two years. Many communications links there have been out of order for a long time. On Shikotan Island, part of the Kuril Islands, they only have heat thanks to kerosene stoves donated by the neighboring Japanese. Not a single ton of coal has been delivered to the remote island, and the stock of diesel fuel for power plants is negligible. There is nothing to replenish it from. Lights are turned on for two hours in the morning and two hours in the evening.

In the northern city of Severodvinsk, Arkhangelsk region, widespread power outages are causing a catastrophe. This city is home to the State Russian Center for Nuclear Shipbuilding, which has already cut its electricity consumption to the emergency level. The city of Voronezh is also in dire straits, as the Voronezhteploset has practically cut off all heating during the cold season; this is of the world's four rocket engine development sites, the Voronezh Design Bureau "Khimavtomatika" (KBKhA). Engines for Soyuz, Proton and other rockets are developed there.

Regular power outages at the Kachkanar Mining and Processing Plant in the Sverdlovsk region led to violations of the technological process on the night of November 2 to 3, 1999, causing a dam to break. A huge area including two cities and many villages were inundated with 12 million cubic meters of water, bridges on the Vyya River were demolished, a gas pipeline and power and communication lines were destroyed, and 200 meters of roadway were washed away. Flooded areas were virtually cut off from the outside world. The sewage, which contains a huge amount of heavy metals, contaminated drinking wells and flooded the food cellars where the villagers were storing food. Environmentalists found an average of up to five dead fish per square meter of polluted land. No statistics are available about the human casualties, since these areas have few communication and transportation links to the rest of the world.

Domodedovo and Krasnoyarsk Airlines have run out of fuel in Primorye, on the Pacific coast. If their planes do not make intermediate landings to refuel, they will be stuck at Vladivostok airport. Air transportation on the Far Eastern lines will simply stop. But while the situation at Vladivostok airport in early August 1999 could be dealt with, the situation just to the north along the coast, in remote Magadan, Petropavlovsk-Kamchatsky and Yuzhno-Sakhalinsk, is much worse. Some flights on local lines have already been canceled. The main carrier in Russia, Aeroflot, has similar problems.

The quality of gasoline in Russia is troubling, especially to owners of foreign cars whose fuel systems are particularly sensitive to poor gasoline. At service stations, more and more cars are showing up with the same problem — their fuel pumps have failed. Everyone knows how pseudo-benzene makes it into the gas stations. For example, in the Moscow region, entrepreneurs buy gasoline fraction at the plant and use special additives to bring the octane level to the required number.

If you buy semi-synthetic oil for your car, for example, from British Petroleum, you may find that you need to overhaul the engine in a month's time. "Branded" oil often turns out to be fake, despite the fact that it is sold in newly designed canisters which appeared on the Russian market only a few months ago. The State Trade Inspection ran an inspection of enterprises selling automobile products, and 40 of the 42 inspected organizations were violating trade rules.

In Russian industry, counterfeit gasoline and automotive oil are not all there is to worry about. The reason why the Ukrainian Zenit launch vehicle failed to launch twelve American satellites into orbit in August 1998 is that the counterfeit chemical power sources (produced in the city of Saratov) that were powering the communications equipment failed. Zenit ceased to obey commands from the ground, and all the expensive cargo on board was lost. It turned out that chemical sources were assembled from substandard components that did not pass factory quality control.

We cannot talk about industry in Russia without also describing the conditions under which such industry exists. For five years, the governor of the Krasnoyarsk Territory, General Alexander Lebed, and the Alfa group close to him — on the one hand, on the other — the aluminum barons Lev Chernoy, Vasily Anisimov and the Krasnoyarsk Aluminum Plant with the support of criminal militants, have been fighting over the Achinsk Alumina Combine, the largest raw material base of the Russian aluminum industry, with varying success. Every day front-line reports arrive from Achinsk: the plant management is alternately stormed by representatives of one or another clan. In turn, there are reports of mines being placed in planes, trains, offices and even lavatories. The Krasnoyarsk plant attracted State Duma deputies from the Liberal Democratic Party of Russia (LDPR) to its side, and Lebed gained the support of special purpose militia forces (assault detachments). According to unverified data, the Achinsk plant was stormed several times by the pride of the Russian army, the airborne troops. Today, the power advantage is on the side of Cygnus and Alpha, and the Krasnoyarsk Aluminum Plant may become the next enterprise brought to its knees. Trains break through the resistance to deliver raw materials as if it were wartime. Every time a train comes in, the police receive a message that it may be mined. Criminal cases have been opened against almost all the managers. Police rapid response units and special forces units are preparing for battle. Exercises are being held at the plant, training personnel how to act in the event armed men seize control. On top of that, an information war is being waged. To underscore its determination, the Krasnoyarsk Plant commissions news articles that it signs with the name of Kalashnikov, while articles by the Lebed support group are signed with the name of Stechkin. Both are the names of world-famous Russian automatic weapons.

Russia occupies a very unfavorable climate zone. The north of Eurasia is the coldest, a vast territory without a developed infrastructure. And although it has huge natural resources, it is terribly difficult to access them. Agriculture in Russia also faces harsh conditions. But the Russians have no other land and never will. Resolving this issue should become a national fixation for Russia. In the meantime, Russia is slowly returning to its primitive state. In many villages, the telephone system is shut down, then the electricity. Light bulbs and televisions go out, freezers defrost, candles are lit in the huts, and the water supply to households is stopped. Often the only connection with the outside world is the dirt road along the river, and the lack of proper roads means traffic is completely paralyzed after a rain. The villages are in this plight because of the protracted negotiations between power engineers and local authorities.

Meanwhile, residents are learning to do without electricity. In the fields where small farmers grow crops for the local farmers' markets, instead of tractors today you may see plows, and plows of a wide variety of designs and modifications. Increasingly, people are being used like draft horses. And not the small farmers themselves, but hired workers. These so-called "barge haulers" have already begun to organize themselves into various kinds of labor communities with a clear division of labor: there is a boss — the owner of the plow, there are "horses," local workers; and, finally, a "manager" who offers the services of such "cooperatives." Prices are moderate: 20–25 rubles per hundred square meters.

Due to weather conditions, Russia regularly faces serious problems with food supplies, and Russia also regularly turns to Western countries for food aid. The country imports not only wheat but corn, soybeans, rice, beef, pork, poultry, milk, vegetables, fruits, and sugar. Both the US and the EU provide humanitarian aid and long-term loans on concessional terms for up to 20 years. Russia's basic food aid is always in short supply. Employees of the Russian Ministry of Agriculture admit in private that they hope mainly for a humanitarian (that is, free) share, which they feel should be about half of the total package of food aid. At the same time, Russian officials are also constantly saying that Russia will not need grain next year. But the yield in the Urals and Western Siberia has fallen sharply in recent years due to delays in harvesting. And it continues to fall from year to year. The cost of flour is about 70–75 percent of the price of bread. It can't go on like this for long. Bakeries eat up the profits accumulated over the previous months. When it's gone, the prices jump again. The government is doing nothing about it, not even getting the surplus grain that grows in the south of Russia, in the Lower and Central Volga region, to the other parts of the country. Thus the situation on the bread market is quite tough. Producers request permission to raise prices on flour and bread every summer, but officials hold out until the new harvest. The main question is who will dare to put his signature on the resolution to raise bread prices. No one wants to take responsibility for this decision. Each increase in the price of bread is discussed long and painfully. But at the same time, producers make no effort to produce cheap varieties of bread.

In previous years, the government decree on advance payments to agricultural producers before the sowing campaign usually appeared in February–March. If the document was not ready by early April, it was considered an unforgivable delay, since in some regions the sowing campaign was already in full swing. By July, all reserves, including humanitarian supplies, are usually eaten up. Some regions periodically switch to limited consumption of bread and cereals. They are forced to seek and ask for grain for food from outside their borders. Cattle that are half-dead already from lack of fodder are finally slaughtered. Other regions restrict grain exports to other regions because sending seeds, flour, and grain to the regions most affected by the drought threatens the food security of their own region. Then, regional and provincial governments issue decrees, police checkpoints are set up on the highways in the border areas, and railway cars are no longer sent for loading grain. Bread trucks "break through" the police cordons with the help of bribes. Existing contracts between suppliers and production enterprise in the neighboring regions may be broken. Because of the regional bans on the export of bread, many customers are not able to bring their grain to the mill. Flour is sent at fixed prices mainly to enterprises in large cities.

But these restrictions apply to far more than flour. The Astrakhan regional government adopted a resolution prohibiting the export of live, chilled or frozen fish products outside their region. It is also prohibited to export fish from the Murmansk region. And you are not allowed to export fruits from the south, vegetables from the middle belt, and other foodstuffs everywhere.

Every year, agricultural experts begin their forecasts by arguing that the future harvest will be adequate to meet domestic needs. And this despite the lack of seeds and fuel, and the reduction of cultivated and irrigated areas. And almost every year the weather brings surprises, forcing the same experts to make significant adjustments to their initial projections. A sowing season that started splendidly fails spectacularly. And large food reserves that do get stored after good harvests simply rot in many storage facilities that are ill-suited for long-term storage. Russia starts almost every new agricultural season with almost zero inventory stored up. Each new harvest is extremely important. But a cold autumn and then a hot, dry summer nullify attempts to set by strategic reserves.

Each crop failure leads to a lack of fodder, and that threatens to significantly reduce the herds of livestock. There is no Russian meat for sale. At the beginning of 1990, there were 67 million head of cattle in the country. At the beginning of 1999, there were 29.6 million. In 1990 there were 38 million pigs, in 1999 there were just over 16 million. Out of 68 million sheep, 16 million remained.

The government only characterizes the situation as "extremely tense," but no one does anything concrete to ensure that the planting season does not fail. In many regions, it is postponed due to floods, adverse weather conditions, lack of seeds, fuel and lubricants, and the almost-consumed carry-over grain inventory. Under constant heat, the grass burns out at the root; there are difficulties with the preparation of fodder. Conditions are even worse with grain crops — the plants begin to ear before they've had time to gain the normal stem height. So, the height of barley ears is usually no more than 10–15 cm. Oats and wheat also begin to ear. It is impossible to harvest them with combines. It is good if you manage to collect at least 30% of the planned vegetable harvest. The farms water the crops intensively, but it is barely enough. The water immediately evaporates without wetting the ground. At the same time, the cultivated areas are overgrown with far from harmless plants. In the collective farm named "Communism," in the Dzhidinsky district of Buryatia, thickets of wild-growing hemp already occupy 2,500 hectares of land. Every year, these unguarded plantations are visited by drug couriers from various Russian cities.

The central authorities are simply shaking products out of the regions. The leadership of the Russian republic of Mordovia was supposed to supply Moscow with 15,000 tons of potatoes. But the problem was that the collective farms had sown only 2,000 hectares of potatoes and the harvest would not have been enough for delivery. Therefore, it was decided to keep the promises made to Moscow at the expense of private farmers, who had allocated more than 45,000 hectares for potatoes. It was decided to take the potatoes by *prodrazverstka*, requisitioning. Exactly the same method used by the Communists in the 1920s. Today in Mordovia each village, each farmstead is obliged to give procurement offices 200 to 450 kilograms of strategic goods, depending on the region. That much was not taken even in the hard war years of 1941–1945. With the sanction of the Mordovian authorities, chairmen of collective farms drive cars along country roads all day long, intimidating independent potatoes buyers with threats that are not provided for in the Russian Constitution. They threaten to confiscate both the potatoes and the trucks, and call the buyers themselves criminals. There have already been cases where drivers' licenses have been taken away over the mere fact that potatoes were found in the back of the truck. But that's not all. Potatoes without a certificate showing that they were grown on a private farm must not be exported at all. And almost no one gives such certificates. In addition, the local authorities buy the potatoes at a ridiculously low price. When villagers try not to sell their crops, officials respond by blocking the roads leading to neighboring regions. In response, the peasants display the Constitution of the Russian Federation, where Article 37, which states that labor is free in Russia, is blacked out. People are forced to remember the ways potatoes were squirreled away during the days of wartime communism. Huge pits are dug right in the potato fields, and the farmers pile the potatoes into them, hoping to dig them out by winter, when the roadblocks are removed. Meanwhile, child allowances and salaries are not being paid in Mordovia, any more than they are in the rest of Russia.

Each new initiative aimed at supporting agriculture actually introduces another extortion from customers and visibly guts Russians' wallets. Using the well-known managerial formula "if you can't solve a problem, create a structure to deal with it," officials have created countless funds to support the countryside. The programs are, as a rule, funded by deductions from the wholesale and retail trade. They do not say exactly what kind of wholesale and retail trade, but they are confident that the population will understand and approve of the measures. But there are doubts about the popularity of such innovation. The problem is not only that no one wants to overpay for potatoes and cereals. According to the same officials, all the funds created for this purpose do more harm than good. The reputation of these special funds for the agro-industrial complex has always been scandalous. The banks servicing the fund constantly accuse each other and the Ministry's management of theft. The Agrarian Party, designed to defend the interests of peasants and farmers, is composed mainly of officials from agricultural departments. The party's webpage on the Internet is a source of great excitement.

The page must have been created for the sake of fashion or entertainment. The site claims that it "defends the interests of the Russian peasantry, rural intelligentsia, and agricultural scientists," contains a dormant "Agrarian Chat" and a giant story by Alexander Laukhin, "On the Merry Adventures of the Tula-Ryazan Agrarian, Told by Himself." It's hard to imagine a peasant leaning over his laptop after a long day's work, waiting for his party's website to be updated or discussing the problems of carrot yields in a chat room. It is noteworthy that the vast majority of the intended audience for the site obviously have no computer, and many of them lack even a telephone.

Because of poverty, many Russian citizens are forced to make do with goods whose prices are not affected by demand. Such products include bread, cereals, and milk. Every time there is a sharp price increase for flour, bread and gasoline, there is panic and people rush to buy food in unprecedented quantities. After that, the buyers disappear from the markets, and everyone waits to see what will happen next. There's no more buying and selling. This phenomenon was only seen in the midst of the civil war and the immediate aftermath — years of devastation, and in the early '30s during the first years of collectivization.

Collectivization was imposed on the country from above, by the Communist Party, and was carried out at gunpoint. Those who disagreed with this policy were exiled to Siberia or exterminated on the spot. And now, by an arbitrary decision, the market economy is "introduced" in the country, collective farms are radically transformed, and the peasant is forced to take land (in the form of a land share), which he does not want to take. People of the next generation are no longer willing or able to work the land on their own. And they don't have tools either, because you can't cut a tractor into pieces, and there are not enough to give one to everyone.

Now there are initiatives again to send volunteers to the countryside to improve agriculture. Those who draft such initiatives say that the economic revival will have to begin with an agricultural revival. Development of this sector will give an impetus to the development of industry: light industry, the chemical industry, machine building; and the extractive industry and the energy sector will become more active. In the thirties, the Soviet power was already sending 25,000 industrial workers to work in agriculture. In socialist times, all the students and workers in the middle and southern strip of Russia were obliged to take part in harvesting, almost for free, as well as in public works. People with higher engineering, pedagogical, medical and other education spent time doing manual labor to "revive" the country's "highly efficient" agriculture and sweep the streets. Those who have already thoroughly forgotten about the traditional autumn trips "to the potatoes" will soon be able to refresh their memories. Some governors, such as Ivan Sklyarov from Nizhny Novgorod, speak at operational meetings about the need to get students and intellectuals involved in agricultural work. It is assumed that this will start out as a voluntary effort. There are constant instructions from the government to ensure timely harvesting with the participation of military personnel from the Ministries of Defense and Internal Affairs. A decree to this effect was also signed by Prime Minister Vladimir Putin as Autumn 1999 was approaching. As a result, everyone was in the fields again: students, engineers, military personnel, and academics, and the country was still hungry, even though its equipment was "unparalleled in the world".

The Russian "Don-2600" harvester won an unusual battle that lasted a full day. It was competing with its American analogue, the Case IH 2366. To the joy of the Rostselmash plant designers, their product outstripped the Case IH by about 10% by every criterion. In 1996 the same harvester beat the Canadian "Western-8570" and then the German "Klaas." And only one small detail overshadows this momentous victory — the American, Canadian and German harvesters came off the assembly line; they are serial models in production, while the "Don-2600" was assembled in Rostov-on-Don five years ago and is still just a prototype. For all these years the machine has only taken part in competitions — and always successfully. In the meantime, crops are being lost and the government is spending a lot of money to buy huge amounts of grain in the U.S. and Canada.

There is a lot of talk about tainted or poisonous food being imported from abroad, but Russian products may turn out to be no less dangerous. Dioxin is found in many domestic chicken feeds. It gets there along with the used vegetable oil. When checking egg producing enterprises in the Perm region, it turned out that 96.6% of them should not be eaten. In this case, not because of dioxin. Eggs are rejected for being beneath market quality and due to the presence of blood inclusions. Among the reasons are the low level of technological discipline and control, careless sorting, marking and poor-quality paint in the inspection stamps. The health service assures us that the meat sold in markets and shops is examined twice, but everyone knows that certificates for meat are easy to buy. More than half of the certificates are fake. Everything in the country is counterfeited. That includes quality certificates, compliance certificates and other papers with stamps, which consumers are supposed to accept as credible. A "mask" of chocolate may cover a bar of something sweet, wrapped in branded packaging, but it does not smell like chocolate. Groups of counterfeiters all over the country buy stale bars in bulk, tinker with them and dress them up again in packaging with a fresh manufacturing date on it, and then sell them for the price of real chocolate. In addition, counterfeiters add flour to cocoa powder, margarine to butter, and even salt has been added to bags of sugar to increase the weight. Approximately half of the goods sold on the Russian market, including foodstuffs, are counterfeit.

Out in the provinces, 90% of the mineral water sold does not meet any food standards, and not a single bottle of mineral water is stored in proper conditions. During inspections of the mineral water storage conditions, the State Health and Epidemiological Supervision concluded that most of the samples are not up to standard. This mineral product not only cannot improve one's health, it can even cause harm due to the way it has been stored.

Russian resellers almost always rely on loans for working capital, and when they are setting their price for a product, they are forced to take into account the cost of the money they use. But that's not all. The pricing process in Russia depends not only on suppliers, on the location of the store, on the cost of the rent, but also on demands from officials from the tax, health and fire departments. Sometimes the wholesale prices for certain products may go down from month to month, but in the stores they move indomitably upwards. The greed of officials whose permits are needed can inflate the prices of any products. As a result, it's not uncommon for supermarkets to sell rotten products at huge prices. Bureaucratic "cheating" on the price increases the cost of products by 100% and more. The average Russian has to spend 80–85% of their income on food.

After that, Russia accuses Western countries of creating a situation where all kinds of strategic resources – natural, material, and especially intellectual, labor – are intensively pumped abroad. Immigrants from the former Soviet Union have significantly enriched the intellectual potential of Israel. They have doubled the number of engineers and scientists there – they are now twice as many per 1,000 inhabitants as in the USA, and three times as many as in Germany. In addition, there are many talented entrepreneurs among the visitors from the former USSR. According to rough estimates of the Center for Strategic and Global Studies, in 1990-1997, the total outflow of resources from the country amounted to about seven trillion dollars, i.e. about a trillion dollars a year. Russia is rapidly losing its position in the world. Because of their own stupidity, the genocide of their own people, the actual contempt of all international and simply human norms.

15. Education and Culture

The average salary of a teacher in Russia today is 80% of the official subsistence level and only 50% of the average salary in industry. But even that amount is not actually paid. For the third time, teachers at several schools are beginning a mass hunger strike because the promised paychecks are months away, and there won't be enough for all of them by a long shot. Only by going on hunger strike can teachers get government officials to pay the money, so they are forced to resort to it again and again. But the authorities are just getting used to this, and a s they become even more insensitive they delay the payments longer and longer every time. Despite the victorious news reports that the arrears on teachers' salaries is being paid down, the facts show the opposite. In 1999, teacher salary arrears were decreased in 23 territories of the country but they increased in 45 territories. Major financial irregularities can be found in almost every public education department, at every level. Plus, at a time when teachers' salaries are being held back on the excuse of a lack of funds, officials grant themselves enormous bonuses and tourist trips, and pay for their children's education abroad. Large sums of money from the budget are handed over to commercial firms that do not exist legally. Teachers are flooding the courts with lawsuits against school principals as their employers. Now, even if the court intends to satisfy the claims, it can only do so at the expense of school property, for example, by selling upholstered furniture from the teachers' lounge. Bailiffs visit schools in search of property that can be confiscated and sold at auction. Bailiffs are not interested in desks, blackboards and pointers, because they do not bring significant money. But the sofa and chairs from the teachers' lounge or the principal's office can pay off about half the school's debt to the teachers.

In addition, the authorities don't keep their promises to provide teachers with textbooks and teaching aids. Classes in the Russian North are starting weeks later than usual because the district utilities are postponing the start of the heating season — mainly due to a lack of fuel and the lack of salaries for utility workers. In addition to all this, Russian teachers are starting to face unemployment, as there has been a sharp drop in the birth rate. Teachers simply have no one to teach. The number of first-graders is steadily declining. The fertility boom of the latter half of the 1980s is gradually fading. If this trend continues, it is predicted that in seven years' time the number of places at some universities will exceed the number of school graduates. Everyone who wants to go to university can be admitted for free, and there will still be vacant places.

The plight of teachers pushes them toward crime. A secondary education certificate is worth only 3,000 rubles on the black market and a higher education diploma, from 5,000 to 10,000 rubles. Fake diplomas and certificates can be bought and sold across the country. In many cities, ads for the sale of diplomas are even posted at bus stops. Diplomas in any specialty and at various levels can be bought — from documents signed by real teachers at a real university to complete fake documents. The buyers decide what grades should be noted in the document, and they can even choose the "graduation" year. Specialties in the humanities are in the greatest demand. Buyers are less interested in technical or medical diplomas, because somebody might get suspicious when confirming their qualifications.

With the introduction of paid education in Russia, bribery among university teachers has become widespread. On average professors charge 1000 rubles for illegal admission to take exams between classes. In Russia bribes are paid collectively in groups of 60 people, especially when studying by correspondence, where the majority of students are very serious people: company accountants, tax inspectors, teachers. Often they are already getting a second higher education. The money is collected and handed over to the teacher, who does not blink an eye and gives everyone a passing grade. The trade in academic degrees has become a highly profitable business, much in demand. In St. Petersburg, a person who has a high school diploma can be confident of getting a PhD or other doctoral degree for about $10,000. All he has to do is complete some formalities and show up to "defend" his thesis, where he will read a prepared text and answer questions that are known in advance. You can add the precious words "candidate [B.S.] in economic sciences" to your name, from the Economics Dept. of St. Petersburg State University, for $3,000 to $8,000. At St. Petersburg University of Economics and Finance it costs $5–10,000.

Here's some food for thought. Every year more and more of the employees in regional government hold academic degrees. Not so long ago, they were first-year students, and just a year later they are becoming PhDs in economics. Putting two and two together, one can imagine what kind of specialists are running the Russian state.

Bureaucrats especially like to study for budgetary money. Every year dozens of employees of various ministries and departments enroll in educational institutions. The well-known laws on state and municipal services, which gave officials numerous benefits and privileges, also gave them the right "to upgrade their qualifications" once every five years. How much does this privilege cost average taxpayers? A year at the St. Petersburg Academy of Public Administration, for example, costs from $800 to $1,400. The education of civil servants involves other expenses, as well. It's not only their studies that are covered, but also their travel and accommodation in hotels. During their absence from the workplace, they receive a considerable salary. So the final figures spent on training for the office workers must be very impressive. There is an additional side to the problem. Having studied at government expense, an official often does not return to the ministry or agency he came from but prefers to apply his knowledge in a more profitable place.

All curricula in Russia are now copyrighted, and certificates are convertible (in different sizes and colors). For an appropriate fee, you can become a laureate of any award, title or order, as well as a prize, medal, commemorative emblem, etc. There is a whole underground industry producing alternative awards. Nominations for awards are not signed by the President (whom you would think might be the only one who has the right to do so), but by Ms. Sazhi Umalatova, who heads the Peace and Unity Party and, in combination, a strange organization called the Permanent Presidium of the Congress of People's Deputies of the USSR (PPSND). In the city of Perm, with the participation of members of the Communist Party of the Russian Federation (KPRF), Sazhi Umalatova presented 80 awards paid for by the recipients. The prices are as follows: 20 rubles for the Zhukov medal, 50 rubles for the Order of the Great Patriotic War, 250 rubles for the Order of Stalin established by the PPSND, $250 for the Gold Star of the Hero. In addition, there are the orders of Lenin and Stalin, the medal "Marshal Zhukov of the Soviet Union," "Admiral Kuznetsov of the Fleet of the Soviet Union," "80 years of the Great October Socialist Revolution".

Many of the experts and analysts who now appear on television programs are academicians and presidents of various foundations, centers, associations and the same academies (usually international ones). Even institutes in Russia no longer have directors, but presidents. President of the Institute for Strategic Assessments, or Global Problems, or System Forecasts, or something else. Such institutions do not have a single vice president or deputy director, or even lesser positions. In fact, most of these establishments consist entirely of their own president, who periodically orders more bilingual gold-edged business cards. On all visible and invisible petitions, appeals and letters of recommendation, the author's surname is preceded by the indispensable title: Academician. Recently, it seems that the absolute majority of the Russian population are academics. Given such a high level of literacy of the general population, then, it is not clear who is pissing in doorways (or why). Recently, this has been happening not only in doorways but already in the embassies.

Since the defeat of socialism, the notion of "shady science" has become firmly established as an activity that does not conform to the norms of truth-seeking and behavior in the scientific community. Genetic engineering, human cloning, developments in ray guns, and a symbiosis between humans and technical devices coexist with mountains of textbooks that contain gross errors but have survived several editions. This happens because of laziness, dishonesty, bribery, and protectionism among reviewers and publishers; it leads to a decline in the quality of science overall.

In order for a scientist in Russia to get any recognition for his discoveries, he must find a high-ranking official who deigns to support the discovery and give permission to put his name on the list of inventors. Naturally, the surname of the official comes first in the list. Only after that do the names of any professors or assistant professors (who are they, anyway?) appear. Here are a few examples. Among the laureates of the State Prize are: Deputy Prime Minister Vladimir Bulgak, who is noted for the latest methods of forecasting and implementation of telecommunications; Minister of Science Mikhail Kirpichnikov, who distinguished himself in the design of protein molecules, not only theoretically but also experimentally; Director of the Russian Space Agency Yuri Koptev, who was awarded the prize for the orbital station Mir, which will be destroyed soon, under his leadership. Also, the president of Chuvashia Nikolai Fedorov became the laureate of the State Prize in Science. The list of laureates includes heads of various academies, directors of institutes, and chairmen of foundations that allocate various grants. Let me suggest that the vast majority of them are actually not even vaguely familiar with what they received their award for. As for real scientists, they are languishing in *de facto* poverty.

I will give some facts that show the state of affairs and describe the level of culture of society. In 1999, a congress of Siberian doctors was held in Tomsk. The first congress of Siberian doctors was held in 1926, so the current one is "the second in a row." The buildings that used to house scientific laboratories are now offices of various companies; everyone is engaged in buying and selling, all the scientists are depressed, people practically do not talk to each other, and they only go to work once a week. One scientist is on his knees, huddled in a dirty corner, making something. Another is selling bananas; he uses the money to buy liquid helium for his experiments. One of the best Russian scientists was killed by a car at a pedestrian crossing.

The intelligentsia in Russia has always put up with the deteriorating financial situation and the loss of the role of the middle class (such as it was in Soviet society) in the name of ideas dear to them. But now they are increasingly shunning the regime under the pressure of facts showing the complete lack of any real reforms, the impoverishment of the people and their conversion to *lumpenproletariat*, and the criminalization of the country. Hence the intelligentsia's attempts to combine democracy with patriotism, often resulting in nationalism. Ethics in today's Russia does not actually exist. No one needs the "good" and "eternal." There are no more positive heroes in Russia.

Due to the all the foregoing, Russia finds itself losing all kinds of strategic resources — natural, material, and especially intellectual, labor — as all these valuable resources are being pumped abroad. Settlers from the former Soviet Union have greatly enriched Israel's intellectual potential, doubling the number of engineers and scientists there. Israel now has twice as many per 1,000 inhabitants as the United States, and three times as many as Germany. In addition, many talented entrepreneurs have emigrated from the former Soviet Union. According to a rough estimate by the Center for Strategic and Global Studies, between 1990 and 1997, the total outflow of resources from the country was about seven trillion dollars, i.e. about one trillion dollars a year. Russia is rapidly losing its position in the world.

And Russia has been enriching the rest of the world with more than scientific and labor resources. There are more than 40 organized groups of former Soviet citizens who have settled in the West and are engaged in smuggling valuable museum pieces out of Russia. This highly profitable trade is thriving thanks to the extremely poor security in museums, which never had such a problem before. They take out paintings and icons, meteorites and jewelry. Customs officials even caught a German citizen who was trying to take out the complete skeleton of a prehistoric cave bear — the only specimen in the world — that was kept in the Geological Museum of St. Petersburg.

A whole separate area of smuggling involves rare books. The rarest works are stolen right in front of the employees of libraries and museums. Robbers, for example, can present the ID an internal affairs officer and take away several old books for an "examination." For obvious reasons, no one wants to get involved with the police.

In addition, like museums everywhere, the exhibition halls can only display a small percentage of the artifacts on hand. Many art objects, sometimes priceless exhibits, slowly deteriorate in basements, attics and storerooms. Often even the museum workers are not fully aware of the value of paintings by medieval masters including Dürer and Rembrandt, jewelry, sculptures, furniture, etc., that are piled up or crammed in boxes.

The rector of the Baltic State Technical University (former Ustinov Military Mechanical Institute) fired four American lecturers after NATO forces began bombing Yugoslavia. They were re-hired thanks to the intervention of the governor of St. Petersburg, but the same rector then approved honorary scholarships named for Slobodan Milosevic. The scholarships are approved as a sign of support to Belgrade and its leadership, headed by Milosevic, who — unlike Yeltsin — was still fighting to preserve the sovereignty of a Slavic country.

What is actually happening in the field of education in Russia? Starting in the mid-1980s, with Perestroika, Russia began to look for ways to incorporate some of the strong points of Western-style education, especially by focusing more on individuals rather than using a standardized approach, and moving away from the strong focus on the maths and sciences to put a greater emphasis on the humanities. Ironically, the US in the 2020s is suffering precisely due to the over-emphasis on soft "sciences" and lack of STEM scholars, and the ever-growing focus on making students feel good rather than actually working hard.

By the late 1990s, the Committee of the State Duma of Russia on Education and Science had some second thoughts and developed a bill that proposed to reduce the study of the humanities and recommended to return to the path of standardization of curricula, to abandon the diversity and competitiveness of educational programs and methods. Teaching methods based on the state educational standard are not focused on the "development of the individual" but on ensuring that the majority of students receives a solid, broad education, without getting entirely sidetracked by questions about the peculiarities of each child's psyche.

The population of Russia is noticeably more bookish than Americans, and the book industry suffers from the opposite types of obstacles. If, in the US, a book can only reach widespread distribution if it pushes the right buttons for those who control the media and is made into a best-seller, in Russia there was a system for distributing books to bookstores nationwide, where the potential readers could decide what they wanted to read. In the early 1990s, the Russia-wide book market collapsed. New literature did not go further than the cities where it was published, since even the transportation costs to get it to other cities did not pay off. There were complaints that for up to 90% of the books published, not even in a single copy reached the stores in many regions. In the US, 90% of new books published are not available in any physical stores at all.

Speaking of the media, however, it should be acknowledged that the penetration of American propaganda has been quiet successful. When asked how they imagine a happy future, 40 classmates from the seventh grade of an ordinary secondary school in Ulyanovsk wrote that they would live in America in their own house on the ocean, everyone would have many children, a dog and a car, they would work at an American job and be American citizens.

16. Mass Media

A population becomes a society only when it has access to information. But despite the proclaimed principles of adhering to international and domestic laws, Russia in its early phases of "capitalism" has adopted the American approach here, as well as in education. Recently there has been a gradual narrowing of opportunities to obtain information. Now it's more a matter of manipulating public opinion through the mass media than about raising public awareness. The main consumers of information today are the government, business, and only then the readership. Many ambitious figures use the media only to shape public opinion and to promote their names, policies, and products. Political elites use the press as a "servant."

Today's pressure on the media comes with the approval and direct guidance of high-ranking officials in the Kremlin administration. When journalists objectively reflect what is going on and how people in society think, they can find themselves running afoul of the authorities. It is not the press that instigates the information war, but the authorities who seek to silence the more or less independent radio and TV stations, newspapers and magazines. The officials use their influence to put pressure on the independent media. In this they may be assisted by the Federal Tax Police Service (FSNP), which "acts strictly in accordance with the letter of the law" and is used to organize special measures "to expose tax violations by printed and electronic media owned by private companies." This is what they call it when the authorities restrict press freedom. The tax services openly state that they have some kind of "plans" for inspections of all the publishing houses in Moscow. The state is evidently mocking Channel One television, of which it owns 51%. The same is happening with regard to another channel, NTV: accounts are being frozen and arms are being twisted. So far, media representatives have no recourse unless they can directly meet with the President and inform him about the situation in an objective and unbiased manner. It is quite possible that this is only the beginning of a campaign aimed at curbing the independent mass media before the parliamentary and presidential elections.

Local television or radio companies that are in opposition to the incumbent governors may find their signal disrupted or face other technical difficulties. A TV channel may get a notice to move out of the building they occupy. Vladivostok authorities blocked the work of the independent radio station Lemma with the help of armed police, who attempted to interrupt the broadcast and seal the station's premises. A radio station may find its electricity cut off. In the regional town of Arsenyev, several issues of the local paper were impounded. Authorities in Primorsky Krai are trying to bring these media outlets to their knees for their independent position. It is not only in Primorsky Krai, on the eve of elections in Russia, that alternative sources of information are being destroyed. The territorially isolated Kaliningrad region may find itself isolated from Russia information soon, too. Governor Leonid Gorbenko has decided to stop operation of the television mast in the city center on the grounds that it required "emergency repairs." This means that in the run-up to the election campaigns, a million local residents will be unable to watch the TV and listen to Russian radio. Almost the same thing, only on a different scale and under a different pretext, is happening in Tatarstan and Bashkortostan.

Criminal outrages are committed against journalists with the tacit consent of the authorities. Journalist Igor Rostov was beaten in Kaliningrad. In St. Petersburg, Valery Dragilev, a TV correspondent for the program "6th Channel News," was beat up by guards at the Russian Congress of Intellectuals at the entrance to the session hall. In Tula, three unidentified men beat up Vladimir Uraev, an employee of the editorial office of Ekho Moskvy. In Belgorod, police officers beat Andrei Egonyants, a correspondent for Komsomolskaya Pravda. The policemen stated that the reason was that his photograph was pasted incorrectly in the his identity card. In Khabarovsk, the editor-in-chief of the newspaper My City, Leonid Kugushev, was beaten up by unidentified persons at a bus stop Not a single crime has been solved. According to experts running the project "Measuring Freedom of Speech in Russia," which took place in 2000, there is not a single region in Russia today with a legislative and political climate that is comfortable for the media. In November 1999, journalists were again beaten up in Kaliningrad, Saratov, Belgorod, Tula, Khabarovsk, Yekaterinburg and other cities. It happens even to foreign journalists.

In recent years, situations have become more frequent when journalists and film crews are arrested and taken away to an unknown location by the police, and the management of TV companies cannot get any explanations for what is happening. However, later the journalists are released (for now) and it turns out that they wrote or filmed reports about things like what happened in October 1999 in Sobinbank. And this is what happened there: the police officers and the special purpose police unit (OMON), having presented an incorrectly worded warrant, gained access to the bank's depository only because the bank's management feared that there might be a provocation on the part of the police. The vice-president of the bank, Yuri Scherling, did warn the police that any attempt to open the vaults would mean an encroachment on the private property of customers. Despite this, the police officers, without a proper warrant to check the safe-deposit boxes, got the owners of the investments and forced them to open the safe-deposit boxes themselves.

The presidential decree on the establishment of the Ministry of Press, Broadcasting and Mass Media "in order to develop a unified information space in Russia, as well as to improve public administration in the field of mass media and mass communications" means that in an election year, the Kremlin and the White House considered the freedom of independent and state media dangerous. In the near future, we can expect the new ministry to clamp down on the licensing of broadcasters and an urgent move to develop provisions for legal penalties against "ideological saboteurs." Neither in modern Russian nor in Soviet history did such an official monopoly on ideology exist. Even in the Soviet Union, they did not dare to create a single Ministry of Propaganda; the State Committees for the Press and for Television and Radio Broadcasting existed separately. Now a single ministry of propaganda has been created.

The Ministry of the Press covers about as many tasks as the Ministry of Truth described by Orwell in his novel "1984," and it is bound to become one of the essential election tools of today's power elite. The new ministry will control: mass media and mass communications, television and radio broadcasting, information exchange, the development of public computer networks, printing, publishing, distribution of periodicals, books and other printed products; the regulation of production and distribution of audio and video products, including registration and licensing; the production of advertising as well as its distribution by the media; measures to develop, build, augment, operate and license the technical base in the indicated areas of activity; regulation of activities using the radio frequency spectrum and the orbital positions of communication satellites for television and radio, the development of mass communications and the dissemination of mass media. The Ministry was instructed to: ensure the development, compilation and maintenance of unified all-Russia registries of mass media and mass communications; and to introduce a unified licensing process for the above activities, including television and radio broadcasting, accounting for all resources used: frequency bandwidth, satellite, on-air, cable broadcasting, community receivers networks.

"Where Lenin tried to take control of the post office and the telegraph, now broadcasting channels have taken their place," said the new minister, Mikhail Lesin, in February 1997. The only difference is that Lenin seized the mail and telegraph offices for non-commercial revolutionary purposes. Things are a little different with broadcasting channels — a lot of money is involved. Television is very important for the projection of presidential power. People involved in TV advertising have considerable influence on the President's inner circle. They have access to all the corridors of power. They do not like to be interfered with from the outside and strongly resist it by relying on their connections in the Presidential offices. Some sources claim that information about the progress of the investigation into the murder of the famous journalist Vladislav Listyev was regularly leaked from top people in the Ministry of Internal Affairs to the very people are suspected of committing a crime. If this is true, then the murderers and masterminds of the crime may well never end up in the dock.

When speaking about the finances of high-ranking Russian gangsters, knowledgeable sources usually say something like this: "We have a lot of information but we cannot disclose it. If you don't have enough power, it's better to keep that information for later on." It's no wonder that such information only appears without attribution: disclosing secrets can cost you your head. Most people are in a state of constant panic, fearing possible persecution, afraid to speak out freely. Everybody is sure that their phones are bugged and any public figure who has ever expressed his opposition to influential officials is sure to feel the breath of external surveillance on the back of his neck. The loudest newspaper articles exposing misdeeds of higher-ups in the government at best only provide fodder for gossip, at worst they cause headaches for the editors-in-chief. But they almost never succeed in generating any legal action: no one is removed from his post, and no one goes to jail. The worst enemies can be made by talking about the heads of the finance departments and the heads of the housing and maintenance offices (which allocate and maintain residential property). By the way, it is they who most often sign the endless letters of complaint, accusing everyone of the collapse of the national economy.

Even the Colombian press still reports on local corruption. In Russia, information about what is stolen (and how) comes from the Western media [which even after the fall of Communism has a special interest in making Russia look bad].

Almost every governor, president and local mayor tries to have some kind of public relations program. Here, too, they are implementing what they have learned from Western and Israeli friends who, despite the evidence of the last 100 years, claim to only have the new Russia's best interests at heart. Politicians, like companies, employ a small group of people who work with the media who are not engaged in journalism but in political technologies, technologies include methods of forced mind control, such as neuro-linguistic programming (NLP). These manipulation techniques are used consciously by the "media contacts" but are deliberately hidden from the public. People exposed to these technologies are not supposed to know about them — like hypnosis, if you are aware of the game, it usually doesn't work.

It's fair to ask whether these techniques are proper from our representatives in a democratic form of government, or are they more like the development and production of weapons of mass information destruction? Aren't modern technologies of manipulating public opinion a further development of the propaganda techniques pioneered by the American Edward Bernays (nephew of Sigmund Freud)? Americans often associate "propaganda" with "Soviet," but it was Bernays who systematized the techniques. He talked Americans into supporting World War I and his techniques are now polished and proliferated worldwide, for commercial and political purposes. All kinds of related "advanced" techniques are constantly being tested on the population. This is how public figures, and candidates, create their images. Newspapers receive advertising revenue or other support only if they help work on someone's image. "Independent" media loyal to local leaders receive support from city budgets. The fruits of this financial support are felt immediately. Newspapers have been publishing "necessary" advertising materials for months. Any independent actions of journalists are immediately characterized as "unpatriotic" and are subject to sanctions. If they try to exercise the wrong kind of independence, they are off the list for good. Some are just abandoned, but some are shut down with accusations of failing inspections by the public health or fire department. The media, in principle, are defenseless when it comes to public utilities that are subordinate to local authorities. And besides that, more than 60% of Russian journalists receive a salary of less than $50 or receive nothing at all. The American alternate media can hardly claim to operate under better conditions.

To shift the public mood, the democratic press stigmatizes Chechens more than it condemns the war against Chechens, just as the press in general directs public sympathy to our own fighting forces and the poor veterans who sacrificed for our good.

In Russia, with the decade of glasnost almost over, Prime Minister Putin canceled broadcasts of government meetings, and prohibited government officials from talking to journalists unless an interview is agreed through the Prime Minister's office. Yeltsin's daughter, Tatiana Dyachenko, one of the "gray cardinals" of Russian politics, also avoids talking to journalists. Almost all of her interviews consist of an exchange of letters between the Kremlin press service and speechwriters on the one hand and the publication on the other. Journalists send their questions and receive written answers of varying degrees of length. The "interviewee" herself, at best, diligently reads the text of her response before it is published.

Although the Russian-speaking community has long been international, and it has business centers in many locations outside of Russia, the Russian press oddly and incomprehensibly stops at the geographic border of Russia. People who exit the country but continue to participate in local business, seem not to count for the Russian press. Quite a lot of people have gone abroad who have a head on their shoulders and have valuable insights into what is going on in Russia, but the press try not to let their independent opinions get into the information space of Russia. It is absolutely not needed here. Western journalists see one set of information, the Russian people see another. Haggling over humanitarian aid, the West is told that the theft of equipment and food is a problem, but among the locals who are responsible there is a different version, referring to potential chemical exposure to Russian residents through this aid ("There is no such thing as a free lunch, right?"). They try not to let foreign journalists visit where the true picture is clear as to where the breakdowns are in society.

An example of the information divide targeting the Russian vs. the international audience can be seen by comparing wot speeches given almost simultaneously, one in Moscow and one in Washington. Russia's chief banker Viktor Gerashchenko told Russians he was indignant that the Americans chose the Russians as "whipping boys" and announced that "The Seven's" new requirements for Russia were "complete nonsense," while First Deputy Prime Minister Viktor Khristenko, speaking in DC, recognized the expediency of the industrial powers' new approach to our country and expressed confidence that IMF lending would certainly continue. After his speech in Russia, Gerashchenko's behavior during a meeting with US Treasury Secretary Lawrence Summers in Washington stood in stark contrast to his angry Moscow-style accusations.

As for the last war in Yugoslavia, of course neither Russian nor American television has ever provided its citizens with objective information. There are two completely different stories, supporting whatever is convenient to the two sides. In one story, small proud Yugoslavia, which was attacked by the army of the world's only superpower and its allies. The strong beat the weak, a big country attacked a little one; 20 countries with a combined population of 600 million people bombed Serbia because they could. In the other story, Albanian villages were burned and thousands of people killed or rendered homeless for no good reason. When the united West turned on the Slavs, , for no good reason. [In neither case is it mentioned that Yugoslavia had the most successful economy in post-Soviet Eastern Europe, and the ethnically diverse population was generally satisfied with the proportional representation offered by their form of democracy. It is not mentioned that Serbia sits on what may be the world's largest lithium reserves, not to mention other highly-prized minerals. It is not mentioned that Yugoslavia's Serbian leader Milosevic proudly called on them to defend their sovereignty in the face of globalist plunderers. It is not mentioned that both sides reported being fired on, by un-known parties, at the outset of hostilities: just like the Maidan in Kiev and so many other "color" revolutions.]

The indignation of millions of Russian TV viewers was natural and justified. They could not understand why all the European countries were going crazy, and only China and Namibia supported Russia in the Security Council. Many countries should heed this cruel lesson of NATO aggression and rely more on their weapons than on the UN and the Security Council — this was the rationale for this information war. The same is happening with information about Chechnya. Therefore, one should not be surprised that the Russians so unanimously demand the continuation of the war in this republic.

17. "COMPROMAT" AND DISINFORMATION

The current government does not shy away from even the crudest electoral tactics. Naïve Russians think that demonstrates an embarrassing distortion of the honorable political system in Western democracies, but they may actually be quite similar. In the Russian information wars, each of the belligerents is supported by a group of newspapers and TV channels. Three or four teams of advertisers and public relations specialists are engaged in the same topic. This is especially characteristic in the shaping of political blocs or parties, whose platform, if any, may change drastically depending on polling numbers. These groups have their own intelligence: professionals, many of whom have advanced degrees in statistical manipulation. They use special computer programs to analyze newspaper materials, identify authors by style, find out which interest group is behind this or that publication, behind this or that story, whose influence dominates in this or that newspaper. Several contradictory information campaigns, as a rule, overlap each other. There is absolutely reliable information, there is reliable information interpreted to give it a specific slant, and there is fiction with genuine details. But if they all start working to promote one message, the result will be even worse.

To succeed in such political battles requires the skills of a master in espionage. Spies operate inconspicuously and lead secretive lives. It is very difficult to find dirt on them. These skills also come in handy in political maneuvers. In the Russian context, experience in the intelligence services does not hurt anyone in a government position. Any time a candidate appears for any office in Russia, a search is underway to find out how he can be compromised. A candidate that you cannot control is terrifying to Russian officials.

Such a person could try to act independently. Digging up or fabricating compromising stories is the domain of highly qualified experts. As a rule, these are people who have held high government posts for a long time and know the tricks of organizing exposé campaigns. For the uninitiated it is can be quite difficult to distinguish fact from fiction.

With a few exceptions dreamt up by talented improvisers, scenarios fitting one of just a few patterns can be used to compromise government officials, bankers, industry leaders and others. Mainly, the goal is to keep open the option of launching a criminal prosecution on one basis or another, regardless of whether there is any grain of truth to the accusations. The first ploy is to create conditions under which, if the need arises, a given individual can be privately or publicly accused of having done something incompatible with the status of a civil servant, of undermining Russian national security, of giving support to extremists, etc. The second is to create the prerequisites for a possible anti-corruption probe at any time. The third is to generate a situation in which a potential victim can be provoked to act in an apparently unethical or immoral way.

Information professionals in Russia consider the media flow to be about half plain information, not being pushed for anyone's interests, and the rest are topics being spun for the benefit of one interest or another. Privatization, conflicts between companies, customs policy, support for domestic producers versus the need to make imported goods cheaper and more accessible, disputes between the governor, mayor, prosecutor, local administration —everyone who is not lazy is lobbying for something. When there is no news, it is "made up." There are all sorts of issues being discussed, for example, campaigns to combat corruption or to combat bureaucratic privileges, which just do not make any sense; but election campaigns have to be fueled by something, and the best fuel is compromising material on rivals. Russian intelligence agencies and security agencies have learned to use Western institutions and media as conduits for information leaks in order to compromise their opponents at home. The current war of kompromat has clearly gone beyond certain limits. All the hostile clans in Russia are fighting with crude forms of bribery and blackmail, at times not even trying to hide it.

Most of the dirt is spread through the press and television. Recently, it has also been spread via the Internet. But some experts consider rumors to be the most effective way of planting dirt in Russia. Rumors are constantly flying, to such a n extent that it is best not to pay much attention. But, nevertheless, it all starts with rumors, which are spread so skillfully that no one can reliably say which of any of the mutually exclusive rumors is more likely to be true. Say, two "passengers" on the subway start to pick apart one of the candidates during an election campaign. Within a couple of days, the gossip is traveling all over town, giving the most incredible details.

Russian experience also belies the notion that such garbage only works within certain limits: that once a limit is reached, voters will stop paying attention. No. One in nine Russians believes that in an election it is acceptable to use any means to achieve victory. These data were obtained in a poll conducted by the Public Opinion Foundation on the eve of the parliamentary election campaign. The amount of filth poured out by Russian politicians on each other was unimaginable. Everything is used. Pitting religious fanatic groups against politicians, smearing politicians with fake prostitutes, allusions to homosexuals and transsexuals, accusing them of selling out their country and having ties to foreign intelligence services, suggesting that they have links to organized crime, smearing relatives, accusing them of being senile and mentally incompetent, potentially bloodthirsty, of being Jewish — or of being anti-Jewish! and much more. Focusing on "issues" like these makes the very essence of elections in a democratic state meaningless.

The game of discrediting one's opponent has shifted from gentlemen's swordplay to a drunken brawl. When discrediting opponents, it's not enough to hint at bad character or an innocent weakness for drink; one has to come up with something quite unexpected and politically murderous. The Interior Ministry has long been aware of Justice Minister Valentin Kovalev's penchant for amusing himself with men on territory controlled by the Solntsevo criminal group. He seems to have had the support of Prime Minister Chernomyrdin and then of President Yeltsin; and it is not easy to dismiss a cabinet member. But when a videotape surface, showing him cavorting naked with naked prostitutes in a sauna, controlled by the Solntsevo crime group, that led to the desired result.

Governor Aman Tuleyev of Kemerovo Region, one of Russia's most promising politicians, was widely accused of having abandoned his faith and converting to Christianity, based on information from an anonymous source; this gave grounds for Muslim fanatics to sentence him to death for apostasy. In a politically, ideologically and religiously electrified country, it is enough to simply make a statement without supporting it with anything. There was no factual information presented: neither the date nor the place where Tuleyev was allegedly baptized was specified. What matters is not credibility, but logic. That is why there is much talk about Tuleyev becoming an adherent of Islam in the early '90s and even making hajj to Mecca. He decided to change his religion because he announced his intention to run for presidency of Russia. Neither of these statements corresponds to the truth. The press who disseminated the falsified information did not bother to print any refutation. After that, the "death verdict" was made public in the Chechen capital Grozny.

Back in the early '90s, a number of newspapers circulated the story that the current chairman of the "Democratic Choice of Russia" party and then-Prime Minister Gaidar was not really Gaidar, but the daughter of the crook Kvakin, who existed in real life and had undergone a sex change operation. Moscow's mayor Luzhkov was said to be a Jew by the name of Katz, and he was linked to kidnappings and organ trafficking. Former Prime Minister Chernomyrdin was accused of hunting poor little bears. One banker asked for open letters from gays to be published in the major newspapers. The gays complained that they were being humiliated in Russia, while among them there are decent, respectable people who do a lot of good for society; it was mentioned that Tchaikovsky was gay, as well as Wilde, and a Russian financier were named, in whom one could easily recognize a political opponent. The famous showman Lisovsky was defamed by use of flyers printed on behalf of "gay" people, urging them to vote for "dear Seryozhenka." Korzhakov, the former head of Yeltsin's security detail, spread a rumor about former CIS Executive Secretary Berezovsky having chronic gonorrhea.

Representatives of the FSB visit relatives of undesirable people at their homes in order to find as much compromising information as possible and to put pressure on the person. In addition, the Federal Security Service and other repressive structures can carry out various kinds of actions against relatives in order to shake out compromising information from them. It has already become a tradition to try to eliminate people through their relatives.

The aging Communist gerontocrats, still in power, are unhappy about the possible arrival of young liberal intellectuals to run the country, in any part of Russia. They are particularly irritated by former Prime Minister Sergei Kiriyenko. In order to compromise him, one night unknown persons plastered posters all over Moscow, presenting Kiriyenko as a Huggies cowboy from the famous children's diaper commercial, with baby hands and feet and a big head.

Often, a leaflet will be glued to car windshields with a strong glue urging one to vote for a specific candidate. Or they call people at home at three o'clock in the morning with the same request. Such "campaigning" certainly turns people against the unfortunate candidate. Or, you may be invited to meet one candidate or another for an "afternoon social, with gifts" at some public institution on the edge of town. When it turns out that no such event was scheduled, you will swear and curse the "deceiver".

The text of real correspondence from the politician may be reproduced in the news with all sorts of nasty things having been inserted. The same thing happens with telephone conversations. Many of the documents appearing in the press are forged by the special services: the forms are real, but stolen, the text is also real, but with the inclusion of kompromat. One common practice is to spread the rumor spread that a politician is a political zero and his wife is doing everything for him.

Fake dirt is also used to counter negative information. When too much dirt has come out on a certain politician, some monstrous bit of information about him is thrown into the press, which of course turns out to be false. The politician may be accused of being a cannibal, for instance, or of being a pickpocket. People are shocked, but then the politician himself appears and proves, with facts in his hands, that the accusation is fake. Voters don't understand anything, and decide maybe it was all fake, and his reputation is restored.

Campaign posters "Let's support Putin in the struggle" appeared in the towns of Kamensky electoral district of Sverdlovsk region. Signatures were collected for the last name Putin, with no initials. In fact, Pavel Putin, chairman of the Sverdlovsk railroad union committee and not the prime minister, is registered as a candidate for the State Duma in electoral district 163, but he lives in Yekaterinburg. The ballots and posters in support of Putin without initials, according to the chairman of the district election commission, are not formally related to candidate Pavel Putin, since they were printed in a Moscow printing house and seem to advertise the current Russian prime minister.

"Dirty" electoral techniques have been known in Russia since 1991. According to some electoral experts, dirty technology is just a moral concept. Now the situation in the legal field is such that it not only presupposed violations of the law, but forces them. The current political struggle has more of a criminal element than any "dirty" technology. The adoption of norms and standards that would somehow regulate the behavior of the political elites is impeded by the elites themselves: they see no benefit in complying with any such framework. As a result, Russia is experiencing "nonsense that has already surpassed the techniques of Goebbelsian propaganda," "spitting on all Russia, all of our society," "filth that only a person who does not respect culture can accept" (Moscow mayor Yury Luzhkov); "information stabbing" (Mark Zakharov, artistic director of the Lenkom Theater); "filth that goes beyond decency" (Sergey Kiriyenko, leader of the Union of Right Forces and former prime minister).

Every political team in Russia has a group of people from the special services to support them, working in analytical centers and various kinds of foundations and associations. They are figuring out how to overwhelm competitors. Thus it is no surprise to see specific methods being used in the current political battles that used to be associated only with law enforcement. Many news agencies specialize in campaigning against prominent politicians and carry out orders from their patrons. At the behest of the relevant departments, they keep on "informing" the public about undesirable politicians. Soon, any discussion of the moral state of society will disappear from Russian journalism. And there will be only one genre left — denunciation and publication of kompromat.

Most of the compromising information comes out at special "closed briefings" of government officials. At a certain hour, especially trusted journalists gather and they are directly told what to publish. Materials that have been known in narrow circles for a long time are shown. This is done without reference to a specific person.

The mechanisms for manipulating public opinion have recently been improved by forging such seemingly innocent things as a rating. By determining the leader in the pre-election marathon, the public opinion poll thus creates it. Everyone wants to vote for the strong one and not for the weak. Thus, one of the most effective ways to manipulate the vote is to "publish" the results of public opinion polls and the ratings. A team of sociologists may come to the province and, for starters, give a true picture of preferences in the region. And then, just before the elections, it slightly, by 3–4%, overestimates the rating of the candidate who hired them. When an inexperienced citizen sees information presented in this way in the media, it doesn't occur to him to doubt their veracity. And so the candidate's popularity actually grows.

New electoral technologies go hand in hand with new technologies of collecting and publishing dirt, which are becoming more and more sophisticated. First, a site called "Kogot" (the Claw) appeared on the Internet, which published transcripts of scandalous telephone conversations. Then came Rumour.ru and Kogot-7. Unlike its predecessors, "Claw-7" was not hosted on the Russian Internet but on a server in the American city of Provo, Utah. That meant that none of the interested parties, much less the individual being slandered in the dubious materials, had no way to get the site taken down. The first sites were online for just a few days, but shortly the operators figured out how to safely and permanently post rumors from the world of politics and business on the Web.

In civilized countries, the state or federal government has been considered the guarantor of election rules. America always took pride in showing the world the honorable spectacle of clean elections; it was something that made people proud to be American. It may be noted, however, that since at least 2000 the presidential elections in the United States have been marred by widespread evidence of fraud and vote tampering, to the extent that the outcome of the last two elections at least remain highly dubious. Russia already had a severely tarnished reputation by the late 1990s, with the state looking like a cheeky croupier, who would set players at the card table and dictate arbitrary rules of the game. The regime starts with elections in a series of regions where the federal center is expected to lose — in order to first create public expectation of the numerous violations of the electoral law, and then, having fixed them, to cancel the results in a given constituency.

Moscow has only one reliable weapon though, when it comes to "dirt" against the President. Evidence of embezzlement or other misdeeds is declared to be just a propaganda effort by the Western media, aimed at undermining the reputation of Russian businessmen. Just as in Washington, the preferred fall-back excuse is always, "the Russians did it."

At the same time, the Russian tax ministry is secretly preparing serious documents that could significantly complicate the lives of undesirable politicians. They envision comprehensive measures to tighten the tax regime, especially with regard to associated economic structures. Under the guise of restoring order, the tax loopholes and tricks that are now used by almost all businessmen are to be eliminated or greatly reduced. If a politician gets out of the net of compromises and accusations, the inevitable decline in the standard of living of the people in the region from which he was elected or governed, and the inevitable rise in prices, will greatly undermine his image. In a concrete and blatant direction on the part of the state, the tax authorities are used as an instrument of political pressure.

If an authoritarian regime is ever established in the country again, it will have at its disposal an army of specialists, a set of proven methods and tools for influencing the masses, adopted and adapted from the West; and it will be able to use them. There can be no doubt that the people will follow the future ruler of the Russian land. The main distinguishing feature of the propaganda professionals — journalists, movie directors, psychologists, education departments, national security officers — is their complete lack of principle. One day these people carry out orders from one party, the next day they collaborate with the opposition. Given their acumen, their ability to communicate and manipulate the audience, you can see that Russia has caught up to the rest of the world when it comes to what is happening on the information front.

18. Human Rights

The widespread acceptance of the idea of human rights was a major European achievement of the 20th century. However, there are some different nuances as to how various cultures define the concept and the hierarchy to follow when one group's rights intersect with another's. Russia does not accept that international law should supersede national laws; that would mean relinquishing the notion of sovereignty altogether, handing over all authority to bodies in Brussels and elsewhere that are mostly dominated by the Anglo-American power centers. Russia holds that human rights violations are an internal matter of the state.

That is why Russia has been concerned about how the Charter of European Security formulates its position. "Humanitarian intervention" may sound like benign charitable action to those doing the intervening; to those taking the brunt of it, the intervention is an act of uninvited interference, an act of war, an outside interference in support of one side of a conflict against another. When does a third party get to decide which side is right in a civil war or regional conflict, and if they believe abuses are ongoing, how much can they or should they do about it??

Within Russia now, early in the transition from the Soviet system to the tentative formulation of a new system, the human rights situation is complicated. Given the abrupt and chaotic privatization of businesses, liberalization of laws and morality, explosion of corruption and opportunism, obviously laws are being ignored and that makes life difficult for the population. Politicians and police are taking arbitrary decisions and actions. Workers are taken advantage of by presumptuous employers, salaries go unpaid, judicial power is unbridled.

Every country has experts on other countries, on economics, politics, weapons systems, and so on. Many such experts are studying Russia, including its approach to human rights. However, they have not been raising any complaints. The fact is that human rights issues come in second place by a long shot when talking about countries that may be tyrannizing some of their citizens but is selling essential resources like cheap coal, oil, gas and timber, metals, fish, diamonds or gold, or that has some other leverage over the leading economies. Just look at Saudi Arabia or Israel. In addition, Russia (like Israel) has nuclear weapons. But as things go downhill in the country, more and more of its decent citizens will flee abroad, seeking to escape the terrible living conditions, and more and more less scrupulous citizens will join the ranks of the mafia, supported at the government level.

All this will lead to problems for those countries that today turn a blind eye to the human rights situation in Russia. They will be overflowing with refugees, their banks will receive stolen money, products will be dumped at below-market prices and the massive dumping of currency and gold by the Central Bank of Russia will destroy their economy. The international community needs to think today of how to prevent such a terrible tomorrow.

In general, the occupation of human rights protection in Russia is not very popular. In part, this is because it is very difficult to achieve justice. And in part, it is because you can't steal from a human rights organization, you can't take anything home with you; you can only get into trouble.

In the aftermath of Gorbachev's perestroika, loudly hailed in the West, the population of Russia slipped back to the medieval level of subsistence farming, just as it had done during the years of the Bolsheviks. This penury and despair limits the level of human development and taints one's perception of the surrounding reality so that everything boils down to the question, What can I get for it? And it's no use pointing to the accomplishments of the military-industrial complex, spaceships and the like. Russia excels the West on a number of fronts, but all this does not really define the everyday life of Russian citizens. You'd better look into the cramped, dark apartments in which the overwhelming number of Russians live, whether in Moscow or Vladivostok. But there are also those categories of citizens who only dream of such apartments, for example, newlyweds who cannot move out of their parents' place.

In the last Chechen campaign, the voice of the human rights community was still heard. Today, there are no more speeches by human rights defenders, and the subject of human rights is of no interest. In public discussions the names of prominent human rights defenders themselves are derided and despised.

Russia managed to sign conventions on human rights with the European Union but they are difficult to translate to the Russian system. According to the unclassified "Instructions on the procedure for issuing, replacing, registering and storing passports of a citizen of the Russian Federation," which can be read only after overcoming all sorts of bureaucratic obstacles, the status of a citizen in his native fatherland records a certain place of residence, and not the fact of birth on Russian soil. It turns out that there is nothing more difficult than proving that you have a right to a passport. Many people simply do not exist in the state archives, so they are not entitled to a passport. Therefore, a person can easily find himself in limbo; a person without a clear place of residence is, on that basis alone, not a citizen. Despite the fact that Russians now seem to live in a new "free and democratic" country and have a democratic Russian Federation, and not a totalitarian Soviet Union, the laws in force date back to the 1930s. Despite the fact that the original decree on persons without a fixed place of residence, the homeless or so-called "bums," and special police-run shelters, was signed back in 1936, no one questioned it even under the democracy of 1997, when the laws were revised. The police are always ready to give iron-clad facts confirming the expediency of everyday inhumanity.

In Russia, everything is measured by the residence permit. If you do not have a residence permit, you are not a person. You won't be able to get medical help or take a book out from the library if you come from one region and live in another. In border areas, a person without a residence permit will not be able to get a job even as a janitor. Therefore, "visitors" prefer to engage in trade. There's nothing else left. But in the markets, local traders put pressure on the directors of the public markets not to give visitors good locations. Thus, if you don't have a residence permit, you don't have access to anything good anymore. Therefore, the issue of registration is not a question of administrative bureaucracy, but a question of human rights. You can't work, you can't study, you can't live, you can't demand answers, you can't be yourself.

During the "market" reforms of the '90s, Russia developed serious demographic problems, but the federal government has no specific approach to solving them. Decades have radically changed the situation in the post-Soviet space, and millions of people have become forced migrants. Just as the developed West has experienced a migration boom far exceeding its historic flow of new-comers, Russia has faced intense migration flows while there is a widespread shortage of affordable housing and there are limited work opportunities — especially for poorly educated people who may not be fluent in the principal language. If a person comes to a Western country and asks for asylum, there are some services set up to help him (overwhelmed as they may be). But who can a refugee in Russia turn to? And where to look for representatives of the UN High Commissioner for Refugees in Russia?

Far more money will be spent on pre-election campaigning than on programs benefiting the population. This is because campaign contributions are a major component of money-laundering schemes, where hidden, stolen money can be invested anonymously in order to support corrupt candidates. That includes funds that were set aside in the budget, or were in the accounts of "bankrupt" banks, or came from international institutions and foreign governments in the form of aid or loans. That money could be used to pay pensions and salaries. The pensions paid out in recent years have been only 60% of the required minimum, and according to official data, on average" wages have not been paid for one and half months. But in fact, the salary arrears range from 3 to 6 months or even more. Some categories of workers have not received their salaries for years. Employees of correctional labor colony No. 17, located in the Komi Republic, have not received a salary for more than a year. The only way to solve this problem is to get fired. At the time of dismissal, the employee is given his entire delayed salary.

In many cities, normal, successful people have been camped out in tent cities for many weeks — teachers, doctors, cultural workers — near the government buildings. Despite claims from the bureaucrats that the situation is stabilizing and the negotiations with the IMF are going well, these people are still desperately demanding that the government pay their salary debts and start paying salaries on a regular basis. These encampments are gradually growing, and delegations of solidarity come from more and more new places. Teachers are no longer demanding their whole salary; they are willing to settle for at least pay for a couple of months' pay so that they can buy food for children and the simplest everyday clothes. The autumn salary of 1999 some employees in Mordovia was issued in food packages containing: millet, sugar, flour, cheese, stew and green peas. Against the background of strikes by starving essential workers, the first match of the all-star hockey teams was held in Novokuznetsk. Each player received a diamond ring worth $1,000. The game ended with a banquet costing $125,000. It should be noted that the Kemerovo region is one of the most disadvantaged, subsidized regions. Kuzbass today owes its creditors about 3 billion rubles. Just a day before the event, which was chic by Russian standards, the arbitration court of the Kemerovo region sued the administration for 32.6 million rubles in favor of the International Industrial Bank from Moscow.

Even outside the country, the authorities manage not to pay salaries to their citizens. In the peacekeeping contingent in Kosovo, where there are 2,900 military personnel of the Ministry of Defense of the Russian Federation and about a hundred employees of the Ministry of Internal Affairs, members of the international police force, the usual Russian situation with a chronic delay in pay is repeated.

Social instability, coupled with the absence of any clear prospects for a better future, has reached its apogee. People whose salaries depend on the budget have begun to break the law. One professor set out to produce and sell fake employee health booklets at his workplace, since they are now in demand among small businesses. Two respected teachers traveled by public transport with fake passes for disabled people, because they have no money to pay for bus tickets. Now even staid professionals are taking to robbing shops and apartments, for example, the head of the toxicological department of one of the hospitals. His wife, a state employee, like him had not received a salary in months, and they had no way to feed their family. In addition, desperate to pay off his debts, a PhD candidate in the medical sciences picked up a sawn-off shotgun.

Employees are being thrown out of factories and shops not because they were poor workers, but in order to clear places for the bosses' protégés. Many people are fired in a needlessly rude and ugly way — they learn about their dismissal after the fact. One wonders how that feels, compared to the hundreds of US employees being laid off in the 2020s by major American companies, without warning, in front of all their colleagues via video conference call.

Young women are under double pressure. Due to the high level of unemployment, it is much more difficult for them to find a job, and in addition, they may face special "conditions" in Russia. Many employers make it clear at the time of hiring that the women they hire on a part-time basis must engage in prostitution in their free time. During the day, a woman stands behind the counter like a saleswoman, and in the evening she has to serve customers personally. However, she receives only the salary of a saleswoman. If you don't like it, don't work here. But there is no other job. Everyone has the same requirements. Older women generally have the least chances of getting a job, even if they have the best qualifications.

Russia is still far behind the West when it comes to birth control and childbirth as well. Russia retains a confident lead in both infant and maternal mortality. An average woman may have five or six abortions during her fertile years. The concept of maternal mortality is also common in Russian maternity hospitals. In public maternity hospitals, no one is held responsible for what happens; improper obstetric care and birth injuries are a common phenomenon.

The system gives the wrong economic incentives. If a mother sends her underdeveloped child to a boarding school, it costs the state 2,000 rubles per month. If a stranger takes guardianship over a healthy child, the state pays him 1,200 rubles per month. Yet women struggling to provide for their own two children receive a government stipend of just 500 rubles. Some mothers give in to the pressures and just have their healthy children committed to a psychiatric hospital, in order to receive the benefit money.

In Yaroslavl, since the municipality is out of cash, they now pay rents with child allowances. At the shipbuilding plant, 24 employees who were looking to be paid the arrears in child support benefits took the city to court, but still no cash was found, so they were offered compensation by writing off the same amount in rent they owed to the municipality. Of course, you can't buy an apple for a child this way. But people have to go along, because the courts have already made hundreds, if not thousands, of decisions upholding this model, and people have not received compensation by other means. The idea of using child allowances to pay utility bills is also of great interest throughout the country. In the worst case, as in the Urals, they offer to pay the benefits in slippers and sets of Christmas decorations. In Yekaterinburg, an exhibition was held of goods that are being issued in the Sverdlovsk region in lieu of children's allowances and salaries. Even in the absurd atmosphere prevailing today, it became the talk of the town and caused a huge scandal.

When it comes to adopting orphaned children, preference is almost always given to foreigners. Although there are thousands of Russian citizens in the adoption queues, more than half of the children go to live abroad. In St. Petersburg, foreigners adopt 85% of children. This is not even explained by the fact that foreigners are better off financially, but by the fact that, seeing what is going on in the country, employees of Russian orphanages and baby homes prefer to give their children a well-fed and calm future abroad, wishing them a happy journey and hoping that these children will recover from all they suffered in Russian orphanages, where sometimes an almost prison-like atmosphere reigns. In Moscow alone, maternity hospitals see at least one case of a mother rejecting a baby almost every day. Scientific research shows that every year the number of "rejected" children has increased by 5–6 percent. According to the president of the Independent Association of Child Psychologists and Psychiatrists Anatoly Severny, 90% of children who spent four years in orphanages need psychiatric help.

A difficult situation awaits almost all Russian children when they grow up. Teachers, unwilling to go on teaching for free, are on strike. Teenagers are brutally beaten in police stations for no good reason, and many of them are forced to confess to crimes they have not committed because the police have targets to meet as to the number of crimes solved. Children are easier to force to confess — they are not so mature, they are easier to frighten, they have more romance in their souls, including, so common in Russia, a romantic notion of imprisonment.

There are two million homeless kids on the streets of Russia, where in 1980 there were none. Russia's interior minister Rashid Nurgaliyev (2003–2012) blamed the situation on "the virtual collapse of the Russian health service in 1991, when the Soviet Union fell, and on the economic misery and moral crisis that affected the country"[1] for years after. On November 20, 1989, the UN adopted the Convention on the Rights of the Child, and Russia ratified it in 1991, but had no resources to devote to the problem. In 2003, the Center for Demography and Human Ecology of the Institute of Economic Forecasting (Russian Academy of Sciences) released a report on homeless children, whose average age was estimated at 12–13; two thirds of them were boys, 50% were migrants (from non-Russian republics of the Federation).[2] Most of the children reported that they had only one — or no —parent to turn to, or that the parents had drinking problems, or that there was violence in the home. Obviously, they are all vulnerable abuse of various kinds, to addiction, and to a future involving detention centers and psychiatric clinics.

When a person reaches the age of majority in Russia, he goes to serve in the army. As of this writing, half of all men who enroll for military service are rejected because they suffer from drug addiction, oligophrenia, nervous diseases, and are significantly underweight as a result of insufficient nutrition. Virtually all of the young men who pass the medical commission on the eve of the draft have dystrophy. In addition, six out of seven young men who have been medically discharged have mental problems. Eighty percent of young people drafted today are fit to serve only in the auxiliary military services, but not the army itself. Information about conscripts who are undergoing treatment is classified and their names are kept private. What happens when a country, including the U.S., needs more military manpower than it can muster? In order to fulfill the enlistment plan, standards are lowered. Then 18-year-old teenagers can be put through the medical examination, as well as other tests, again and can be admitted to serve despite their being unfit.

The fondest dream of Russians of conscription age is to obtain a "clean" but fake military ID, exempting them from the draft. These are widely available for an average of 15,000 rubles. An elementary feeling of self-preservation says that it is better to buy a fictitious paper for a lot of money than to trust your luck. During the first Chechen war, the leadership failed in its promise not to send untrained recruits to the front. Families from far out in the provinces were most affected, as they had no high-level connections, lawyers, or

[1] https://www.bmj.com/content/330/7504/1348.3
[2] https://imrussia.org/en/society/245-besprizorniki?start=1

money and, moreover, these people are the most inexperienced and easily fooled part of the population. Three hundred and fifty lawsuits filed in 1995 in the Presnensky Inter-Municipal Court of Moscow were pending for four years; these cases were filed by mothers from all over the country, whose sons-soldiers died in the Chechen war. Almost none of the famous people in Russia responded to the request of mothers and journalists to help in the investigation of this case.

The press secretary of Nobel Prize laureate Alexander Isaevich, the famous author who was imprisoned as a dissident in earlier times himself, refused to accept even a fax about the controversial Chechen war. He said that the Chechen topic was of concern to Solzhenitsyn, but it was unlikely that he would agree to help. Solzhenitsyn essentially defended Russia's position. The writer, who claimed to have become the "conscience of Russia," recalled in an interview the Chechens' history with Russia. According to him, they had sided with the Bolsheviks after 1917 and destroyed the Cossacks, another minority group in the south. Clearly, when it comes to hurling accusations of government injustice towards one group of citizens or another, it is all too easy to form a quick impression based on emotions. These are complex matters and all this touches the national, if not nationalistic attitudes of the "new great Russia." Except for General Lebed, there was not much official response to the appeals of the soldiers' mothers.

Some Russians think their country has a high rate of incarceration; however, their rate is just two thirds that of the US, which is by far the highest in the world. In Western Europe the rates are, indeed, low, as violent crime is relatively rare there. In 1999, about 1,035,000 people were being held in detention camps and prisons in Russia — 0.730 per cent of the population. In 2012, according to World Prison Brief, the U.S. incarceration rate was 629 per 100,000, while the Russian Federation's was 322.[1]

A number of judicial/prison reforms were introduced, but as Evgeny Primakov (then Prime Minister) said, "All of the amnesties planned in Russia are needed to make room for those who have committed 'economic crimes,'" which is a very flexible notion in Russia. And indeed, the transition from government-owned resources to crony capitalism (or gangster capitalism) did end up creating boundless and jaw-dropping opportunities for those who were ready to take those resources into private hands. The turmoil and the state's efforts to fight back remind some of the days of Stalin.

---

[1] https://www.prisonstudies.org/highest-to-lowest/prison_population_rate?field_region_taxonomy_tid=All

At the end of October 1999, First Deputy Prime Minister Y. Maslyukov rejected in principle the concept of public oversight over places of detention, so that members of the public should not have access to detention centers and evaluate the conditions and the treatment of prisoners. He called such public scrutiny "unacceptable interference in the activities of public authorities and their officials." Thus, he blocked efforts to ensure that prisoners' rights were properly observed, as well as the establishment of an institution of trusted experts (doctors, lawyers, psychologists) who would assist public inspectors.

A visa regime for Moscow has been re-introduced, which breaches a number of articles of the Constitution. Absent the official declaration of a state of emergency, and with no end date established, this illegal initiative was taken solely on the basis of a personal order from Luzhkov, the Mayor of Moscow.

His personal order also abolished the freedom to protest and demonstrate, although the Constitution guarantees everyone the right to hold such public actions. Pacifists opposing the Chechen campaign and members of the port workers' trade union alike were denied the right to picket.

At police stations, people from the Caucasus republics, Central Asians including Kazakhs, and others, especially those with darker skin, may sit for five hours or more waiting to be "processed." In the newspapers' police blotters they never mention race when the suspect is Slavic, but only when he is "Caucasian." When human rights activist Sergei Kovalev offers his observations on the excesses of the Moscow police against immigrants from the Caucasus, his comments are simply cut out by all the newspaper editors during the editing process.

In fact, the Mayor's Order No. 1007-RM (dated September 13, 1999), "On Urgent Measures to Ensure Registration of Citizens Temporarily Staying in Moscow" is entirely illegal. It contradicts the International Covenant on Civil and Political Rights of 1966 (Article 2), which states: "Everyone lawfully staying on the territory of a State shall, within that territory, enjoy the right to freedom of movement and freedom of residence... The above-mentioned rights shall not be subject to any restrictions..."; Protocol 4 to the European Convention on Human Rights (Article 2); nine articles of the Constitution of the Russian Federation; and the Code of Administrative Offenses of the Russian Federation (Article 178). According to the Constitution of the Russian Federation, no limitation of a citizen's rights and freedoms can be imposed except on the basis of a federal law. Therefore, any person who is expelled from any region for lack of re-registration theoretically can and should assert his rights in court. Nevertheless, the authorities have already prepared a corresponding draft amendment to the federal law, which will be submitted to the State Duma as a legislative initiative. Most likely, this will be some kind of decree. Everything is done decrees now, not by laws, which can be quite easily issued or revoked. Imagine if you could build your domestic and foreign policy on this basis. It is very convenient: if you want, you can enforce it; if you want, you can cancel it. No Constitution can tell you what to do. And no one will be able to pick on you.

The Ministry of Justice is trying to come up with a new version of the law, which would include the possibility of introducing a special regime, the essence of which is "restrictive measures, but somewhat less than those imposed by the state-of-emergency regime. The "special regime" would not mean the cancellation of elections or the suspension of political party activity, but it would tighten registration measures, place strict controls on the movement of people and vehicles, allow for extensive inspections of vehicles in transit, and introduce curfews.

Regarding freedom of expression, we can say the following. Political organizations are free to operate comfortably only when they are under instruction from Moscow at the highest level to "create," "develop" a program, etc. Government officials give instructions to whomever necessary, and a meeting of constituents is quickly assembled, at which a well-known candidate is elected — in advance. This person alone distributes the funds. Leaders or their family members are paid. No democracy. When this happens, it creates the prerequisites for corruption and theft. The upper echelons are annoyed if anyone tries to object, to express their own point of view. In addition, these figures cannot be forced out, no matter what dirt turns up — even if there are serious grounds to suspect one of them of contract killings, even if it makes the headlines, even if a criminal case is opened against him.

An official Human Rights Prize has been established by Oleg Mironov. The new prize will be awarded annually on Human Rights Day — December 10 — to an individual, a group of individuals, an institution, or a non-governmental public organization in recognition of an outstanding contribution to the cause of human rights. Who is Oleg Mironov and what are his contributions to protecting human rights in Russia? On May 22, 1998, Oleg Mironov moved directly to the position of Commissioner of Human Rights from his job as a prominent bureaucrat in the Communist Party of the Russian Federation (CPRF). On June 5, 1999, anniversary celebrations began in Moscow — a conference to mark the 60th anniversary of day "democratic Russia's" main official human rights defender was born. And, the celebration was announced as a double one — the anniversary was timed to coincide with the anniversary of the Commissioner's assumption of office. To ensure a massive turnout for the celebration, they brought in cadets from one of the military schools in the capital. Western journalists were fooled again. But not Russian journalists — they could tell by the uniform haircuts and the way they carried themselves. Nevertheless, the cadets refused to talk: "Sorry, we were forbidden to talk to the press and to name our educational institution."

In his "Report on the Activities of the Human Rights Commissioner in the Russian Federation," made public at the conference, Oleg Mironov stated the following: "The Ombudsman's office is still in the process of formation.... The process is being held back due to the fact that the status of the Office's personnel, as public servants, has not been resolved." In other words, human rights cannot be protected until all sorts of benefits are provided, for housing, medical care, and pensions. The "Report" consists of 54 pages of various grandiloquent pronouncements, and only 5 pages are devoted to "pressing problems of ensuring human rights in the Russian Federation," in fact, nothing more than tables based on the results of opinion polls conducted in various places on various occasions. This is despite the fact that there are millions of Russians behind bars, millions of disabled people and pensioners on the verge of starvation, millions more unemployed, hundreds of thousands of refugees and internally displaced persons, and thousands more orphans. An impressive staff of about 80 people work diligently to process the one thousand letters and statements a month (according to the commissioner) from suffering citizens. They are organized into dozens of departments, including several secret ones.

All the Ombudsman can boast of is that during his service the organization was granted an office on Myasnitskaya Street, a historic and picturesque street in Moscow. The renovations went on for about six months. Several business trips were made around the country and abroad to exchange experience "within the framework of expanding international cooperation." At the same time, having flown to Cuba, Mironov publicly announced that human rights were fully respected there, and he saw this with his own eyes. This is not surprising, since the best friend of our Commissioner for Human Rights is a like-minded person named Kondratenko, the governor of the Krasnodar Territory, known for his anti-Semitic and racist views. Having gone to one of the military units, the Plenipotentiary reported that the problems of the army were exaggerated (see chapter "Army"). Not in any organization — neither in the Moscow City Court, nor in the Committee of Soldiers' Mothers of Russia, nor in the Foundation "Mother's Rights" (assistance to the parents of dead soldiers), nor in the queue of refugees waiting to be processed and admitted, will you find a single person who needs any help from the Commissioner for Human Rights. So it turns out that the institution of the Commissioner in Russia is just another lie, a smokescreen and only an imitation of activity. Nothing more.

Minister of Justice Valentin Kovalev personally organized the "Foundation for Public Defense of Civil Rights." When Andrei Maksimov, General Director of the Fund, who was also an assistant to Minister Kovalev, was arrested on June 30, 1998, it was found that only about 10% of the money spent by the Fund had been used for statutory purposes. The remaining 90% had been spent on completely irrelevant activities, including trips to Slovakia, Switzerland, Iran, Australia, Indonesia, etc., by the Minister, his family, his aide, and some "useful" people. At the same time expensive real estate was purchased for personal use. In the village of Sukhanovo near Moscow, Valentin Kovalev bought an estate, the total market value of which is close to $600,000. Kovalev's 33 personal accounts at Montazhspetsbank held $255,000 that were not listed on any tax returns. Another $160,000 were found in Rato-Bank. The minister withdrew almost $2 million from his personal accounts in Russian and foreign banks. Is this the salary of a human rights activist and a civil servant? The minister began to think about civil rights only once he was in prison, after he was accused of corruption and embezzlement. While there he wrote: "I consider it an act of intimidation to place the former chairman of the interdepartmental commission of the Security Council of Russia to fight crime and corruption in the Butyr prison, crowded with people accused of criminal offenses, patients with AIDS, syphilis and tuberculosis".

The real human rights defenders are housed at 4 Luchnikov Pereulok, Moscow. For many years now, this site has been the headquarters of some of the most prominent and active human rights organizations such as the Union of Committees of Soldiers' Mothers, the Mothers' Rights Foundation, the Public Center for Assistance to Criminal Justice Reform, the Moscow Research Center for Human Rights, the Independent Psychiatric Association, and the Right to Life and Civic Dignity Society. Beaten and humiliated soldiers often make their way to Luchnikov Lane with one goal in mind: to stay alive (over the years, thousands of them have been saved from death). This space was given to human rights activists when the authorities were flirting with international organizations. Now, when adherence to the democratic course has been practically rejected, human rights defenders are being kicked out of the premises. The official documents related to the eviction of human rights defenders were signed by Mayor Luzhkov and the Presidential Administration. A certain Foundation for Legal Problems of Federalism and Local Self-Government, which is to be given the premises, is headed by none other than Ruslan Orekhov, the former all-powerful head of the Main State Legal Department of the Presidential Administration and long-time opponent of human rights and civil society activists. It was Orekhov who worked so hard in his day to ensure that, for example, the Commission for Pardon and Human Rights did not remain under the President's authority.

A few more details on the human rights situation in the country. Russian society still holds to traditional values in many ways. Homophobia is rampant. In Chelyabinsk, seven gays were murdered in 1998, and an attempt to start their own club was met with opposition from the police. The society tries to ignore persons of non-traditional sexual orientation, and if they draw attention to themselves, the response generally includes indignant calls, angry letters and public appeals to higher authorities. What used to be called "deviance" still rankles those who seek to preserve "moral purity"; they believe that an article about people of unconventional orientation in a newspaper is offensive, has a corrosive effect on the younger generation, and distracts people from the righteous struggle against decadent Western influence. The Duma acts as though its deputies will soon vote for the introduction of censorship and for the execution of homosexuals without trial.

If a Russian citizen finds himself in a difficult situation somewhere abroad, he cannot actually rely on the support of his consulate or embassy. They exist as if for themselves, so that their employees can receive double salaries, dream of a future diplomatic career, or, of course, provide appropriate services for large bribes. They simply won't talk to you and tell you to get out.

As for animal rights, the situation is just tragic. For example, Krasnoyarsk, a city in Siberia, has recently become the center of the "dog business." Stolen pedigree dogs are shipped here from all over Russia for onward shipment to China, where the law that banned keeping pets has recently been repealed, and acquiring a dog is now a sign of wealth. In Krasnoyarsk, the animals are resold to wealthy Chinese; some end up in local restaurants as specialty meat. In various parts of the city, in small rooms, basements, garages and sheds, hundreds of emaciated, starving dogs are kept waiting for their fate. People have called on the authorities in Krasnoyarsk but the police have done nothing about it: there is no *corpus delicti*. Gradually, this business is spreading to other cities of Eastern Siberia. Local "dog dealers" either buy dogs on the cheap or steal them. Often, owners are intimidated and forced to sell their dogs for next to nothing, or the pets may be snatched from the hands of children during walks. The traffickers easily find helpers who are willing to provide fake veterinary certificates, pedigrees and documents to enable them to get the animals through customs.

19. Ecology and Health

People in the former Soviet Union have gotten used to a profound degradation of the environment, even radiation and chemical pollution. After
the Chernobyl accident in Ukraine (1986) , some three million residents in
Russia alone woke up to find themselves in an area of radioactive contami-
nation. A federal program was set up to relocate victims to clean areas. But
today thousands of Chernobyl victims, not having managed to settle on unfamiliar land, without sufficient state support, go back to their native villages,
covered with nuclear ash.s

And it's not only the territories closest to the Chernobyl disaster area
that were contaminated. At the Krasnoufimsk storage facilities of Uralmo-
natsit, a state enterprise, there are drums containing 84,000 tons of monazite
sand, brought in from China and North Korea in the 1940s by the order of
Lavrentiy Beria, the head of the Soviet nuclear program. These barrels emit
2000 micro roentgen per hour. The monazite sand contains 10% radioactive
thorium, as well as rare earth elements.

Thorium was needed to make the atomic bomb. But it was impossible
to extract this element from monazite, and the idea was discarded and the
hazardous sand was piled into wooden grain storage barns on the bank of
the Ufa River. Guards were placed there — and it was all forgotten. In the
course of half a century the sheds rotted away, and the rains mercilessly
poured through the leaky roofs the radioactive raw materials, which were
stored in ordinary wooden crates and even paper sacks. No one gave any
serious thought to the health of the local residents. Later the monazite sand
was transported to Krasnoufimsk. And nobody knows what to do with it
further on.

The northern regions of Russia have also been contaminated. There are, in fact, seven vessels with nuclear reactors on board — six nuclear icebreakers and one nuclear-powered lighter carrier — in the city of Murmansk, with a population of half a million people. Despite all the scandals and denials, Russia continues to pour radioactive waste into the northern seas, especially in areas adjacent to the Novaya Zemlya archipelago, as well as into the Sea of Japan in the Far East.

There is not a bird in the sky over the city of Karabash, in the Sverdlovsk region. There are no trees on the land. You can't breathe the air here, and you can't drink the water. You really can't live in this city. But people do live, knowing that they are condemned to disease and early death. Local residents continue to plant vegetable gardens, catch fish in poisoned rivers, and slowly die — from lead poisoning. Karabash means "Black Head"; it is located near a copper smelting plant built before World War II. In Karabash, they fear the rain and the wind, close the windows tight, and do not walk the streets in the evenings. Karabash has earned notoriety in the international community. The United Nations declared it the most poisoned city on the planet, marking it on maps with a black dot. Acid rain here leads to the death of vegetation; the radiation level exceeds the critical level 15 times. There is also an orphanage nestled on the dreary outskirts of the city, home to fifty young children from 3 to 15 years old who have never heard the chirp of birds or known the taste of clean water. Until a few years ago, the orphanage was in a dilapidated school building without heat, hot water, or medical care.

Excess chemically harmful substances can be obtained in Russia not only in the rain, but also from almost any food. Fields in the USSR, in order to combat pests, were for many years massively pollinated with pesticides containing a substance 24-D, "rich" in dioxins. The same one that the Americans sprayed during the Vietnam War. And only after the Vietnam War, the use of this substance stopped. However, thanks to the long-term and generous sprinkling of this drug on the ground, Russians still face the problem of poisoned vegetables and fruits, which is practically hushed up at the government level.

The quality of drinking water in Russia deserves a separate conversation. About a third of the Russian population, consuming water, is quite at risk. Every third water sample does not meet hygienic and sanitary-chemical requirements. And every fifth reveals the presence of any bacteriological infection. The pollution of seawater in some areas exceeded the norm by 400 times according to bacteriological indicators. Oil products in the water recorded ten times more than the regulatory limits.

According to Greenpeace, the Cheboksary Reservoir, outside of Novo-cheboksarsk, contains dichlorophenolacetic acid (weed killer) and penta-chlorophenol (wood preservative), which indicates the presence of dioxins. In addition, the content of heavy metals like copper and zinc exceeds the maximum permissible concentrations established for fishery reservoirs by two to thirty times. The water of the Kichiginsky Reservoir in the Chely-abinsk region is unsuitable for human consumption. It contains large quantities of phosphorus, organic matter and heavy metals: zinc, copper, lead, cadmium. These are the findings of a scientific study by the children's ecological association "Rostock" from Yuzhnouralsk.

Excess chemicals are found in the rain, but also in almost any food. Fields in the USSR were mass sprayed for years with pesticides containing 24-D, "rich" in dioxins, in order to control pests. The same substance that the Americans sprayed during the Vietnam War. The chemical was still being used until after that war, and by then, there was so much of it soaked into Russian soil that people still face the problem of poisoned fruits and vegeta-bles, which is basically hushed up at the government level.

The quality of drinking water in Russia deserves a separate discussion. Approximately one-third of the Russian population takes great risks when drinking tap water. Every third water sample fails hygienic, sanitary and chemical tests. And every fifth one reveals all sorts of bacteriological contam-ination. Even the seawater in some areas is contaminated by bacteriological indicators exceeded the norm by 400 times. Petroleum products in water were ten times the normative limits.

The concentration of dioxins in Penza's tap water is so high that it can cause serious poisoning. This was established by the Swiss Green Cross, which conducted a water study. The reason is that the Sur Reservoir is surrounded by chemical landfills, where concentrations of dioxins are up to 200,000 the maximum permissible levels. In the late 1950s, ammunition with mustard gas, lewisite, phosgene and prussic acid were destroyed there.

Malfunctions in sewage treatment plants and water supply systems in the villages and towns of Karelia, which stretches from just north of St. Petersburg to the Finnish border, have led to a surge in intestinal infec-tions. In October 1999, nine water supply accidents occurred in the village of Nadvoitsy and 106 people were hospitalized with acute intestinal infection. In the Loukhsky district, a quarter of the students at the Kesteng boarding school were diagnosed with dysentery. In the Medvezhyegorsky district, the number of intestinal infections increased from 86 in 1998 to 331 in 1999. In the district center, the sewage discharge into the river is less than two kilometers from the water intake. The treatment facilities of Velikaya Guba and Poventsa fell into disrepair long ago.

The public water system in Altai Krai system is in such a deplorable state that it poses a health hazard to the population. None of the pipelines from surface water sources has proper treatment facilities so that water disinfection and purification are inadequate; 50% of the water and sewerage networks need repair and that number goes up every day. Some 40% of water wells are out of order or are in emergency condition.

The reservoirs are drying up, too, as elsewhere in the world. As Rybinsk Reservoir gets shallower and shallower, big troubles are ahead for three regions of Russia. One is Cherepovets, the largest city in the Vologda region. Fisheries and one of the largest steel manufacturers, Severstal, a joint-stock company there, are suffering. But most importantly, cattle killed by anthrax were buried in the Cherepovets and Kirillov districts of the Vologda region, and now the remains are exposed as the water evaporates. Yes, all this time the population of the three regions were drinking water from the reservoir where several burial sites were hidden.

An ecological catastrophe that occurred on the Irtysh and Ob rivers may have more terrible consequences than Chernobyl. The course of the Irtysh River cuts closer to the waste dump of the local biofactory, where an anthrax vaccine was developed and had been manufactured for about a century, by one and a half to two meters every spring, and today it's only five meters from the embankment to the official edge of the burial site during floods.

In Tver, within the city limits, there is a similar burial of cattle infected with anthrax that is practically exposed in the open. It was built here 50 years ago. The city had no money to pave over the site, so they simply put up concrete wall.

In Moscow, the Kuzmin Forest Park is a popular holiday destination for Muscovites. There is another cattle farm there where animals who have died of anthrax are buried. All the sanitary regulations were violated at the time of burial: the livestock was not burned, the burial grounds were not covered in concrete, or fenced off, and no sign was put up. The same cattle breeders are located in many places around the capital and Moscow suburbs. New suburbs are being built on sites of former farms, including such animal burials. Meanwhile, no one knows how long the germs can live in such conditions.

Moscow is polluted with mercury waste. The soil is being polluted, and toxic substances are getting into the water supply. Lamps containing mercury, which until recently were used in Russian homes, were simply thrown away at the nearest garbage dump. As a result, increased background mercury is found in every landfill near Moscow. Mercury lamps are also found in 824 medical institutions of the Russian capital.

Based on all of the above, it is not surprising that in many areas of the country, there are hundreds of cases of congenital genetic abnormalities in newborns. In the Russian Republic of Buryatia, in Siberia, for example, up to 150 such cases are registered annually. Most commonly, these are extra fingers, elongated coccyxes (tails), increased hairiness, and extra mammary glands in girls. Doctors report that the same reason is behind a case that is quite unusual in clinical practice: a resident of Ulan-Ude grew "horns," meaning large, hard growths on the sides of his head.

Demographic destruction came as a result of the chaotic transition to a market economy. There has been a catastrophic drop in, among other things, the number of people getting married, much less deciding to have children. The reasons include a general loss of hope and sense of security due to economic instability, rising unemployment, and the collapse of the social system.

The current economic and political transition has also cost the lives of 6 million Russian men. Middle-aged men are dying out at an alarming rate, and those who have survived are suffering from disease, depression, and alcoholism, with rising poverty, unemployment, and crime at their core.

UN reports on Eastern Europe have noted that while life expectancy is rising worldwide, it is stagnant or falling in the former Soviet Union and Eastern Europe. The data on life expectancy for Russian men are the most dire. It is the lowest in the region, at 58 years — ten years less than in China. The gap in life expectancy between women and men in Russia has reached an unprecedented 13 years for developed countries.

Medical care in Russia has long been divided into two categories: first there is the so-called elite medicine, intended exclusively for the leadership of the country, region, and city, and financed from the corresponding budgets, plus a special form of commercial medicine which consists of elite medical institutions.

The commercial sector includes the bulk of the funds and supplies and technical equipment of the entire national medical network for the majority of the population, but all this is used exclusively in the interests of a narrow group of people, primarily those same officials again.

In the public health care sector, the fixed assets are obsolete and worn out, technically already depreciated by 80% or more, and the buildings and communications systems are continually deteriorating. Health facilities charge the general public for everything used: alcohol, syringes, paper, x-ray film, and other things. The reason is that the municipal budgets provide beggarly salaries to the doctors (and even those payments are made only irregularly), some food for patients in the hospitals, and the minimal provision of medicines. The Compulsory Medical Insurance Fund prefers to spend money on countryside mansions for the top officials, foreign trips "for the exchange of experiences," and payment for the needs of the families of the Fund employees.

Pharmaceuticals for the population represent one of the wildest sectors of Russian life. The profits from the super-profitable business of medicines exceed even the profits from oil and vodka. Deputy Prime Minister Valentina Matvienko, who studied this area, concluded: "This area is completely corrupt. Patients are given lists of drugs that they have to buy at their own expense, and the elderly and disabled are denied the benefits they are entitled to by law." In a number of hospitals, basic drugs have disappeared. People are not prescribed the medicines they actually need, but the cheapest and outdated ones on the government order list. In fact, people are officially treated with the wrong drugs!

Serious diseases are becoming more widespread. Here is some data from the Ministry of Health of the Russian Federation, describing the morbidity rate per 100,000 people from 1992 to 1997. The rates of tuberculosis increased from 35.8 to 73.9; syphilis, from 13.4 to 277.3; malignant neoplasm, from 271.6 to 294.3; drug addiction, from 3.5 to 28.4; mental disorders, from 274.3 to 348.2; HIV infection, from 0.05 to 2.7. At the same time, during the same period, the number of hospital facilities went down from 12,600 to 11,500; the number of beds available to the population decreased from 130.8 to 121.0.

Diseases such as tuberculosis, anemia, and poliomyelitis — long considered defeated worldwide, are again rampant in Russia. Tuberculosis was not unknown in Moscow even in the 1980s, but its rapid spread now threatens to affect the rest of the world. The Russian Ministry of Health announced that in 1998 about 25,000 people in Russia had contracted tuberculosis, three percent more than in 1997, and it was spreading 2 to 4 times faster than in Central Europe. One million one hundred thousand Russians in prison and HIV-positive people are the most at risk of TB, but heavy smoking doesn't help, either. One in ten prisoners suffers from serious forms of tuberculosis, while almost one in three suffers from lung tuberculosis.

Desperate people are taking extraordinary measures in hope of extracting money from the state, at least via disability benefits. Russian TB dispensaries are rapidly developing an industry of tuberculosis self-infection for money. Patients who have been declared second-degree invalids sell their sputum full of Koch's bacilli to "less fortunate" colleagues in misery. Desperation pushes the latter to buy a test tube of pathogenic bacilli for a hundred rubles and use it for subsequent self-infection. According to the testimonies of "pseudo-invalids," this works without fail. After swallowing the sputum, the patient returns to the TB Dispensary a month later with a 100% guarantee of testing positive for lung blackouts.

AIDS became a severe problem in this period and the number of AIDS cases registered in Moscow has increased significantly. Russian officials are seriously afraid that in the absence of prevention programs and public information, there will soon be a real epidemic. Mikhail Narkevich of the Ministry of Health cited the following data: as of the end of June, 4,085 out of 15,819 cases of HIV infection in Russia were registered in Moscow Region. The epidemic is taking on threatening proportions in the provinces as well. For example, in Ryazan, 30–40 new cases are recorded every month. The vast majority of HIV-infected people are intravenous drug addicts. The Ryazan Center for AIDS Prevention and Control does not have the capacity to handle such a large number of patients and needs additional specialists and equipment. Many regional budgets do not provide any funds for these needs.

The main reasons for the rapid spread of AIDS are increase of prostitution and drug use, which is aggravated by ignorance of the population about the disease itself and methods of prevention. In Russia, there are more jokes about AIDS than information on how to protect oneself from it. According to Vadim Pokrovsky, president of the Russian Academy of Medical Sciences and head of the Research Center for AIDS Treatment and Prevention, "We are told that many more people die in shootings, so we need to fight crime, and AIDS can wait-perhaps until the real epidemic breaks out."

Meanwhile, the population remains sexually illiterate. Ironically, 13-year-old Russian boys learn about sex from Kama Sutra chewing gum inserts. In Novosibirsk, a scientific center in the heart of Siberia, authorities passed a decree restricting the circulation of sexual products, closing the doors of kiosks and supermarkets to condoms. Now you can buy condoms only in pharmacies (so far without a prescription), and at a very decent price. The fact that condoms are hygienic rather than erotic does not embarrass the Novosibirsk deputies. They declared that from now on condoms will be sold only under appropriate sterile conditions.

In the last five years the sale of drugs in Russia has increased more than fivefold. The number of people who use drugs is up to six million. There are people who start taking drugs at the age of seven; 86% of drug addicts are young people between the ages of 15 and 25. It has been predicted that by the year 2000, the number of drug addicts will double.

According to the Research Institute of Psychiatry, one out of four people in Russia now needs psychological help. And according to the forecasts of the Scientific Center for Mental Health of the Russian Academy of Medical

Sciences, the number of patients with mental disorders caused by social stress in the country will reach 10 million in the coming years.

Even with the closure of the dreaded prison psychiatric hospitals of the USSR Ministry of Internal Affairs in 1988, there has been no dramatic change for the better in Russian psychiatry. No one has apologized to this day to his own people for the abuse of people's mental health in the Soviet state. The truthful history of Soviet punitive psychiatry is hushed up. Individuals seeking rehabilitation find that the relevant government agencies are blatantly unwilling to deal with their cases. Most former prisoners of psychiatric dungeons are simply afraid to face it again. There are no judges, courts, or attorneys dedicated to protecting the rights of persons with mental disabilities. In the emergency departments of psychiatric hospitals, people who are admitted on an emergency basis are pressured (with threats, intimidation) to give their consent to hospitalization in order to spare the doctors from the judicial procedure. The problem of the legal competence of a citizen to establish his or her sanity has not been solved.

Patients in psychiatric clinics, who spend months and years in hospitals, are harmed by the low level of funding, which is purely symbolic. Such patients are allotted 8 rubles a day for food. What can we feed an adult person for that amount of money? That is why one diagnosis is accompanied by another — dystrophy. It already became normal years ago for patients in hospitals to weigh in at 30 to 40 kilograms (66–88 lbs). But going to the hospital also implies receiving treatment. For that, 58 kopecks (about 2 cents) a day are allocated.

The atmosphere in psychiatric hospitals is one of boorishness and cruelty. Social and psychological factors are not taken into account in the treatment of patients. Psychiatrists do not view the mentally ill as individuals and therefore do not bother to communicate with them. Most psychiatrists rely on medication-assisted treatment, which involves the use of psychotropic substances, including the drug LSD, electroshock, and lobotomy. In the Angarsk psychoneurological boarding school, mentally ill women are simply and without further ado sterilized.

Psychiatric hospitals with strict supervision are located separately from other psychiatric hospitals, and their activities are completely isolated from public observation. There is data that reveals the existence of secret shelters. The former Seraphim-Ponetaevsky Monastery in the Nizhny Novgorod region contains several hundred women injured in chemical industries. The departmental affiliation of this mysterious shelter has not yet been determined. There are suspicions that the people contained in it are considered as objects of testing new psychotropic substances and organ donation.

20. The FSB

When the FSB officers declare that their basic goals are to ensure the security of the individual citizens, the society and the state, it is the state that takes priority in this list. They should say that they ensure the security of the state, society, and individuals, in that specific order. Any attention that remains after taking care of the state is turned to society, but almost no one is concerned with personal security in Russia. Unless we mean turning their attention to identifying threats from individuals side to the security of the state in order to neutralize them promptly. At the same time, instead of the presumption of innocence, we see the presumption of guilt, which they considered justified back in the bloody 1930s. You are guilty already because you live here. "Think about the ordinary people, improve the life of the ordinary people" — these are the most cynical, but also the most often used words uttered by the FSB leadership

Here is how much the ordinary people matter. Two vice-mayors of Omsk — the head of the Department of Economics Yuri Fedotov and the head of the Department of Finance Vladimir Volkov — made a joint statement published in the newspaper *Vremya MN*. The vice-mayors were told that their phones were being tapped, and they themselves saw signs that the special services were watching them closely. They warned the public not to be surprised if "drugs" or "weapons" were found. They might also be accused of organizing an attempt on the first vice-governor of the Omsk region.

On November 28, 1998, the newspaper *Kommersant* published an open letter from the oligarch and politician Boris Berezovsky, in which he accused former FSB director Nikolai Kovalev of colluding with a number of FSB generals who had incited their subordinates to kill him when he was the

CIS executive secretary. Also, Alexander Litvinenko has repeatedly stated that his boss, General Khokholkov, had instructed him to kill Berezovsky. Litvinenko[1] was immediately accused of abuse of office.

Russia's main Military Prosecutor's Office claims that it has data that Litvinenko widely practiced so-called "forceful methods": he broke into premises, beat people, and also extorted bribes. At the same time, the prosecutor's office notes that Litvinenko's criminal case is absolutely unrelated to the scandalous Berezovsky v. FSB case.

Pressuring the press has become an everyday practice in political life. In fact, elements of censorship have been reintroduced. Both the FSB and the ruling party thought that the press should all adhere to a certain uniform order. Analytical articles are to be written by officials from the department concerned, not by outside observers. It is not known who will perform their direct duties at this time. These articles will be "posted" in the media — mainly in regional newspapers. That is, regional newspapers must print only what the center tells them to print. The number of journalists from news agencies and television companies accredited at the government center should be greatly reduced. It's a problem when not enough information is given out, but too much information is even worse.

The FSB says that the government is not interested in press conferences. The Prime Minister met with the heads of newspapers and news agencies, and that is enough. The most one can hope for is that an analytical article will be issued by some official in cases that are "expedient for the government." If the situation obviously gets out of hand and the government has to cancel the elections, the media will be even more needed to justify its actions. The government is insulated from the press.

In order to make sure only "the right news" is broadcast to Russians, "bad" television stations will have to be shut down and "harmful" newspapers closed. And also the "agencies" seek to get "their" people into all media outlets. In the US, it is interesting to see how many broadcasters have completely changed their stripes over the years, from "independent" to Party-line mouthpieces, whether Republican or Democrat, and changing the definition of "liberal" or "conservative" whichever way the wind blows.

---

[1] This is the FSB lieutenant colonel who defected to the UK, signed on with MI6, and later was poisoned to death in London. Needless to say, this crime was pinned on Russia, but it is obvious that such a trick would backfire. This and related transparent false flags against double agents, designed to smear the victim country, are debunked by Nicholas Kollerstrom in his book *The Novichok Chronicles: A Tale of Two Hoaxes* Veterans Today, at https://www.veteranstoday.com/2021/06/11/the-novichok-chronicles-a-tale-of-two-hoaxes/

Russian phones may be tapped and there is no way to control it. This would still sound scandalous, if it weren't for the AT&T scandal of 2013, when "AT&T was voluntarily selling phone records to the CIA."[1]

As the Internet and messaging apps become more popular, these too are monitored in both countries — ostensibly for offensive content involving terrorists, con artists, foreign spies, drug peddlers and pornography distributors; but as in the US, politically inconvenient information is also filtered out and made "undiscoverable," one way or another. As for personal data, in 2006 AT&T was found to have warrantless wiretap rooms for the NSA — a permanent set-up for funneling internet traffic data from its switching station in San Francisco directly to the NSA.[2]

Internet providers in Russia are required to provide the FSB with a connection that is at least as fast as the connection for any other client. And that's not all. The Federal Security Service has come up with the so-called the System of Operative Investigative Measures-2 (SORM-2), proposing unrestricted control over electronic communications in Russia. The previous SORM project (or now we can say SORM-1) provided for full control over telephone conversations. SORM-2 eliminates the need for the FSB to obtain a court authorization to "wiretap" someone. It seems to bear some similarity to aspects of the US PATRIOT Act of 2001. There are no technical limitations, as well as no obligations to disclose any aspects of this activity. SORM-2 is not a law, but a departmental act. Neither the Parliament nor the President has any say over it; and it will not be made public.

Nothing should escape the watchful eye of the heirs of the KGB — from matters at the federal level to the personal problems of ordinary citizens. Together with the Ministry of Communications, the FSB aims to directly regulate the content of websites (that is, to decide what you can write on your site and what you can't). In this sense, nothing has changed in Russia; the soldiers of the invisible front are still on duty. Obviously, all the work to install eavesdropping and spying apparatuses is paid for using taxpayers' money. People end up paying more for their connection and use of the Internet. At the same time, the FSB has no plans to disseminate information via the Internet. The Defense and Interior Ministries' websites are still

---

[1] *North Carolina Journal of Law & Technology*, November 12, 2013, Kelly Morris. https://ncjolt. org/blogs/att-sells-phone-records-to-the-cia-insisting-its-lawful/

[2] "AT&T has asked a court to suppress documents leaked to the Electronic Frontier Foundation by an ex-employee detailing how the company indiscriminately diverted domestic and international traffic to the National Security Agency for warrantless wiretapping," https://boingboing.net/2006/04/12/att-built-warrantles.html. Cory Doctorow, April 12, 2006.

"under development." Official Moscow practically ignores the World Wide Web.

Here, the Russians seem to have been ahead of the Americans, who only installed George H.W. Bush as President in 1989. The Russian authorities developed a pattern of appointing former FSB chiefs to the post of prime minister or president. The last three Russian prime ministers came out of the depths of the security services. This has nothing to do with their desire to continue any reforms. All the PM has to do is to discredit and neutralize his opponents, and who better to do this than an experienced member of the security services who is well versed in behind-the-scenes machinations? Moreover, the Kremlin is interested in former policemen and secret-service workers, inflexible people who can be absolutely ruthless to their opponents. They write forecasts, analyze the situation in the country. They organize influence campaigns against opponents, including in the press. They can organize harassment and legal or physical persecution. They have a knack for such things, and they are well trained for this.

Vagif Huseynov, a former chairman of Azerbaijan's KGB, works as an advisor to Moscow Mayor Luzhkov and heads the firm Region, a subsidiary of Sistema, which is responsible for providing information and analytical support for the Moscow mayor's political activities. President of Azerbaijan Heydar Aliyev is demanding that Vagif Huseynov be extradited to Azerbaijan because he is considered a national criminal there. The former chief of security of Georgia, Igor Giorgadze, also works in agencies close to Yuri Luzhkov; he, too, is considered at home to be a dangerous criminal, accused of organizing an attempted assassination of Georgian President Eduard Shevardnadze. Giorgadze got a job in Moscow thanks to his friendly relations with Joseph Ordzhonikidze, deputy prime minister of the capital. Former deputy chairman of the KGB Bobkov works as an adviser to millionaire and media tycoon Gusinsky. Kryuchkov, former Chairman of the KGB, and Shebarshin, his successor, also found suitable jobs. With such people no one will be able to avoid *kompromat* and persecution. This means there will be further gutting of the government agencies: business, industry, finance, media, etc. Just look at the utterances of the *siloviki* ("strongmen," veterans of the security services police and armed forces — the term *siloviki* became commonplace under Yeltsin in the early 1990s). For example, Stepashin, former head of the counterintelligence service, former Justice Minister, former interior minister, and former prime minister, has publicly stated that "expediency may be more important than legality."

Stepashin, a lifelong member of the "agencies," played a decisive role in the outbreak of the Chechen war, and his influence in the conduct of hostilities was also enormous. This war cost the lives of 100,000 people, mostly civilians. The Kremlin considered Stepashin an expert on national issues. He also participated in the 1989 operation to restore order in Fergana, Uzbekistan, an operation ordered by the Political Bureau of the Central Committee of the Communist Party of the Soviet Union (CPSU), where the agencies also displayed great brutality.

Appointing people from the FSB to leading roles in the government is intended to intimidate regional leaders, whose influence has significantly increased in recent years. The FSB knows all their background and can use this information to discredit them. Politicians who came out of the FSB/KGB do not serve a specific person or even the state, but their own ideas of expediency and order. The mindset and the soul of such people goes with the peculiarities of their field of work. Hence, the habit of not looking into their interlocutor's eyes, deliberate impassivity, isolation, ability to impose their will and break it on the "target." The reason why Prime Minister Putin's rating has gone up is that he emerged as a political leader while remaining a cipher: his economic views, personal qualities and even hobbies remained unknown. In addition, he is secretive and ambitious, and since his student days he has avoided noisy company. If such people get their hands on power, the era of "liberal" liberties will come to an end. Power in Russia has never promoted the moral center of the individual. Proclaiming the image of Russia's future leader with the face and psychology of a KGB investigator is the surest way to unmask Russian so-called democracy and Russian so-called liberals and show the country, the world, and ourselves what Russia is really about.

A large number of former intelligence officers got jobs in the State Duma [parliament] as assistants to deputies, in committees on security and international politics. Hundreds of former KGB officers are now working in business organizations and public associations as lead consultants or managers. Many KGB officers are at the head of firms, like the former chief of illegal intelligence, Yury Drozdov, whose job was to train "illegals": the deep cover spies who would live in foreign countries completely blending in as natives. Others are listed as advisers to banks; they knock money out of failed clients, using all their arsenal of intimidation.

21. The Police and the Tax Police

The post-Soviet impoverishment of the population has driven more people back into the class of the lumpen proletariat. [Yes, in the 1970s and 1980s people generally felt secure.] Now, many people are forced to go and work wherever they can and still somehow get paid and, most importantly, actually receive the money they earn. The police are paid, but they do not have to deal with the best of people. The poorer the people, the more of them are just squeaking by. But what is unique to the Russian situation is that police officers are among the latter group.

A person who serves in the police is no longer a person. For the people, he's a "cop," an undefined, angry, uniformed individual who makes every effort to show you his power, to shove you into a jail for the slightest reason, and, if you complain, to beat you up too, threatening to "pin a case against you" — that is, to accuse you of committing one of the unsolved crimes, of which every investigator has plenty to check off on his list.

Many members of the police force are returning veterans. Many policemen are obviously below average intellect, and many of them are also alcoholics. In the auxiliary police units one can see even more signs of retarded development — it is not unknown for employees to have completed only two grades and to be registered in a psychiatric hospital.

It is strange that there is no question about the fact that these people are allowed to carry weapons. By comparison, during active combat operations in Dagestan, a militiaman who wished to defend his village could only obtain a weapon after presenting 12 certificates from law enforcement and medical institutions. Guards at private companies constitute a class of their own who carry out a significant proportion of armed attacks and beatings of citizens. Mentally unstable and armed, after serving in Afghanistan, Abkhazia, Tajikistan and Chechnya, they may beat their family members. But they are considered "real tough guys." Until the first big scandal involving robbery or brutal abuse.

Sometimes police officers, who are not entitled to free public transporta-tion, get caught by controllers. What do they do then? Very simple. They call for help from their colleagues, who take the controllers out of the bus or trolley and beat them up in the nearest alley, taking away their IDs and telling them not to show up around here again. Therefore, controllers prefer not to mess with people who might, based on their appearance, be members of the police services and limit themselves to harassing passive citizens, such as women, teenagers and the elderly.

The powerful international NGO Human Rights Watch prepared and published a report entitled, "Confession at any price: Torture in the Russian police," in 1999. After two years of monitoring and collecting material, they concluded that the police in Russia systematically practice beating and torture even in trivial cases, for example, in order to get a person to confess that he stole a jacket.

[The idea of planting evidence or entrapping someone in order to "solve" a nagging open case or to enhance the performance statistics is not unique to any one country. The US is Number One in police brutality worldwide,[1] beating Russia, China, Haiti, even Somalia and North Korea. But the sheer visibility of policemen and police cars, on peaceful suburban streets as much as on the "bad side of town," is quite American. Maybe because, as the saying goes, "that's where the money is" and fines are easily collected without any risk of exerting oneself. And let's not even mention the abusive cases of Maria Butina, Julian Assange and others.

[In the Wild West that Russia became in the 1990s, there was certainly an astounding breakdown of civility in many ways. Despair gave rise to huge increases in drunkenness, casinos popped up like mushrooms, pornography and prostitution were everywhere, and gypsies roamed the streets to pick pockets and steal. Desperate poverty led to abandonment of children, who roamed the street without a sufficient "social safety net" to take them in. None had been needed before. There would have been plenty of legitimate work for the police, but they, too, were caught up in the mayhem and general breakdown of discipline and social norms that accompanied the political and economic chaos.]

---

[1] "Countries With The Most Police Brutality: The numbers in these countries are alarming..." in *The Richest* [online], https://www.therichest.com/shocking/15-countries-with-the-most-police-brutality/, Rhiannon_D, Nov 21, 2016

Law enforcement officers, accustomed to permissiveness within the police state, "short-circuit" much more often than normal people. Policemen get drunk and go on a rampage in cafes, restaurants, on the streets, breaking furniture, insulting people, harassing women, and demanding free service. Anyone who dares to object suffers brutality, even torture. And FSB special operatives have no control whatsoever. They can even pick on police officials, if they cross the wrong man. This actually happened in the prestigious waterfront resort city of Sochi, where Commissioner Kasinov of the Department for Combating Economic Crime was viciously attacked.

Also in Sochi, the entire staff of a café, "Charm," was beaten up by the FSB's special Alpha team. Over 10 masked men beat them with batons, first on the street and then they dragged everyone inside. This "Alpha" detachment is based in Sochi, which is not only a casino town but is located at the strategically-important edge of the Caucasus Mountains. And the Alpha Group just can't get enough of the hot spots in the Caucasus. The unit already has its own Hero of Russia. These brave guys, picked from all over the country (and one girl who lost all her loved ones in Chechnya) train day and night. They can do things that no other squad of the police can do, including kidnapping and torture without a trace of sympathy for their victims. They really are "special." They don't hold any psychological talks with the squad members, and they don't need to. They are raised as vicious hounds, ready to bite at the first command from their master.

Vehicular traffic has increased significantly in recent years, and the ambitions of the Traffic Police have grown proportionately. Inspectors of the State Traffic Safety Inspectorate (GIBDD), have unprecedented authority. In practice, they alone arbitrarily determine the amount of the fine for a traffic violation. They name such sums that it is always easier for a driver to "agree" with the inspector than to pay the maximum. Earlier in Russia, there was a point system of penalties, which everyone knew. In order not to lose their license for a few minor violations, everyone was ready to pay off the annoying man-with-a-baton, if at least he did not put the ominous points on the ticket. Nowadays, the traffic police can also take away one's car for almost any violation of traffic rules. This law appears to be related to a new policy of the Ministry of Internal Affairs to use administrative measures to reduce the traffic flow by at least 20%. Now the inspector has the right to detain a car and send it to the impound lot if it is not properly registered, up to date with inspection, or has any defects that, according to the traffic rules, require it to stay off the road. In sum, based on the road traffic rules in force in Russia, almost any car, even a brand new one, can be declared unfit for operation. This unambiguously opens up enormous opportunities for bribes and abuses.

$ Material evidence against the police — records, papers documenting abuses — disappear into the bowels of the police headquarters and the prosecutor's office without a trace. It doesn't cost much to get someone in a prison cell eliminated: sometimes just some minor privileges for certain prisoners. At the well-known cafe "Elephant" in the center of Moscow, investigators and other police officers gather, and they meet with guys they know among the criminal and official realms to discuss the details of various sensitive cases. And sometimes they simply reduce the years for a verdict, for cash, at the prevailing rate. Both the upper and the middle ranks of the law enforcement agencies have employees with ties to the criminal world.

In this long period of transition to "a better future," whatever form that may take, the people of the country are tired of waiting for positive changes that will show an improvement in their lives. Right now it is simply impossible to improve the economy significantly, in ways that ordinary citizens can see and appreciate, due to the current methods of economic management. [For some insights into the role played by experts from Harvard, helpfully guiding the transition, see David McClintick's article, "How Harvard Lost Russia."[1]] But any institution has to justify its existence to average citizens. This includes law enforcement agencies. When they have to sacrifice someone in order to "show results," they have their own hierarchy of potential targets. They need to identify murderers and corrupt officials, and get the sentenced, because otherwise the guilt is not proven. But there's a problem with that. Officially, the judiciary, FSB and police consider many high-profile murders solved, but no one has heard about any convictions. In order to maintain the prestige of the departments, to bring at least one case to trial, and to make the sacrifice so eagerly awaited by public opinion, the law enforcement agencies actively fabricate political cases under the guise of criminal cases.

In the summer of 1998, a criminal case was opened against the State Statistics Committee (now the Russian Statistical Agency). The investigation resulted in charges of embezzlement totaling more than $3 million against seven high-ranking employees of the committee. Initially, however, the head of the statistical agency, one of Russia's most professional economists, Yuri Yurkov, was accused of underreporting real data, thereby increasing the size of the shadow economy. This level of accusation speaks to the political

---

[1] The best and brightest of America's premier university came to Moscow in the 1990s to teach Russians how to be capitalists. This is the inside story of how their efforts led to scandal and disgrace. *Institutional Investor*, January 13, 2006, at https://www.institutional-investor.com/article/b150npp3q49x7w/how-harvard-lost-russia .

background underpinning the entire case, which was later covered up as a mere criminal case. It says a lot that in Russia, all major cases are primarily political, and so are the sentences. When criminal charges are levied against high-ranking officials there is hidden revenge, envy, and the active use of the FSB patronage. There is no point in counting on a fair verdict.

In one well-known case the head of the Main Department of Police on Execution of Punishments was arrested, accused of taking a bribe of several hundred thousand dollars. This money was supposedly paid to him in order to get someone who was in prison punished using traditional gangster methods, but not by the methods of state justice. This was done, in part, in order for everyone to understand that even in a maximum security prison you cannot escape from the long arm of the state mafia. This speaks volumes. Unless, of course, it is just another blow-up case against the same head of the Main Department of Police for Execution of Punishments.

The government constantly threatens to take even tougher measures against crime. But despite all the agencies, offices and institutions devoted to security, the internal affairs bodies, the armed forces, and the rest of the law enforcement agencies, has managed to suppress (much less prevent) encroachments on state power: terrorism, insurgent incursions, and assassinations of high-ranking officials. After the explosions in the high-rise buildings, the FSB promised to take all 30,000 residential buildings in Moscow under their control, but this is not realistic, given that the authorities are unable to cope even with everyday crime. Nationalists and fighters for the faith are raising their heads. International financial scandals involving the country's leaders are undermining their reputations. Laws in Russia are in utter chaos — at first glance they it looks perfectly fine, but it is simply impossible to reconcile the various laws, bylaws, and official instructions. Any instruction can be interpreted completely arbitrarily by any authority.

The Russian Ministry of Internal Affairs tried to take into account the requirements of the UN in the training of the of personnel

The All-Russian Institute of Advanced Training of the Ministry of Internal Affairs of the Russian Federation has approached the training of its personnel in the light of United Nations requirements. There's a hitch, though: One of these requirements is proficiency in English. It is understood that, in performing international tasks, a police officer must maintain relations with his foreign colleagues. But inside the country, the idea is laughable. Russians know their police too well. The image comes to mind of some policemen beating up some drunk in the police station at night, swearing in English.

Many senior law enforcement officials are increasingly politicizing and ideologizing their activities, putting pressure on the investigation process, including directly and indirectly influencing the investigation of criminal cases. The Minister of Justice was given the task of identifying violations of the law by any means necessary so that reprisals can be taken. When giving the directive to prohibit or deny access to something, the authorities list, point by point, what violations must be found. But they are not interested at all in what is really going on. There is, in fact, no investigation. Everything is known in advance. The orders of the authorities are to be executed unconditionally.. The Ministry of Internal Affairs is able to "mercilessly screen out" candidates for the new State Duma on the basis of "criminal" criteria. It may even publish operational information in the press and on television. Thus, the ministry becomes the second Central Election Committee, only with much greater power, and is actually going to determine the degree of criminalization of this or that candidate for the State Duma.

The current Minister of Internal Affairs, Vladimir Rushailo, has been notable for his increased cruelty since his time at the Moscow Regional Directorate for Organized Crime. It is said that there was no place more terrible than his department. Those who got there are in for trouble. They are treated as if they were not only outlaws, but not human at all. Many in the government turn a blind eye to this, believing that Rushailo can operate on the edge of the law, as long as he fights terrorism effectively.

Victor Malaya, the head of the Bibirevo district of the capital, was arrested right in the military hospital. He was astonished to learn from the investigator that he had been under round-the-clock surveillance for two years. Two hidden video cameras were working in his office day and night, and 140 special cassettes were recorded. He was charged with bribery. As the operatives themselves say, such close surveillance applies to either high-flying criminals or foreign spies. Every minute of such surveillance costs the state a lot of money. It is not known exactly how much the taxpayers shelled out for watching this official, but the indictment says that this dangerous criminal received a bribe of, first, 1500 rubles, then another three times in the same amount, and finally gave a bribe of 450 rubles himself. Against the general background of corruption in Russia, this looks ridiculously petty, to say the least.

Yury Lushnikov, a former prosecutor of the Stavropol Krai, Lieutenant General of Justice, who has been give the awards of Honorary Prosecutor of the USSR, Honored Lawyer of Russia, and who did not receive a single reprimand in 28 years of service, openly spoke about corruption in the Prosecutor's Office and the criminal activities of Nazir Khapsirokov, the office manager. He was thrown out in the street in a flash.

Meanwhile, several criminal cases were opened against Nazir Khapsirokov in connection with Yuginvest company, the Federal Food Corporation, and the renovation of the building of the St. Petersburg Prosecutor's Office, which were immediately shut down once he appeared in the Prosecutor General's Office. It is not known how many tens of millions of budget dollars were stolen in these scams. While working as a case manager, he built himself two luxurious mansions in the Republic of Karachaevo-Cherkessia, territorially part of Stavropol Krai. With his assistance, Deputy Prosecutor General of Russia Skuratov Rozanov and Demin bought government cottages for $60,000 and $70,000 respectively, although cottages like these cost much more than that. This happened at a time when there was no financing available for the regional prosecutor's offices. In particular, in 1996–1998, the Prosecutor's office of Stavropol Region has not received a penny for these purposes. However, on July 29, 1996, the krai prosecutor's office paid 70 million rubles for his and Skuratov's personal flight from Mineralnye Vody to Yekaterinburg on demand of Hapsirokov. In just a few months of 1999, the Prosecutor General's Office "scraped through" Moscow banks 1.3 billion rubles and did not pay salaries to its employees for months.

For the most part, law enforcement is financed from the budget and they suffer from a chronic shortage of funds. The only source of funding is from fines imposed administratively by internal affairs departments. Corruption is rampant among the police, whose salaries are too low. Many moonlight as security guards for criminal leaders. And now they also protect the Russians from the "nigger invasion," as they themselves say. Slavs are ten times less likely than those with dark skin to have their passports checked on the streets, simply because their faces are Slavic. And this despite the fact that the vast majority of criminal gangs in the country are made up of Slavs or Jews. At the same time in Russia they say there is no propiska [residency permit], only registration, and no chauvinism, but only healthy patriotism.

The police do not hide their pleasure when their chief is nominated for any state office. At this time there is a lively and businesslike atmosphere in the Interior Ministry. Telegrams are sent out all over the country in which the heads of the departments are instructed to cancel vacations, leaves and business trips for their personnel until further notice. Each new head of any law enforcement ministry of Russia (Interior, Defense, Tax Service, Intelligence, etc.) removes previous chiefs from key positions in the ministry and appoints his own people. In this case, the merits of the existing officials are not taken into account. It is like in the times of the pharaohs in ancient

Egypt. Serious purges in all branches of the ministries are primarily designed to ensure the personal power of the new head, who, like President Yeltsin, is trying to hold on to his post forever. As for serious political technologists and analytical PR centers, there are none in the police department. Through the Ministry of the Interior and the Tax Police, the authorities are attempting to block the activities of commercial entities that fund unsatisfactory governors. But most of the militia, though subordinate to the Ministry, live in the regions under the same governors. So tax administrations can do better, because to influence financial flows, you have to at least be able to do that.

The US Internal Revenue Service (IRS) is proposing a joint investigation of the Bank of New York scandal. The Tax Service declares that it is ready to cooperate. Apparently the FSB and the Home Office are in constant contact with the relevant authorities in the United States, and they are constantly exchanging information. But let's see who the Americans are working with and what the Federal Tax Police Service (FSPP) is doing in Russia.

Vladimir Avdiysky is the right hand of Vyacheslav Soltaganov, the head of the tax department. Avdiysky was commissioned as an advisor to the director, but immediately presented to the appointment of the deputy director. Avdiyski is a career police officer. Like Soltaganov, he fought against the theft of socialist property for many years. Then he joined the tax police. He rose to the rank of head of the Tax Audit Office, received a major general. But in December 1995, he resigned from the Federal Tax Police Service because he came to the attention of the intelligence agencies. He was charged with a "quick investigation" on suspicion of corruption. As a result of the research, a lot of interesting things came to light. It turns out, since 1989, Avdiysky was registered with the KGB of the USSR as the leader of a criminal Azerbaijani group named Adik. For a long time he worked in Baku, participated in work with Baku criminal groups. When the Tax Police inspected the firm "Living World," the head of Zhurkin's firm explicitly stated that "the strategy of specific financial transactions was carried out personally by Avdijsky." According to the merchant, he also directed the company's accountant. However, when a criminal case was started over the concealment of the firm's profits, on a large scale, something unexpected happened: the head of "The Living World" Zhurkin was killed. The End of the road.

Valery Yampolsky, former first deputy director of the Federal Tax Police Service (FSNP), was also suspected of having links with organized crime. There were materials suggesting he had contacts with groups of smugglers. In 1995, the FSB decided to detain a group of criminals smuggling cash. They caught everyone red-handed at the airport — the smugglers were carrying

$150,000 from Hungary. But right at the gangway of the plane, General Yampolsky met the couriers and personally led them through the VIP lounge. Subsequently, it turned out that the VIP for smugglers was paid by the tax police. That is the Russian treasury. The capture team did not dare to contact the first deputy director. Subsequently, Lieutenant General Yampolsky was forced to resign, but not for long; there are rumors that Soltaganov intends to bring Yampolsky back.

The authorities of the Moscow tax police extorted $300,000 from the commercial bank "National Credit Partnership," which the bank had accepted from its client in repayment of a loan. According to the tax police, the money belonged to a charitable foundation supporting the tax police themselves. This was accompanied by threats, the appearance of special forces in the bank, promises to arrange a "beautiful life" personally for the bankers themselves and a few of their clients. The tax authorities modified their demand and only required that bank employees had to bring $300,000 in cash to the tax police building. When the vice-president of the bank asked how he could just take this money out of the bank and cash it, and stuff it into suitcases, Migunov, head of the bank control department of the Moscow tax police, replied: "We will remove the verification protocol and we will not touch you."

An attempt to bring suit against the tax police by the State Duma Anti-Corruption Commission and the Moscow City Prosecutor's Office received responses that re-characterized the overt blackmail and threats by the police as simply "tactless behavior." All this shows that the department clans (that is, police, prosecutorial, tax, army) have the same status in Russia as "gangster" clans. The mafia is given a state status, in which the fight against corruption becomes meaningless. If it goes on like this, soon individual criminal groups will announce the initiation of criminal cases in Russia "according to the rules." This is the most dangerous trend in Russian society. I wonder who gets the money from funds such as the supposed foundation to support the tax police?

The heads of the State Tax Inspectorate divisions steal almost openly — who would dare to check on the head of a group endowed with such control and punitive functions? It has gotten to the point that the bosses simply order the chief accountant to issue money from the cash desk and write it off as being spent on various household needs. The accountants comply — otherwise, they can say goodbye to their job.

Ordinary tax audits can be carried out by armed police. By assigning this job to the tax police, the government actually recognizes that it is impossible to collect taxes in a civilized way in Russia. According to the police, business owners are driven by criminal instincts; and according to the majority of the Russian population, it's the tax system that is abnormal. Lawyers add their own view: Russian tax rules are such that "violations" could be found by anybody at any point, if they wanted to. The tax police can crack down on anyone; this makes them a weighty tool in the political struggle. On the eve of the elections, one of the most important people is the director of the tax police. A lot depends on him: he can influence any business and state structures however his "masters" require. Their most important weapon is the seizure of documentation. When it comes to seizing documentation, it does not even matter if the company was certified by the head of the State Tax Service the previous year.

We should add to all of the above a few words about the Russian customs office. Russian customs works according to a plan, with targets, just like the police. This includes the collection of duties, proceeds from confiscated goods, and paperwork. With every new plan, they need to confiscate more, and draw up all sorts of new documents. Many of the border crossings have long been recognized by foreigners and Russian tourists alike as legalized nests of thieves, where travelers' wallets are lightened by the friendly efforts of border guards and customs officers. At Russian Customs there are continuous levies. Most fines and car seizures are illegal. If the customs officers calculate that you are carrying a bit more than the rules allow or something else does not comply with one of their other strict rules, then you will not be let go. And you will have no recourse. The issue will not be solved by going through lawyers; you will be forced to give up some of your property or pay a bribe. Customs officers circulate around the rows of trucks, pick out any vehicles they think they can get some money from, and block them from entering Russian territory. The barrier lowered and they offer the drivers one solution: to accept an escort vehicle, appointed by customs, which will follow the tractor trailer anywhere across the expanses of our homeland, whether to Moscow or to Vladivostok. Where they will have to be paid. Or you can pay less, but pay it now, up front. The constantly increasing pressure to increase duty collection plus the growing appetite of bribe-takers standing at the border will soon be completely impossible to fulfill.

22. The Military

[When Vladimir Putin came to power in 1999, his two most daunting challenges were to turn around the social and economic decline and to yank the military forces back into position #1. It has been said that the Russians had a 25-year plan to overhaul their military and to come up with weaponry based on technical innovations using properties of physics that were not yet well understood.

[By 2018, international experts were noting that the Russians had developed fighter jets that could out-perform anything in the West, in every parameter from maneuverability to evading radar, and their new missile systems practically defy belief (at an exponentially lower cost than what the US produces). And most of Washington, to this day, does not believe it, although the evidence has been shown in technical data and in practice. Arguably, Mr. Putin's team has succeeded, while the West thought it was all bluff.]

Optimally one sets both long-term and short-term goals, but from Mr. Sidorov's perspective, normal countries would base their military policies on the real needs and capabilities of a particular nation at a particular time, not on vague notions of "geostrategic interests." This is what he saw in the late 1990s.

The "new Russia" has neither the strength nor the means to handle a new confrontation based on ideological conflict. After working fiercely for decades and winning the arms race by the late 1970s, it already fell behind again. As of the late 1990s, Moscow has nothing to counter the United States, which is taking advantage of its superiority. Therefore, Russia has adopted the tactics of vague nuclear threats. Russia is trying to present itself as a reform-oriented country (in the hope of an early IMF loan and still expecting to be accepted into the Western "club" since it dropped both "communism" and empire), but it is obviously very vulnerable right now and so it never misses an opportunity to shake its military arsenals, which have not melted away. Both militarily and politically, Russia is too weak to play the role of a European regional power except in cooperation with NATO.

Russia has long recognized the North Atlantic Alliance as a competitor, but even so it has invariably participated in joint military contingents intended to monitor compliance with the conditions set by NATO. Moscow has long felt that the expansion of NATO to the east, drawing in more and more of the former socialist countries that had been part of Russia's alliance, represents an aggressive intent on the part of NATO despite their constant assertions of only being defensive in nature. This trend belies the West's smiling reassurances, as they not only enrolled Russia's neighbors in NATO but moved in with military trainers and set up "pro-democracy" groups and a wide range of organizations for political influence.

The State Duma considers that in the army now: "There are only 12 combat ready regiments in the Combined Arms formations. Their weaponry is dominated by outdated missile systems, and there are practically no modern anti-tank missile systems. A significant part of the fleet of armored vehicles consists of outdated models of tanks and armored personnel carriers. Combat, transport-combat and transport helicopters in service with the ground forces do not meet modern requirements. Many of them are in a faulty condition and require repair."

In the Russian Air Force, no more than 55% of the aircraft are serviceable. The service life of their strategic nuclear weapons is expiring. In 2001, the operational life of air-launched strategic cruise missiles ends; by 2003, only about 1,000 warheads will remain in the composition of Russia's strategic nuclear forces. Already at present, the capabilities of the strategic nuclear forces of the Russian Federation are 2.5 times lower than the nuclear forces of the United States. Along with this, a significant part of the personnel, scientific, technical and industrial potential has been lost [in large part, through recruitment/emigration to higher paying countries], the reproduction and modernization of elements of strategic nuclear forces have practically stopped.

In the Navy, over 70% of strategic missile submarines need factory repairs or other work in order to maintain their combat readiness. Of the existing 26 nuclear submarines, almost half are morally and technically obsolete. On the remaining submarines, 75% of the warheads should be removed from operation by 2003. The servicemen have found themselves in an extremely difficult social situation. As of October 12, 1998, the Ministry of Defense received only 36.8% of the approved budget, so that salaries, housing and maintenance costs, medical care for military personnel were all left grossly underfunded. Due to the systematic delays in the payment of allowances and wages, a significant deterioration in the social and living situation of servicemen in the troops, morale and discipline have fallen sharply, the number of dead servicemen and suicides has increased.

According to the International Peace Research Institute in Stockholm (SIPRI), the Russian armed forces currently number 1,200,000 soldiers and have impressive arsenals of weapons and ammunition, in particular, 10,000 nuclear weapons and 40 tons of toxic substances. The report published by SIPRI claims that for Russia the reforms of the military-industrial complex are not just a way to bring it into line with the new international situation that has developed since the end of the cold war. Rather, it is about preventing the collapse of the Russian military-industrial complex.

For eight years the Defense Ministry has done nothing but "optimize" the Armed Forces "in accordance with modern military-political realities." President Yeltsin set the task of reforming the army, but he did not say anything about reforming the entire military system of the state. The results are clearly visible in Chechnya and Dagestan: this approach has brought the army to such a state that it cannot conduct even a local war. The bureaucracy and budget are disastrous. To military professionals, this is not surprising. They can't manage their troops in a war, even if they really want to. In addition, there is a constant open confrontation between the General Staff and the Ministry of Defense.

It is in this context that the first Chechen War broke out.

The financial crisis of August 1998 and the subsequent economic downturn halted the already weak reform process in the army. Nevertheless, knowing how vulnerable this weakness leaves Russia in the face of continued Western pressure, the leadership is assiduously focused on developing new technologies in order to prepare novel military responses to the Western countries.

A secret meeting of the Security Council on 29 April 1999, formally dedicated to the issue of nuclear weapons systems, turned out to be very radical. First and foremost, the discussion revolved around modernizing the nation's nuclear arsenal. A change is being made to Russia's military doctrine, rejecting the principle of non-first-use. (After all, the United States and NATO never did agree to a no-first-use policy; they keep their nuclear arsenal on hair-trigger alert.)

The main point is that in a case of life or death for Russia, then facing a Western opponent Russia must be prepared to use any available defense, including nuclear weapons. This was stated by the Chief of the General Staff, Army General Anatoly Kvashnin, and the chairman of the Duma Defense Committee, Major General Roman Popkovich. The Russian Security Council adopted Viktor Mikhailov's concept, from the Ministry of Nuclear Industry of Russia, which reads: "Today, the consequences of using nuclear weapons are understood to be so horrifying that no one will dare to use them. As a result, a real nuclear war has become impossible in fact. Nuclear pressure will become an effective tool of politics once again, if the threat of nuclear strikes is made more real. To this end, we need to be able to deliver 'pinpoint' low-yield nuclear strikes on military facilities anywhere in the world. At the same time, it is assumed that such a 'pinpoint' strike will not lead to an immediate global nuclear war." [NATO and the US refuse to pledge "no first use,"[1] and the US has used tactical nuclear weapons in Iraq and Afghanistan, at the very least.[2]]

The idea is not new; the only creative element in Russian doctrine is the introduction of the concept of a "pinpoint nuclear strike." These ideas are supported by social movements organized by the former military, for example, the "Combat Brotherhood," headed by Boris Gromov. General Boris Gromov, a deputy of the State Duma of Russia, once sent a letter to Serbian President Milosevic with assurances that he "can always count on the help and support of Russian veterans of local wars and military conflicts."

According to the generals, Russia's voice has been rendered mute on the world stage, and in order to be heard once again Russia needs to restore the military superiority it had achieved by the late 1970s. It needs to develop serious nuclear options not only for the land forces but also the naval and aviation components. First of all, we need a program to support and develop the defense industry, the restructuring of the military-industrial complex and the development of high-tech industry (primarily for military needs).

The concept of a limited nuclear war ruffles the feathers of idealistic peaceniks, but history has shown that the US and its Western allies are

---

[1] "The U.S. Air Force deploys an estimated 100 [tactical nuclear gravity bombs] at six NATO air bases in five countries. The remaining 130 nuclear weapons are stored in the U.S. for possible overseas deployment." Center for Arms Control and Non-Proliferation, Fact Sheet: United States Nonstrategic Nuclear Weapons, updated March 2022, at https://armscontrolcenter.org/u-s-nonstrategic-nuclear-weapons/.

[2] "USA Used Tactical Nuclear Weapons in Afghanistan and Iraq," *Oriental Review*, 09/04/2012, at https://orientalreview.org/2012/04/09/the-usa-have-used-tactical-nuclear-weapons-in-afghanistan-and-iraq/ ; "US Used Small Nuclear Weapons in Iraq," by Sue Arrigo, MD, at whale.to/a/arrigo2.html; "The USA Have Used Tactical Nuclear Weapons in Afghanistan," Strategic Culture, at https://www.strategic-culture.org/news/2012/04/09/usa-have-used-tactical-nuclear-weapons-afghanistan-iraq/

always ready to cast aside its inhibitions when opportunity strikes. It would be irresponsible for Russia to ignore the evidence and fail to protect its national interests. Thus, a redistribution of defense budget funds is needed in order to boost the Ministry of Nuclear Industry. Influential forces in Russia have set a course for the priority development of the military-industrial complex. The emphasis is on financing the military-industrial complex and on the creation of five new defense agencies that will create industrial concerns.

This new strategy also seems counterintuitive to those observers who believe in the good intentions of the West, who are [in the late 1990s] providing credit and agricultural aid,[1] and who are most disturbed by the real military conflicts brewing on Russia's eastern and southern borders. Countries in the Middle East are seeing an onslaught by guerrilla groups fighting their governments. The pro-West contingent cannot conceive who might be funding and organizing such de-stabilization on Russia's borders, but they argue that rather than focusing on the main adversaries Russia should first pay off the army's debts, feed and clothe the soldiers, repair the barracks and officer accommodations, and increase salaries. However, the strategic leadership remains most concerned with the eventual need to stand up to those who are behind the destabilization movements. Theoretically, there is a debate between those who focus on the end goal and the short-term thinkers who think high-precision weapons alone and the priority financing of the military-industrial complex cannot achieve much, unless they also solve the everyday issues of the army.

[Casual observers miss the fact that NATO expanded to 13 more countries after the fall of the Soviet Union in 1990, erasing any pretense that its purpose was to protect Western Europe from the Soviet Union and erasing, at the same time, the buffer of neutral countries between Russia and the West. NATO training centers were immediately established near Russia's borders, and weapons poured in.

Russia's doctrine adopted in 1999 focuses on two essential provisions. The first is the time allotted in it for a retaliatory nuclear strike, which becomes unpredictable. In other words, now the Russian military doctrine has a provision that resembles the NATO military doctrine of the 60s–70s. In

---

[1] It is a common error to think that the US sponsors everything from food deliveries to arts programs out of a good heart, without looking to see which corporations and which government agencies are actually funding such programs. USAID, for instance, and the USIA, are related directly to the State Department and the intelligence services, that is, to bolstering pro-US sentiment among the common people and the elites alike while providing avenues for infiltration. Recruiting support, weakening patriotic allegiances. And favored corporations end up being subsidized by the US taxpayer. .

those days, NATO held that if they were unable to contain the enemy's offensive with conventional weapons, NATO troops could use tactical nuclear weapons *to retaliate*. At that time, the USSR called this extremely irresponsible. Finally, Russia itself has borrowed this position. In the previous doctrine, there was a provision stating that Russian nuclear weapons could only be used as a retaliatory strike against a nuclear attack.]

The new Russian concept of national security emphasizes the role of the US and NATO, who "claim to be the sole decision makers of the destinies of Europe and other continents." The new doctrine contains two essential provisions. The first is the time allocated in it for a nuclear retaliatory strike, which is becoming unpredictable. In other words, a provision has now appeared in the new Russian military doctrine reminiscent of NATO's earlier military doctrine. In the 1960s and 1970s, NATO stated that they could use tactical nuclear weapons to retaliate if they were unable to contain an enemy offensive with conventional weapons. At that time, the USSR called this idea extremely irresponsible. Given the West's unremitting encroachment, Russia itself has been forced to adopt this position. In the previous doctrine, there was a provision that Russian nuclear weapons could only be used in response to a nuclear attack. Second, the doctrine reverts to the old Soviet rhetoric of a "bipolar world." As in Soviet times, it refers to the US, NATO, and Western Europe on the one hand, and Russia, China, and India on the other. Who can say they are wrong?

Russia is bristling again. It has a visible enemy again and is therefore ready to build up its armed forces. Russia still has a third of the world's uranium enrichment capacity. An analysis of the long-range aviation exercises conducted in recent years shows that the Air Force is working out tasks corresponding to the new military-political situation. The Command of the Russian Armed Forces considers Long-range aviation as a means of launching demonstrative nuclear strikes, which should, without causing significant destruction and casualties, show Russia's determination to thwart the plans of a superior enemy. This represents a new round in the nuclear arms race.

According to unofficial information, these are the main points as far as countering the West:

1. Tactical nuclear weapons are being deployed in Belarus again.
2. Russia is withdrawing from agreements with the United States regarding the supply of weapons and military equipment to Iran.
3. Cooperation with NATO within the framework of the Partnership for Peace program is being curtailed.

4. The Russian peacekeeping forces will come under sovereign control again, and will carry out only the instructions of the Russian General Staff, not orders from NATO generals. Imagine the United States ever agreeing to be ruled by instructions from non-US, non-NATO generals!
and 5. Russia reserves the right to provide military assistance to countries that have been subjected to NATO aggression.

Already in 1991, during a time of popular euphoria about the new apparent American–Russian rapprochement, some experts in Russia were warning that there were still prospects of an upcoming clash with the United States, perhaps as soon as 1997–98. Only someone who knew the real state of affairs at the ideological level could have guessed that. In fact, his forecast was made just a few days before the coup attempt in Moscow in August 1991.

Service in the Russian army is still a compulsory civic duty. More than a third of its current composition —approximately 450,000 military personnel — are conscripts, with 90% consisting of men aged 18–19. The most vulnerable end up in the army: those who cannot write to someone higher up or pay off someone who can help. Boris Yeltsin signed a decree on the eve of the elections in 1996, aiming for: "On the transition to recruiting" for privates and sergeants on a professional basis, but it was not implemented. There was an effort to recruit service members, but 50% of the contract soldiers turned out to be women — the wives and daughters of officers. After the crisis of August 1998, a third of contract soldiers parted ways with the army because of the beggarly wages, and the position of Russian "pros" began to be considered "women's work." As a result, as of 1999, service in the Russian army is still a compulsory civic duty.

Maintaining stability in the post-Soviet space is a challenge in areas where there is a danger of ethnic clashes. The "collapse" of Yugoslavia is a lesson in how ethnic groups can be turned against each other to destroy a working partnership. At this time, the country faces the danger of regional conflicts more than a direct threat from NATO.

Some regional leaders, especially the presidents of the ethnic republics within the Russian Federation, who have gradually become an independent and powerful force, act in very ill-considered ways and only aggravate the situation in the country. This can bring nothing but trouble, and there is always the possibility that they will be used by foreign interests to stir up trouble. Leaders have already been identified, whose actions are constantly destabilizing the situation, which could lead to the country collapsing into smaller, even weaker parts.

It so happens that the most corrupt part of society at this time is the army generals. They even wormed their way into deals involving the sale of military equipment from the former Soviet units in Germany, Poland, Czechoslovakia, Hungary, even in Afghanistan, and later in Chechnya, Georgia, Moldova and other countries. With equipment being sold off, including aircraft and cruise missiles, the armed forces would not be able to face anyone with modern weapons and the defeat would be complete.

And the credit for that would belong not only to the enemy generals, but also to Russia's own. Now the picture looks simply terrifying. Russia cannot even defend its capital, let alone distant frontiers.

Meanwhile, in 1991 the United States had demonstrated that it was to their advantage to help former Soviet republics dismantle their nuclear arsenals. They passed the Nunn-Lugar program to offer funding for that purpose, targeting particularly the Typhoon nuclear submarines, the largest in the world. Each of them was designed to be capable of destroying half of America with one salvo of 20 RSM-52 ballistic missiles, with a dozen warheads on each of them. In total, 6 Typhoons were built in the USSR in 1980–88. However, as of this book's writing, no more than 2 Typhoons were still seaworthy.

Russia dragged its feet when it came to the actual dismantling of nuclear installations, despite certain promises. The funds from the United States were quite welcome and were not explicitly tied to this work. Various US officials including US Secretary of Defense William Cohen visited in 1998 and 1999, having been offered a visit to one of the military shipyards where the submarines were to be disposed of. They were shown very little, but promised to continue financing the work.

No one knows who the demoralized and sold-out army will support in the conflict between the branches of power in Russia. Most likely, "their people" in the security forces will not be particularly concerned about human rights and compliance with agreements with their ideological opponents, and will not worry about showing a great deal of humanity towards the civilian population. It is even possible that a military junta could come to power in the near future, consisting of generals and high ranks of the KGB/FSB, slightly diluted by police, tax, customs, liaison officers and other special officers. That is how well the West's strategy is paying off, undermining the country socially, morally, economically, and politically.

23. Searching for a "Miracle Worker" and a "Wonder Weapon"

Russia's experience in the 1990s left the public demoralized and divided. Capitalism and the new social free-for-all bankrupted the human soul and the nation as a whole. On top of sorting out the new economic relations, Russia now had to formulate a national idea to bolster social cohesion, and rebuild the military to recover its international security.

As late as May 2022, after all Ukraine's military installations were wiped out in a couple of months, such "scholars" as Volodymyr Zelensky still make fun of Russia for "trying to find its wunderwaffe."[1] Russian Deputy Prime Minister Yuri Borisov may be more on target: "Russia has successfully tested a new weapon...the 'Peresvet', which can blind satellites up to 932 miles away....[T]he weapon also has the capacity to destroy drones."[2] As this book is about to go to press, that is what the evidence points to. Russia is generations ahead of the West in hypersonic missiles and other technologies. But in the 1990s, this truly seemed like pie-in-the-sky.

National-religious exclusivity became one of the rallying points. The Kremlin and the Russian Orthodox Church worked together with the public to re-affirm the benefits of conservative family values, morality and culture. Patriotism and national cohesion came along as a result of successes starting in the 2000s.

---

[1] Oliver Browning, "Zelensky mocks Russia for 'trying to find wunderwaffe' amid use of laser weapons," *The Independent*, May 19, 2022, at https://news.yahoo.com/zelensky-mocks-russia-trying-wunderwaffe-082225421.html

[2] Monique Beals, *The Hill*, "Zelensky: Russia's search for 'wonder weapon' illustrates failure of invasion." May 19, 2022, at https://thehill.com/policy/international/3493936-zelensky-russias-search-for-wonder-weapon-illustrates-failure-of-invasion/

In some cases, the military experimentation entailed not only the laws of physics but psychic activity as well. Thus, in parallel, exotic mental/psychological and scientific avenues were being explored. As Yekaterina Sinelschikova has observed, "Not long before the breakup of the Soviet Union, the country was gripped by the occult. The pendulum had swung and the previously atheistic state plunged into religious ecstasy."[1]

A chaos of religious cults burst onto the scene. The new openness was a gift from above to "religious" cults, international corporations and wheeler-dealers of all kinds. Officials and parliamentary deputies, anyone in a position to "open doors," might profit immensely by allowing access to decision makers and potential clients. The sharply reduced standard of living made many people especially vulnerable to bribes.

Leaders of various totalitarian cults, from Aum Shinrikyo to L. Ron Hubbard's Scientologists are said to have had contacts with highly ranked government figures and the President's administration. Such contact could have been granted not only in exchange for huge sums of money, but also because the Secret Services have always showed a great interest in ideas related to mind control. [Here, the infamous and copiously documented American program of MK-ULTRA comes to mind. The psychic "technologies" used by these sects have been studied by all sides.]

For these reasons, various sects were allowed to freely function on the Russian territory. A considerable example is Shoko Asahara, who was supported by the former Parliament's speaker Ruslan Khasbulatov and by the former chief of the Security Council Oleg Lobov. It is known that Shoko Asakhara bought weapons and observed exercises on "closed" military training grounds. Shoko Asakhara was permitted to preach and sing his "hymns" on the state radio channel.

By 2011, the Scientologists seem to have been in retreat worldwide. But for years they had a network of training-centers and business colleges in Moscow and other towns and cities in the Former Soviet Union. They were helped to establish connections in business and political elite by General Rutskoy, by the former Parliament speaker, the chief of the Ministry of the Inner affairs and later FSB chief — Stepashin, and by former prime minister Kiriyenko.

Then there is Sun Myung Moon, the South Korean prophet. A number of famous reformers and journalists as well as Gorbachev, Shushkevitch, and Popov visited the USA and South Korea, their trips paid for by Moon.

---

[1] "Why has Aum Shinrikyo been banned in Russia only now?" Oct. 4, 2016, in *Russia Beyond the Headlines* at https://www.rbth.com/politics_and_society/2016/10/04/why-has-aum-shinrikyo-been-banned-in-russia-only-now_635553

University rectors, professors and teachers from all over the country spent a week at a health resort in Crimea in 1992 on the same account.

The Russian Orthodox Church also had contacts with some of the foreign cults. An ecumenical conference was held in 1989 using Moon's money with the participation of Archbishop Philaret, a chief of the Patriarchate's Department of foreign affairs The Moscow Patriarchate also received $50,000 from Aum Sinrikyo to publish the Bible.

The former State Duma's Chairman of the Committee of National Security, Viktor Ilukhin, had a personal web-page (no longer available) at http://www.gull.ptt.ru/Iliuhin/index.htm. Thus the orthodox communist placed his web-page at the site www.gull.ptt.ru, belonging to a group calling themselves "The Gray Angels." Casting themselves as "little gray sparrows," "from hell," they consider themselves a security service of God, and Mr. Ilukhin, their inspiration, a kind of spiritual leader and "a punitive hand of the God."

Nationalistic esoterics and prophets of all kinds frankly confess that they are waiting for natural cataclysms, a pole shift or a comet falling into the Atlantic Ocean, as predicted by different interpreters of Roerich, Nostradamus and Edgar Cayce. Such an event is seen as destroying Russia's strategic opponent — the USA and Western Europe. They say that this will leave Russia as the most powerful country in the world.

In the West, much of this was not taken seriously. Their main concern was a challenge in the fields of nuclear, bacteriological, rocket and other technologies. In spite of the assurances of the Russian authorities, it seemed quite possible that for the right price, bad actors could be given access to the ordinary, chemical, nuclear and other types of weapons. Even leaders of cults.

The overwhelming majority of the Russian elite shares the opinion that Russia must stick together with the East against the West if a new world war or even local wars break out, because that is the only possible way to regain its former power and station. Russian politicians are trying to engage China and India in this idea. But these countries, having inherited a legacy of stratagems of their own, were in no hurry to accept this suggestion. [By 2022, we see that both China and India are inclined to maintain at least a neutral stance if not to support Russia outright. Russia's long-term strategy is bearing fruit, as both China and India resist being drawn to America's side in Russia's military action in Ukraine.]

Organizations dealing with practical parapsychology technologies and other esoterical groups are proliferating, under names that give no indication of their real essence. For example, the Institute of Venture Research, the Academy of New Thinking, the Academy of Informatization; a Military

Laboratory of Reincarnational Problems was even established by the Military Medical Academy in St. Petersburg. Its former chief, Yuri Shevchenko, has recently been appointed a minister of Public Health, recommended by highly ranked people from the Russian security service. The ex-prime minister Sergey Stepashin commented that public health would be strengthened by the new appointment. That means just one thing: resources were being poured into parapsychological elaborations.

In the 1970s and 80s, people having any parapsychological abilities or esoteric knowledge were allowed to teach only KGB members. A special department was established at that time. Yoga, chi-gun, and the martial arts were under special prohibition. Karate was to be taught only to the KGB and militiamen. All people of this kind, as well as the priests, specialists on bioenergy, and most of the staff of the Eastern Studies Institute were officers of the secret service.

A current of fearful ideas was circulated among the upper echelons: that the Russian genotype was to be destroyed via humanitarian aid, "gifts" processed with special bio-chemical preparations; that people's minds were to be influenced via special impulses from Western satellites passing over Russian territory, and so on. The activity of different Western religious and humanitarian missions and their public announcements were seen as encoded influence of some special kind.

[Such "fearful ideas" have been revealed to be correct. Hundreds of US-funded experimental biological labs have been operating at the borders of Russia practically since the moment the other republics broke away. In Tbilisi, Georgia, just south of the newly expanded showcase resort town of Sochi, the Russian Foreign Ministry noted in 2020 that the Lugar lab is conducting studies on the spread of dangerous viruses through insects. "The United States has already patented unmanned aerial vehicles to disperse infected mosquitoes in the air. In addition, a patent was issued for the production of ammunition into which toxic substances or infectious agents will be loaded."[1] On top of that, PCR testing — practically-enforced by the CDC — enabled them to collect each patient's DNA (although they claim that was just collateral to their intent). This goes hand-in-hand with the nearly worldwide injection of experimental genetic-modifying serums that were acknowledged to be only in the "human trial" phase. The notion that the US is preparing biological attacks tailored to genetically different populations seems well-founded.] In Russia, the development of new secret

---

[1] "'Infected mosquitoes from an American plane' " — Moscow demands inspection of Lugar lab in Tbilisi, JAMnews, May 27, 2020, at https://jam-news.net/moscow-demands-inspection-of-lugar-lab-in-tbilisi/

weapons based on previously unknown physical and psychic principles began a long time ago. In 1956 Anatoly Stavitskiy came up with a vacuum device, a *polythron*, intended to register diffused fields. In the 60s there was the Petrov secret department in the scientific center Novosibirsk. That organization has studied the question of telepathy 18 different ways. At that time the Ministry of Defense was intrigued with the idea of being able to send a telepathic signal to a submarine. Since the end of the 60s, the Scientific-Industrial Association "Vympel" and a number of other secret scientific institutions were working out P. Avramenko's idea of a plasma weapon. He had ideas about how USV-radiation could affect rockets, or be used by rocket designers, to affect the course of a rocket in the atmosphere. That sounds far out, but indeed by 2003 both the Americans and the Russians were well along in studying the plasma field generated by supersonic rockets and testing what to do with, or about, it.

Back in 1987, another seemingly far-fetched line of speculative scientific investigation came to light when the academic Evgeny Alexandrov, a deputy of the chairman of the scientific department in the State Optical Institute, received a secret report from the Ministry of the Defense Industry. It suggested a universal theory that could serve as a basis for creating a super-fast delivery means for nuclear weapons, a hyper-engine, which could also make it possible to develop a generator to improve crop productivity as well as other applications.

Apparently, many people thought this was crazy, but in 2021 Russia demonstrated to the world its unique Zircon hypersonic missiles.[1] No other country is close to having such a weapon — or a means of detecting it in time to defend against such a strike.

The scientific-technical center "VENT" was thriving in 1988–89 under the wing of the Soviet State Committee on Science and Technologies. It had the support of the Ministry of Defense (military subdivision # 10003), the Ministry of Nuclear and Energy Industry and of the special Innovation Council of USSR. All of VENT's specialists were working on far-out theories related to torsion (spin) or microleptonic fields,[2] which are invisible and

---

[1] The 3M22 Zircon or the SS-N-33 is a maneuvering anti-ship hypersonic cruise missile... [Its] estimated range is 500 km at a low level and up to 750 km at a semi-ballistic trajectory, but the state-owned media in Russia reports the range as 1,000 km." MDAA, 2020, at https://missiledefenseadvocacy.org/missile-threat-and-proliferation/todays-missile-threat/russia/3m22-zircon/

[2] "The principle of operation is that the device reflects a non-ionizing microleptonic radiation and it fades in the mobile phone. Electromagnetic radiation, which provides communication, does not change its parameters." Tesla Screen, *TheWaveMatrix*, at https://thewavematrix.net/en/products/tesla-screen/ ; and some discussions at "Theory Of Entropy Logic," *Biophilia NLS Bioresonance Diagnostics* at https://www.biophilia-tracker.

which existing apparatuses were not able to register, although ostensibly the human sensory organs could detect them.

By the time the USSR was going to pieces, the scientists experimenting with and inventing the new weapons had to find new "homes" for their activity. Many new academies popped up, usually headed by the military or by KGB officers. The inventor of the torsion weapon, Akimov, was given a place in the Section of Noospheric knowledge and technologies of the Russian Academy of Natural Sciences. He became an academician and set up an International Institution of Theoretical and Practical Physics. In 1997, the military men paid pretty well for his research on torsion communication lines intended to enable the immediate transmission of information to a definite subject in any part of the world. The unique appeal peculiar to these lines was that the information transmitted was impossible to intercept. Akimov also received funding from the military institutions in Soviet times. Money for this kind of research has always been found.

The military subdivision #10003, camouflaged under the military corps and managed by the military department, was actively engaged in extrasensory perception, occultism and the study of UFOs. The Federal budget allocated funds for conducting different experiments on human beings, on esoteric information, looking for evidence of extra senses and inventing new weaponry. The military worked on ways to change the weather: to cause rain, dissolve the clouds, or shift cyclones. They created a special process for precipitating smog out of the air, and received four patents. They have also attempted to develop climatic and geodesic weapons, the latter referring to the ability to create a resonance on the opposite side of the platform with enough frequency to destroy the enemy's infrastructure on another continent when the bomb is exploded. They have even identified a site in northern Siberia which, if a nuclear explosion were triggered there, would move the geotectonic plate. That would probably cause sufficient global climatic and geographic changes to bring on a new world order. Their test data suggested that Russian territory, especially its eastern part, would not suffer, while America and Western Europe would be completely destroyed.

The head of subdivision # 10003 is Major General Alexey Savin. Experts in his organization have been involved in active research on occult teachings, psychic practices and methods of extrasensory influence, have developed special devices, and tried to identify previously unknown reserves of human abilities.

com/Theory-Of-Entropy-Logic-For-Hunter-4025?layout=full&content=grid&page=1&l imit=75; https://www.rialian.com/rnboyd/Shpilman/cover-contents.htm

PsyOps use very similar tactics to cults. Thus, they studied the subtle psychic technologies used by different sects and cults, mostly the totalitaristic ones.

They use human test subjects and one of their goals was to create a substitute for the old national idea—a general all-encompassing idea that everyone could identify with, suitable for all society levels. # 10003 has different departments—medicine, philosophy and others. They have been looking for people working out nontraditional theories and inventing new things, studying telepathy, clairvoyance, levitation, chakras and energy meridians in the human body.

General Savin often meets the other high ranked generals and officials, politicians, even a prime-minister and their spouses in the office, which is situated not far from the Ministry of Defense. All of them are interested in being tested on special, extremely expensive German equipment. This is the way the lobbing group is being formed. The policy conducted by General Savin asserts that the more people are involved in the structure's activity, the stronger it becomes. So, several specialists from 10003 have been assigned to manage affiliates groups at outstanding universities all over the country. A goal would be laid out by 10003 and given to one of the affiliates, who were empowered to use the specialists by contract. They were funded by the Ministry of Defense, and the "Institute" managing those means at its own discretion would find scientists able to solve the problem. The finished project was sent back to #10003.

Some of the experiments involving psychotronic and torsionic fields produced results. While professional physicians recognized only four types of interaction, they identified a fifth and set up huge program to see how it could be turned into a "wonder-weapon." For example, it might be easy to turn an enemy's whole army to a dull, impersonal mass in one moment and at any distance using a specially formulated psychotronic weapon. It is also possible to spread panic among the population and the army. Now there are serious physicians who admit to the existence of the "fifth force," but they consider it as something outside the frame of physical experience.

The torsion theory was aimed to develop Tchizhevsky's ideas about direct influence of the cosmic processes on humanity. Torsion fields carry universal information. These fields represent interrelations as yet unknown in physics. The word "torsion" or torque generally refers the twisting force associated with rotation. It is said that while an electron goes from one orbit to the other, it produces not only electromagnetic fields but torsion fields as well (made by its own rotation). It represents nothing but a memory of the previous rotating. The author of the theory, Akimov, declares that the impulse of its own whirling, the so-called *spin*, can come off and determine universal processes without any influence.

Scientists say that it is possible to change a substance's properties using a torsionic generator invented in their laboratories. For example, if you influence hot metal with the torsion field coming from this generator while producing armor, you can its strength increases several times over. What is more, there is no defense from torsion radiation because it penetrates through all objects and events in the material world.

There are military models of a spin-torsion generator in Russia. Its influence can wreck the instruments, change crystals and "switch off" people's minds. The generator radiates craterlike torsion rays of rotation. This tremendous weapon was created to combat the US Space Defense Initiative (SDI, or "star wars"), announced by President Reagan in 1983.

There are no limits for torsionic influence; in comparison with other types of radiation, it cannot be stopped either by water or earth. Besides, primary torsion fields are the mind's transmitters. The human mind is a system of "spin" fluctuation of the particles composing the brain. That suggests it can be used to influence and direct the brain's activity.

It was also suggested that if copper, when crystallizing from alloy, were processed by the torsion field, its electro-conductivity would be much higher. An industrial plant and special factory for processing "torsionic" copper were built and they started conducting experiments from the 1970s.

In 1987, soon after *perestroika* began, Nikolay Ryzhkov, Chairman of the Ministry Council, approved it. From 1989 onward, testing on the torsionic delivery of information has gone on under the state's and Ministry of Defense instructions.

By late 1994–95, they compiled a huge amount of esoterical information. Then A. Savin had a meeting with the chairman of the Security Council Oleg Lobov, the same Lobov who had helped Shoko Asakhara and Aum Shinrikyo's activity. An exhibition was arranged for him at "The Laboratory of Nontraditional Means of Teleportation in Space" in Monino, Moscow Oblast. They showed him reports (from 1993) with the results of experiments. For one, using extrasensory perception people from Savin's group within the Major Staff managed to find a depot of arms and ammunition hidden in Moscow, and some covert members of the opposition in the Supreme Council. The Ministry of Defense thanked them for their work. After Savin persuaded the Deputy Chairman of the Main Military Administration, General Anatoly Kvashnin, to meet several the extrasensory experts, they predicted he would attain the position of the Chief of the General Staff. Kvashnin seriously doubted that, but when became chief indeed, he called to Savin and had a serious talk with him.

The only way to test the new psychological methods is to test them on people. That has been the other field of activity for #10003, alongside forecasting. In 1994–95 two specialists from the "College of the Informational Technologies" (an affiliate of 10003), Elena Klimova and Elena Nevzorova, conducted seminars on methods of self-regulation: self-anaesthiology, self-immobilization and the like, with the Spetsnaz corps (highly trained Russian commandos). Some 10–15 soldiers were ordered to participate in the experiments.

Meanwhile, experiments to reveal previously unknown psychic abilities have been discovered among the students of the Dzerzhinsky Military Academy — a prominent institution preparing staff for the militia and KGB. In 1995, I. Lebedev, a managing director of the Association of Military Psychologists from the Defense Ministry Military University, signed an agreement with V. Baranov, the chief of the psychophysical center "Edineniye," to test a number of psychophysical methods in addition to those elaborated in the center. The activity of "Edineniye" is based on belief in the Absolute and aimed to develop a human ability to fly, teleport and live forever. The association "Army and Society" has invited everyone to work together on self-regulation. If a person got a chance to work with a group, as so-called "human material," he was hooked.

Today the military institutions are still seeking to invent new types of "wonder-weapons" on the basis of "new" laws of nature. Discovering new defensive technologies is essential to the preservation of Russia. All this experimentation is considered top secret, needless to say. However, such secrets tend to invite corruption. Huge amounts of money are spent to discover something unknown. But no one can publicly verify the results because everything, obviously, has to be kept top secret. This is a gold mine for enterprising people and a pretty good opportunity to siphon money from the budget.

The General Staff do not want any information somehow connected with parapsychology to leak out. This leads to another problem. People involved in any way with such research can disappear without a trace. There have been numerous cases. So, the Ministry of Defense goes on tinkering with measures for countering the intrigues of Western intelligence; the Ministry of Public Health, the FSB, and the State Duma are perfectly aware of the scientific- and quasi-scientific research going on, as well as the experiments on people. In fact, this activity is completely outside the public view.

Just like the American MK-ULTRA program,[1] there exist no certifications, licenses or oversight from the public side. What is most disturbing is that these technologies can be used for military/defensive purposes but in everyday life as well.

In early 1998, representatives of Russian intelligence, the Scientific Military Administration of the Major Staff and #10003 reported to the President about progress in the field of esoteric experimentation. It was said that Russia needs to accelerate its activity in this field, lest in the Americans gain the upper hand. It has also been written that foreign secret services were interested in Russian specialists in bioenergetics.

In the early 1990s, Boris Yeltsin (the Head of the State as well as Supreme Commander) demonstrated a great interest in a project for extracting energy from stone. Fascination with the idea of a "wonder-weapon" was prevalent in the Kremlin for years. And then there was General Georgy Rogozin who worked in the KGB for military counterintelligence (not to be confused with Dmitry Rogozin),[2] and then became a key figure in the protection of the President of Russia. He actively worked in worked on telepathy, clairvoyance, hypnosis, applied psychology, parapsychology, telekinesis, and astrology, and enthusiastically spread these ideas among the President's circle. In his last few years General Rogozin would check the horoscope while pondering financial–budgetary and economic problems. He even created a "positive energy field" around the President and placed his bed according to the energy flow, from north to south.

This Georgy Rogozin also got involved in political consulting and influence peddling. Under the cover of a company named "The Agency of Economic Security," he helps certain high-level criminals, those cowboys of casino-capitalism who managed to grab whole industries when the state monopolies on essential resources and enterprises were hastily privatized. These über capitalists (now called "oligarchs"), having obtained their wealth, now want their offspring to attend Harvard and Oxford, and enjoy life without problems. A prime example is Anatoly Bykov, who seized control of the aluminum market in Siberia using bribery, threats, and murder. (He was charged in a murder case in 2002 but the European Court of Human Rights over-rode the Russian court. In September 2021, Bykov was sentenced for 13 years in connection with a number of murders in 1994.) The main idea is this:

---

[1] The CIA's secret mind-control projects involving torture and the covert use of biological and chemical materials, including LSD, on kidnapped civilians including children. See https://www.cia.gov/readingroom/search/site/mk%20ultra

[2] No apparent relationship to Dmitry Rogozin, the former deputy prime minister in charge of the defense industry and, since 2018, head of the aerospace program Roscosmos which enables American astronauts to reach the International Space Station.

Any guy who manages to get out of so many tight spots is no fool, criminal or not. Even if the newspapers refer to him as a "godfather," maybe we can use him.

General Georgy Rogozin has also been involved in programs using narcotics to program peoples' minds. According to his own words, the American intelligence in Afghanistan was deceived by the Russian security. The Americans were completely sure, that Russians had not used either hypnosis or narcohypnosis when extracting information from captive soldiers and officers. They imagined that only chemicals such as caffeine-barbiturate were used. So, the Russian intelligence has still been using these mistakes in the structure of their decisions. This is a high-class work giving good results, he says. The moral of this conflict is classical and there is no place to ethics, they say. After Rogozin's departure from the Kremlin at the beginning of 1998, a new institution was created — the Center of the Temporal Problems headed by P. Sviridov. Its main task was to make political prognoses using processed astrological charts for high officials of the country.

There are just a few facts about the military's esoterical quests in Russia. The political sector has also taken note of the utility of subconscious messaging. Studies have shown that 90% of information is accepted on the subconscious level, and consequently it is essential to influence the subconscious mind. A crucial point for society is that under pressure, say, when the media are blaring on about various emergencies, people are incapable of making logical choices or even formulating the most important criteria to consider. As a result, in tough situations the electorate ignores logic and behaves according to unconscious choices.

From NLP it is known that people can be divided into several groups according to their way of perception: visual, audial and kinesthetic. The specialists notice the main mistake made by politicians: they give mostly auditory information, which is based on logic. But only 20% of people are able to process and retain it. At the same time, more than 60% of people are visuals, people who can effectively learn information through vivid video-clips.

It is said that each nation has a mental image of the ideal politician. These archetypes are fit to the real political figures. There are twelve of them: Protector, Teacher, Painter, Priest, Servant, Ruler, Scientist, Parent, Fool, Collector, Executor and Child. The strategists and image-makers are dealing with the problem: who does the electorate want right now? A Ruler, Fool or Protector? They search for a prototype able to capture any audience, even a monkey flock. Karl Gustav Jung, the founder of analytic psychology, said 40 years ago that "All nations have an archetype of a Ruler and an archetype of a

Fool, but only in Russia they are so close that it will not be surprising if one day a Fool becomes a Ruler."

Evgeny Zotov, an outstanding doctor of physics and mathematics having officially begun to heal with NLP-technique, now has become one of the leading specialists in psychotronic weapons. In addition, the following people were involved in research of torsion fields: Lubov Petrova — a doctor of physics and mathematics, a scientific member of the International Institute of Theoretical and Applied Physics (this Institute has been dealing with psychophysical elaborations for 8 years); A.V. Moskovsky — a scientific member of the Institute of Theoretical and Applied Physics; Petr Goryaev — a president of the Institute of Quanta Genetics; Vladimir Isakov — a chief of the juridical medicine department in Military Medical Academy in St. Petersburg; Valery Antonov — a military doctor. Gennady Dulnev, a doctor of technical sciences, studies technogenic psy-influence in St. Petersburg.

All the above-named people are closely interconnected by an invisible network of members of KGB/FSB and scientists. For example, one of the elaborators of the torsionic theory, Gennady Ivanovitch Shipov, has been combining several positions: a director of the Scientific Center of Physical Vacuum, a chief of the Laboratory of the International Institution of Theoretical and Applied Physics, a president of the Scientific Institute of Venture and Untraditional Technologies and an academic of the Academy of New Thinking.

The Jehovah's Witnesses are managed by the Frunze Military Academy, "The Church of the New Testament" — by an FSB colonel general in St. Petersburg (and one of the main positions is taken by the teacher of the Military Academy, a colonel and doctor of science).

Military experts are mostly interested in the psychological mechanisms of esoteric practices, because this knowledge promises insights on how to control social processes, social groups' behavior and helps to build a unique hierarchy with little disagreement and dissatisfaction. They study the possibility of influencing people with hypnosis, how to make people spy against their will (making the subject a kind of bio-robot), how to create an agent to send into the future.

Mysticism is accompanied by ideology. It is notable that astrologers and mystics were in great favor with Adolf Hitler. Luckily, he did not have a nuclear weapon. Speaking of national fascism, we should note that it has an unsettling tendency to show up in partnership with a revival of paganism and occultism, with strong repressive organizations based on esoteric concept, similar to SS in fascistic Germany (or in Ukraine since the US-led coup of 2014). A certain degree of nationalism, the normal human tendency to identify with one's own group, is one thing. When it is weaponized against others, it is a problem.

A current of extreme nationalism showed in Russia in the martial paganism that appeared on the political stage during the transition period. The Russian National Unity Party founded in 1991 by Alexander Barkashov was specially trained by the Russian security agencies. They urgently needed someone able to fulfill the need for a "Russian national idea." A special group from the President's administration had been thinking about it for a year. They had in mind a special group that would fulfill unofficial orders from the security and governance institutions. Later, that group was put at the disposal of the police, but they could not keep it under control. The national movement that was let loose found a stable social foundation. That was also an experiment in selecting and artificially crafting an ideology based on the achievements of the military psychologists. Now, Russian National Unity is managed by former KGB people who, in fact, have still been maintaining contacts with their *alma mater*. These retired members, having access to good opportunities and money, have set up their own numerous associations, where military men, young people, scientists and those with acute extra-sensory abilities can work on practical aspects and methods for promoting ideological and psychological goals.

The time for setting order in Russia has come. A passion for mysticism has always been a sign of decay of any social structure. In the eras of ancient Rome and of fascistic Germany, such fixations had spread widely. Soon after that the empires' existence came to an end.

Here are just some examples of religious-national and messianic thinking among developers of new secret technologies, government astrologers, and so on and so forth. We won't make any editorial comment: reader can feel for themselves what lies at the heart of this philosophy.

This presentation was given by Anatoly Akimov, Director of the International Institute of Theoretical and Applied Physics, in Moscow:

Reflection of the spiritual role of Russia
in the development of earthly civilization:

"...In the age of Aquarius, in the era of the formation of the 5th race, Russia is doomed to greatness, to a leading role in the evolutionary development on Earth, no matter how paradoxical these words sound in the conditions of our modern reality ..."

"...With the formulation of a new scientific paradigm and with the creation of a sum of torsion technologies, Russia has begun to fulfill its space mission as a leader the age of Aquarius and Russia will lead humanity into the third millennium..."

"...The race that meets the following requirements can be the leader. This list is far from complete, but these items reflect what is most important: the first is the radicalism of transformation, the second is the will to achieve one transformation after another until the achievement of the final goal, the third is tolerance in the process of re-educating people who stand aside from the global process, the fourth is conservatism for the preservation of enduring values, the fifth – collectivity, conciliarity, community in the implementation of the global process in the name of a common goal, the sixth — the ability to follow cosmic laws.

You can name many countries or nations that have *some* of these qualities. For example, the conservatism of Great Britain has become a byword. There is the radicalism of China with its revolutionary bent, etc. But only one nation — the Slavic people — and, above all, Russia, possesses all these qualities at once, and together these qualities constitute the spiritual essence, the spiritual imperative of the Slavic nation and, above all, Russia. The highest spiritual essence of Russia allows modern civilization to turn a technological breakthrough exclusively for the benefit of humanity and in accordance with cosmic Laws ..."

"...The concept of a new history born in Russia has already given Russia the opportunity to begin fulfilling its mission. Humanity will have to realize the importance of this fact — we have been living in the 21st century for 15 years. And his march began here in Russia. And this is a historical fact..."

(Report presented at the international socio-scientific conference "The Spiritual image of Russia in the philosophical and artistic heritage of N.K. and E.I. Roerich," Moscow, 1996)

And from another article:

"...The torsion field of the universe must inevitably have an outlet to the collective unconscious, which ultimately determines social processes and changes on our planet. Through messiahs, prophets, gurus and deputies of the State Duma (?!)...".

It is not unreasonable to say that almost every astrologer in St. Petersburg is involved in cooperation in the development of new methods of military analysis and forecasting through numerous academies, associations and institutes. They also fully share the above-mentioned ideology.

[Lunacy or prophecy? Twenty years ago, this may all have seemed preposterous. By the time the United States and NATO started shelling the Russian population in Donbas in February 2022, forcing Russia into a counter-attack on Ukraine, much of it seems to be on target.]

Here are some excerpts from Albert Timashev's article "Russia is the Last Hope (an astro-political forecast)," June 23, 1999, that foreshadowed what many observers are saying in 2022.

"...Russia is in fact the last hope of the unconquered portion of humanity to get rid of the American yoke. And if Russia perishes as a power in the next year or two, it may take more than a decade before the American military machine, and with it the entire American system of economic parasitism, will collapse and be destroyed by the forces of the peoples who rebelled against the American dictate..."

"...It is not typical for Slavs to wage aggressive wars, but if 'someone comes to us with a sword, he will die by the sword'; it has always been so, and it will continue to be so. Russia has never staged genocide against other peoples..."

"...Throughout its history, America has profited from the grief and suffering of others..."

"...The first war in the history of the United States was an undeclared war of extermination against the Indians, the native Americans. The American Constitution, now extolled as an example of the highest manifestation of democracy and being the national pride of every American, in fact, until the middle of the XIX century, equated Negroes and Indians with animals, legislated slavery and the policy of genocide against native Americans, considered Negroes and Indians as goods and property of "free citizens." This is the whole essence of American foreign and domestic policy to this day: the rights and freedoms of US citizens must be protected in every possible way, no matter what crimes against non-citizens would have to go for this. This is a typical ideology of a criminal group — a mafia clan..."

"...most major countries of the world will simply have no choice but to engage in hostilities on one of the sides: either on the side of the United States of America at the head of NATO, or on the side of Russia at the head of the union of states opposed to the new order..."

"...the military experience of the United States is not comparable to the experience of Russia and the peoples inhabiting it..."

"...It is now clear that the Third World War has begun. Sooner or later, all the major world powers will join it, this is also beyond doubt..."

"...It is important for Russians to understand now that they will have to fight and Russia will have no choice in this matter..."

"...Yeltsin should be removed in disgrace from the post of President of Russia... during the war, such a commander-in-chief will bring us more harm and losses than all the NATO strategists combined..."

"...Yeltsin, suffering from senility, will hesitate for a long time, and invaluable time will be lost ... to be ready in time...to begin an emergency restoration of Russia's defense capability..."

"...Russia... will simply stop supplying electricity, gas and oil to Europe. The entire European economy will be paralyzed in a matter of hours. The same thing will happen to the US economy, which will collapse overnight if China presents them with all its dollar reserves for payment. In the course of one day, the dollar will become a worthless piece of paper. There is no doubt that embittered America, and with it Europe, will be ready for anything, up to a nuclear war, just to take revenge on their ravagers by completely wiping them off the face of the Earth..."

"...Obviously, Moscow and St. Petersburg will be the first to be subjected to nuclear strikes. There is very little hope that the Russian air defense forces will be able to completely block these strikes. The epicenter of the strike on St. Petersburg will, most likely, be to the west or southwest of the city, somewhere in the area of Kronstadt or the Leningrad Nuclear Power Plant... Perhaps NATO will not need to use a nuclear bomb on St. Petersburg, since all one has to do is to blow up the NPP by conventional means to produce a similar effect..."

"...When America starts bombing Russian cities, there will be no question of what to do. We have to do what is necessary — to give a worthy rebuff to the enemy — that's the harsh truth of life. Therefore, Russia now has one single and over-arching task: to gain as much time as possible before entering into hostilities, and to use this time to the maximum to restore the combat capability and tactical and technical training of its armed forces, to bring them into full combat readiness and ensure Russia's defense capability, which can now be expressed only one way — readiness at any minute to repel any NATO strike, including a nuclear one. Our losses, and ultimately the outcome of the Third World War, and the fate of Humanity as a whole depend on how we cope with this task in the coming months..."

"...After the end of the Third World War... the moral advantage, without any doubt, will be on the side of Russia and its allies, since America, destroyed, bankrupt, and the first to use nuclear weapons, will be completely discredited in the eyes of the world community, and in many respects the heavy burden of restoring order and peace on the land scorched by nuclear fire will fall on the shoulders of the surviving Russians..."

Below, we have the Program of The People's Movement "Towards God-Power." (Much of it, indeed, consists of an obscure disquisition on the esoteric framework and a particular religious interpretation, but we can focus on certain ideas that in retrospect appear to reflect useful insights, albeit often couched in oblique terms. One of the kernels of reality here is the suggestion that lending for interest, "usury" as it used to be called, is at the heart of one of humanity's greatest problems. Just look at countries trying to repay Western loans today. By "biblical," this document apparently means the Old Testament, the "Jewish Bible," and the author continues to use euphemisms.

The movement was registered on April 23, 1997 as No. 1693 by the Moscow Regional Department of Justice. Chairman of the Council of the movement — K.P. Petrov, members of the Council — M.N. Ivanov, V.A. Zaderey (editor–in–chief of the newspaper "Knowledge — Power!"), O.V. Petrov (Chairman of the Leningrad Regional Organization), G.A. Vyshchipanov. In Moscow, the movement publishes the newspaper "The Law of Time," editor–in–chief S.A. Lisovsky.

"The main goal of the movement is the dissemination of scientific and conceptual information about global governance, the creation of a human resource base for the salvation of Russia and how to extract all mankind from a deep socio–ecological crisis."

Excerpts:

3.4. We are an occupied country. But it is a lie that we lost the Cold War. We have lost ONLY one of the battles in the "cold" war, which has been waged for centuries by the world's mafia financial clans to establish their "world order".

In essence, all of us, all the people, are faced with a choice:

- Accept defeat and turn into a herd of slaves who will be pastured on raw material plantations by the new masters of the world;

- Or, having realized the essence of the information war, master it and go on the offensive.

There can be only one choice. "We are not slaves! We are not slaves!"

3.5. To win the information war, you need more powerful information than the enemy, you need to master it, and you need the same unbending spirit and, as in a conventional war, the same faith in the Just Cause.

3.6. We have the most powerful information necessary to win the war imposed on us! This is the Concept of Russia's public security in the global historical process, which outlines the plan for the life order of Russia in the new millennium. [This plan] passed parliamentary hearings in the State Duma of the Russian Federation in November 1995.

3.7. It was proposed for implementation to all political leaders, both the ruling party and the opposition. All of them shied away, once again proving that they are only puppets in the hands of all the same "masters" and it is through them and with their help that Russia is being destroyed.

3.8. There is no hope in "leaders"! Responsibility for the implementation of the Concept of Saving Russia is assumed by the people.

III. Program goals of the Movement

1. Goals of social policy. Each of these goals is *unachievable as long as our country lives according to someone else's concept.*

> 1.1. We are for everyone to have the opportunity to exercise their right to work.

> 1.2. Every worker is to be adequately paid.

> 1.3. Everyone, regardless of social and financial status, is to have the opportunity to receive any education and realize their abilities.

> 1.4. Everyone is to have the right to free medical care and all the conditions for a healthy lifestyle.

> 1.5. Every honestly working person should feel calm and secure in old age.

> 1.6. The soldiers standing guard over the Motherland are to have everything they need, and their service is surrounded by honor and respect.

2. Conceptual conclusion:

The implementation of these inter-related goals of the Concept of Public Security in Russia will allow the country to be taken out of control according to the biblical concept, while parasitism on Russia by the global Zionist–Nazi Freemasonry will be stopped.

This will be done based on:

> 2.1. enlightenment of the peoples of the USSR about the true causes and culprits of the supposedly "Russian" revolutions and unrest, all crises and wars, cataclysms and restructurings, all the oppression of the national cultures of all the peoples of the USSR.

...2.3. creating conditions for building an integrating culture in a single multinational superconcern state and the free development of people, regardless of their social origin and nationality;

2.4. forceful methods are not to be used in achieving these changes but rather moral, educational, cultural, economic and social security of the population;

2.5. building the credit and financial system of Russia on the principle of increasing the purchasing power of means of payment, provided by:

- outpacing growth of the country's energy potential in relation to the money supply in circulation;

- lending on an interest-free basis;

- limiting income and accumulation in families to a level that is obviously sufficient for life, but does not allow parasitizing on someone else's labor.

- Live in a family: honor parents; nurture the younger generation; inherit the experience of ancestors with understanding;

- Strive for the truth ...;

- To work together, conscientiously from the generosity of the soul, and not to do someone else's work for pay or for fear, contrary to conscience;

- To live, protecting the Fatherland, sacredly protecting it from enslavers, but showing hospitality to guests; repay traitors with contempt and blot out them and their deeds in life, but be merciful to those who make mistakes.

...

2.8. the formation of a new world order based on fair, excluding national cultures, cooperation of all peoples in various fields of activity, in order to ensure the stability of the planet's biosphere, of which all people are a part.

3. A fair system of life has not yet taken place in Russia — the USSR, since the ruling "elite" did not want it, and the people did not want to think for themselves how to build it, but in many ways envied the higher consumer opportunities of "their elite" and "the crowd abroad." The people wanted a leader who would lead them to a brighter future. But no one is allowed to enter paradise on someone else's hump. The future grows out of all the results of the past: what you sow, you will reap a hundredfold, in the future. So think before you sow something, so as not to cry from impotence when it all comes up.

Author's Conclusion (1999): What's Next?

What, in the end, is the real meaning of the words "national idea"? Religion and patriotism can always be abused.

The head of the Central Spiritual Administration of Muslims of Russia and European CIS countries, Sheikh-ul-Islam Talgat Tajuddin, made a paradoxical statement at the 5th World Russian People's Council, which was held at St. Daniel's Orthodox Monastery in Moscow. He said that Orthodox and Muslims together should make sure that Russia always remains "holy Russia." This term came out of Orthodox Messianism, which no longer deifies individuals but the whole country and harshly rejects any freedom of religion. On this basis, back in the early 20th century in Russia, it was possible to receive not just church condemnation but state penal servitude for changing one's religious confession. Today, the idea of holy Russia encourages some politicians to declare that only those who have been baptized can be elected to the State Duma — only they can be considered truly Orthodox people. At least an interesting statement was made by the head of the Muslims of Russia. The heads of both the Orthodox Church and the Spiritual Administration of Muslims are actually engaged only in politics. This is distinct from the way those of Jewish heritage play their hand in Russia: their political power comes via gangster capitalism, without reference to any spirituality at all.

In a time of national collapse, is it normal or wise to seek help from a country's historical opponents? What happens when reformers are trying to return to power, only this time with foreign help? In any other nation, this would be seen as treason and tantamount to political suicide; not in Russia of the 1990s. But while the West supports certain politicians in order to prevent communists and nationalists from coming to power, too explicit support will only harm these politicians, because they will all be seen as corrupt. One of the latest indicators is the activity of Viktor Chernomyrdin. Having earned the gratitude of the world community for his role as a peace-maker in Kosovo, he did not gain fame in his homeland.

Chernomyrdin followed in the footsteps of Mikhail Gorbachev, who, for all his popularity in the West, has a bad name in Russia. He has firmly entered history along with the concept of "perestroika," which is remembered in the bitterest terms. Having destroyed the Soviet Union, Gorbachev essentially defected to the West[1] — that's all that can be heard about Gorbachev in Russia now.

When a person who has enjoyed circulating in the upper echelons of power leaves politics, the usual refuge is to secure a position as an adviser in pro-government monopolist firms, where he can continue to do what he's been doing. Yeltsin also intends to stay in big politics after his presidency. During his meeting with the security forces, Yeltsin casually said: "I can't just do nothing. I need to find some kind of social work." Foreign Minister Igor Ivanov, who was present at this meeting, was the only one who did not flip out. He cheerfully advised the President, with a wink, to create and head a Council of Wise Men in Russia by analogy with the Council of Elders in the North Caucasus. Yeltsin liked the idea.

The biggest difference between Russia and the Western democracies is that there are no public organizations working to poll the public for feedback (and to shape public opinion).[2] The activities of political parties and blocs, even the activities of the so-called Russian democratic parties, are mostly virtual. Parties do not reflect anyone's interests, if we are talking about the people. No stratum of the people will win if any of the currently existing parties wins the elections. Therefore, none of them will gain a majority of votes. While there is still an opportunity, while there is still a generation alive that has been accustomed since Soviet times to swallow and accept any information as the pure truth, former communist functionaries are trying

---

[1] Although he was given a government-owned and -maintained house outside of Moscow, he almost never appears in Russia and it is believed he resides in Germany, where he owns substantial real estate.

[2] As noted earlier, this was quickly rectified by Western organizations who leapt into the void to launch pro-democracy initiatives of all kinds. The Levada Center, Russia's "only independent national pollster," for instance, has partnered with entities funded by the U.S. Defense Department, as admitted by Prof. Theodore P. Gerber, Director of the Center for Russia, East Europe and Central Asia at the University of Wisconsin-Madison. He has worked with the Levada Center on 20 survey projects since 1998, funded by a variety of U.S. government and private sources. *The Washington Post*, September 17, 2016, at https://www.washingtonpost.com/news/monkey-cage/wp/2016/09/17/the-kremlin-blamed-our-work-when-it-declared-russias-most-respected-polling-firm-a-foreign-agent/ .

their best to advertise themselves in the media. This explains why there is such a fierce battle going on for newspapers and television in Russia.

Russia's issues are not resolved at the state level, because officials can always agree among themselves. Even if it is not peaceful, they will still come to agreement. One official who has a lot of compromising material will simply show it to another, and they will come to terms. Because everyone steals. Almost everything, with the rarest exceptions. As long as there are pocket parties and trade unions, as long as all matters are resolved in a narrow circle of officials, the authorities do not feel much discomfort even with the almost military situation in the country. Neither the executive nor the legislative authorities have concrete proposals for the country's recovery from the crisis. Russian citizens can only count on themselves. It does not matter which government will be in power. As long as the existing system of values is in effect, nothing worthwhile will arise in Russia. The Russian elite is poisoned by the poison of national exclusivity and is completely deaf to the urgent demands of life. Although she admires the achievements of Western civilization, in her country she admits the existence of these achievements in a kind of truncated form, arguing that the West is not worth worshipping.

Most of the public foundations or funds that are kept afloat, including human rights organizations, were created by former high-level criminals and exist on criminal money. The charter of such foundations mention tasks such as promoting the study of public opinion, the development and support of civil and social programs, charity events, giving food to the elderly, holding concerts and domino tournaments. But in fact, police officials are being paid off, fed money from the funds by way of sponsored vacation trips and valu-able gifts to police officers. The permanent representative of the Govern-ment of Khakassia to the President of Russia and the founder of the Civil Initiative Foundation, Sergey Gruzdev, has asserted that he "feeds" about four thousand employees of local law enforcement agencies in this way. But the policemen do not remain indebted, either. They all pretended that no one noticed anything when, having taken up the position of permanent representative, Gruzdev first of all paid for his new villa in Florida from the republic's budget. And it was of no interest to them at all that Gruzdev had been previously convicted, and repeatedly, for bribes and abuses. But that's not all. All the data on Gruzdev's criminal record disappeared from the City Department of Internal Affairs database when he began his active political activity. Three years ago, Gruzdev became chairman of the Moscow City Boxing Federation. Then he became a member of the public council of the City Department of Internal Affairs of the Moscow Region.

It is not difficult to make forecasts for the development of the situation in Russia. Methods have not changed lately, when there was a need to rally people who could only find common ground with the authorities if they felt the nation was under siege by enemies from all sides. These measures have always included: the rejection of everything that is not national, the oppression of private property in favor of the development of strategic industry, the widespread mobilization of the population for strategic work and other duties. [As is true of war-time situations anywhere. "Democratic" systems are a luxury available from time to time for countries who are militarily and economically secure.]

The executive power was transferred from Boris Yeltsin, the "first president of Russia," to his successor, Prime Minister Vladimir Putin, on New Year's Eve, December 31, 1999. Or perhaps we should call it the staged spectacle of the transfer of power. It was apparently choreographed according to all constitutional canons, but where, in what democratic country, has the power been transferred by the incumbent president to a new head of state by his own decision rather than by the will of the people?!

It is no coincidence that a few months later Putin was formally elected to the post of President of Russia (March 2000). By the end of 1999, the greatest impact of the ruble's devaluation after the financial crisis of 1998 was pretty much exhausted, and from here onward, Russian financial analysts were predicting that world oil prices would start to go down. These two factors allowed the Russian state to make ends meet, and now they could afford to allow a serious crisis to follow, one that would provoke a serious "crackdown" by the state. In addition, in the first quarter of 2000, Russia was scheduled to pay $3 billion to international creditors. This amounted to a quarter of the country's gold and foreign exchange reserves, a rather serious test for the Russian economy.

Sooner or later, President Putin will be forced to start eliminating those who brought him to power, as they are sure to constantly interfere with the establishment of a stable regime. Dyachenko, Voloshin, Berezovsky, Abramovich and others will soon become a liability for Putin. The "strong hand" must distance itself from the oligarchs who have stained themselves with financial fraud.

But this will not happen right away, maybe in five or six years. For now Putin depends on the Kremlin puppeteers, as he is their own creation. It was they who turned an unknown KGB colonel into a national hero in a few months, taking advantage of their monopoly on the media and using the war as a propaganda tool. At first, Putin will be busy learning about various monetary frauds and political twists. And only then, when the studies are over and all the political and economic methods of restraining the country's decline have been exhausted, the opponents can be removed.

POST SCRIPT: A SHORT TIME LINE SINCE PUTIN TOOK OFFICE

Dec. 31, 1999 to 2022[1]

- 1999: Putin becomes President. Putin's first challenge is in Chechnya, where the Russians crush the jihadist insurrection in the Caucasus.

- 1999: Three former Soviet allies in the Warsaw Pact (disbanded in 1991) are added to NATO, breaking a 1990 promise from Sec'y of State James Baker to Gorbachev that NATO would not expand eastward.[2] By 2020, fourteen countries are added to NATO and several former-Soviet republics and direct neighbors express a desire to join.

- 2001 June: The SCO is formed, which leads a panicked Rockefeller Empire to activate a military move into Central Asia via the events on September 2001 — 9/11.

- 2001, a state takeover of media seized the television networks previously owned by the oligarchs.

---

[1] Sam Parker produced this excellent synopsis in his "Russia/Putin & the West Part 1," published online May 21, 2022, at *Behind the News Network*, and edited by Algora Publishing at https://www.algora.com/Algora_blog/2022/05/21/has-russia-already-won-is-it-game-over-for-the-rothschild-rockefeller-empire

[2] "Soviet leader Mikhail Gorbachev was given a host of assurances that the NATO alliance would not expand past what was then the East German border in 1990 according to new declassified documents." Dave Majumdar, "Newly Declassified Documents: Gorbachev Told NATO Wouldn't Move Past East German Border," *The National Interest*, December 12, 2017, at https://nationalinterest.org/blog/the-buzz/newly-declassified-documents-gorbachev-told-nato-wouldnt-23629

- 2003 March: The US invades Iraq — Putin helps the Iraqi Resistance with military equipment, including the Kornet anti-tank missiles.

- 2003: Just as Washington had taken over Iraq, Putin orders the spectacular arrest of Mikhail Khodorkovsky on charges of tax evasion. Putin then freezes shares of Khodorkovsky's giant Yukos Oil group, putting it under state control. Khodorkovsky had been negotiating to sell 40% of Yukos to 2 Rockefeller oil companies, Exxon and Chevron, Oil. This would have ended Russia's economic and financial independence.

- 2005 May: The CIA moves forward with its Color Revolutions along Russia's periphery and launches a coup attempt in Uzbekistan. The leader, Karimov, cuts US ties and closes a US base next to the Afghan border. Uzbekistan moves closer to Russia, while the US is out.

- 2007 February: Putin's speech at Munich shocks "the two families," the Rothschilds and the Rockefellers — now the gloves are off.

- 2008 August: Georgia invades Russia — and is defeated within 3 days.

- 2008 September: Financial crash

- 2010 December: Arab Spring

- 2011 March: Destabilization of Syria begins

- 2012: Xi Jinping becomes President of China — and the US "pivots" East

- 2013: Since Putin's arrival, Russia's GDP more than doubles, inflation drops from 36.5 to 6.5%, Forex Reserves grow from 12.6 bil USD to 511 bil USD and national debt is reduced from 78% to 8% of GDP.

- 2014: The Maidan coup in Ukraine. US & NATO "advisors" and "trainers" start to pour in. After February 22, 2014, the Kiev coup regime began to wage a war of extermination and ethnic cleansing of Russian-speakers in eastern Ukraine. This was still ongoing in 2022.

- July 2014: As Putin is returning to Russia after the BRICS summit in Brazil, his plane flies above Ukraine. The CIA targets his plane, but the wrong plane is shot down — Malaysian Airlines MH17.

- 2015 September: Russia goes to help Syria.

- 2018: Putin unveils Russia's advanced military hardware — the Pentagon has a cardiac event.

- 2021 September: Belarus color revolution fails against Putin ally Lukashenko. A huge military buildup takes place within eastern Ukraine.

- 2021 November: Putin sends a demand to Washington that peace requires three guarantees: Ukraine to be a neutral state. No nuclear missiles to be stationed in Ukraine. Ukraine will not be a member of NATO. Weeks pass, but Washington does not respond.

- 2021 December: Russian intelligence thwarts a coup attempt in Bishkek, capital of Kyrgyztan. NATO missile systems in Romania and Poland about to become operational.

- 2021 December: Vladimir Putin notes that Ukraine has refused to honor the Minsk Accords for seven years, and he announces that if NATO does not provide binding guarantees to curtail military deployments in Eastern Europe and to bar Ukraine from membership in the alliance, he will be forced to consider a military response.

- 2022 January: Russia puts down an attempted CIA/MI6 coup in Kazakhstan

- 2022 February: The Ukrainian military intensifies its shelling of the Donbass, practically non-stop. Zelensky announces his intention and readiness to deploy nuclear weapons on Ukrainian territory. Two days later, Putin recognizes the sovereign independence of the Donetsk and Lugansk People's Republics (Donbass), then Russian forces begin to assault military installations and NATO centers in Ukraine.

Printed in the United States
by Baker & Taylor Publisher Services